Theo Angelopoulos

PHILOSOPHICAL FILMMAKERS

Series editor: Costica Bradatan is a Professor of Humanities at Texas Tech University, USA, and an Honorary Research Professor of Philosophy at the University of Queensland, Australia. He is the author of *Dying for Ideas: The Dangerous Lives of the Philosophers* (Bloomsbury, 2015), among other books.

Films can ask big questions about human existence: what it means to be alive, to be afraid, to be moral, to be loved. The *Philosophical Filmmakers* series examines the work of influential directors, through the writing of thinkers wanting to grapple with the rocky territory where film and philosophy touch borders.

Each book involves a philosopher engaging with an individual filmmaker's work, revealing how it has inspired the author's own philosophical perspectives and how critical engagement with those films can expand our intellectual horizons.

Other titles in the series:
Eric Rohmer, Vittorio Hösle
Werner Herzog, Richard Eldridge
Terrence Malick, Robert Sinnerbrink
Kenneth Lonergan, Todd May
Shyam Benegal, Samir Chopra
Douglas Sirk, Robert B. Pippin
Lucasfilm, Cyrus R. K. Patell
Christopher Nolan, Robbie B. H. Goh
Alfred Hitchcock, Mark William Roche
Luchino Visconti, Joan Ramon Resina

Other titles forthcoming:
Leni Riefenstahl, Jakob Lothe
Jane Campion, Bernadette Wegenstein

Theo Angelopoulos

Filmmaker and Philosopher

Vrasidas Karalis

BLOOMSBURY ACADEMIC
LONDON • NEW YORK • OXFORD • NEW DELHI • SYDNEY

BLOOMSBURY ACADEMIC
Bloomsbury Publishing Plc
50 Bedford Square, London, WC1B 3DP, UK
1385 Broadway, New York, NY 10018, USA
29 Earlsfort Terrace, Dublin 2, Ireland

BLOOMSBURY, BLOOMSBURY ACADEMIC and the Diana logo are
trademarks of Bloomsbury Publishing Plc

First published in Great Britain 2023

Copyright © Vrasidas Karalis, 2023

Vrasidas Karalis has asserted his right under the Copyright, Designs and
Patents Act, 1988, to be identified as Author of this work.

Cover image: Landscape in the Mist (1988), dir. Theo Angelopoulos
(© New Yorker Films / Photofest)

Bloomsbury Publishing Plc does not have any control over, or responsibility for,
any third-party websites referred to or in this book. All internet addresses given
in this book were correct at the time of going to press. The author and publisher
regret any inconvenience caused if addresses have changed or sites have ceased
to exist, but can accept no responsibility for any such changes.

A catalogue record for this book is available from the British Library.

A catalog record for this book is available from the Library of Congress.

ISBN: HB: 978-1-3502-4535-8
       PB: 978-1-3502-4536-5
       ePDF: 978-1-3502-4537-2
       eBook: 978-1-3502-4538-9

Series: Philosophical Filmmakers

Typeset by RefineCatch Limited, Bungay, Suffolk
Printed and bound in Great Britain

To find out more about our authors and books visit www.bloomsbury.com
and sign up for our newsletters.

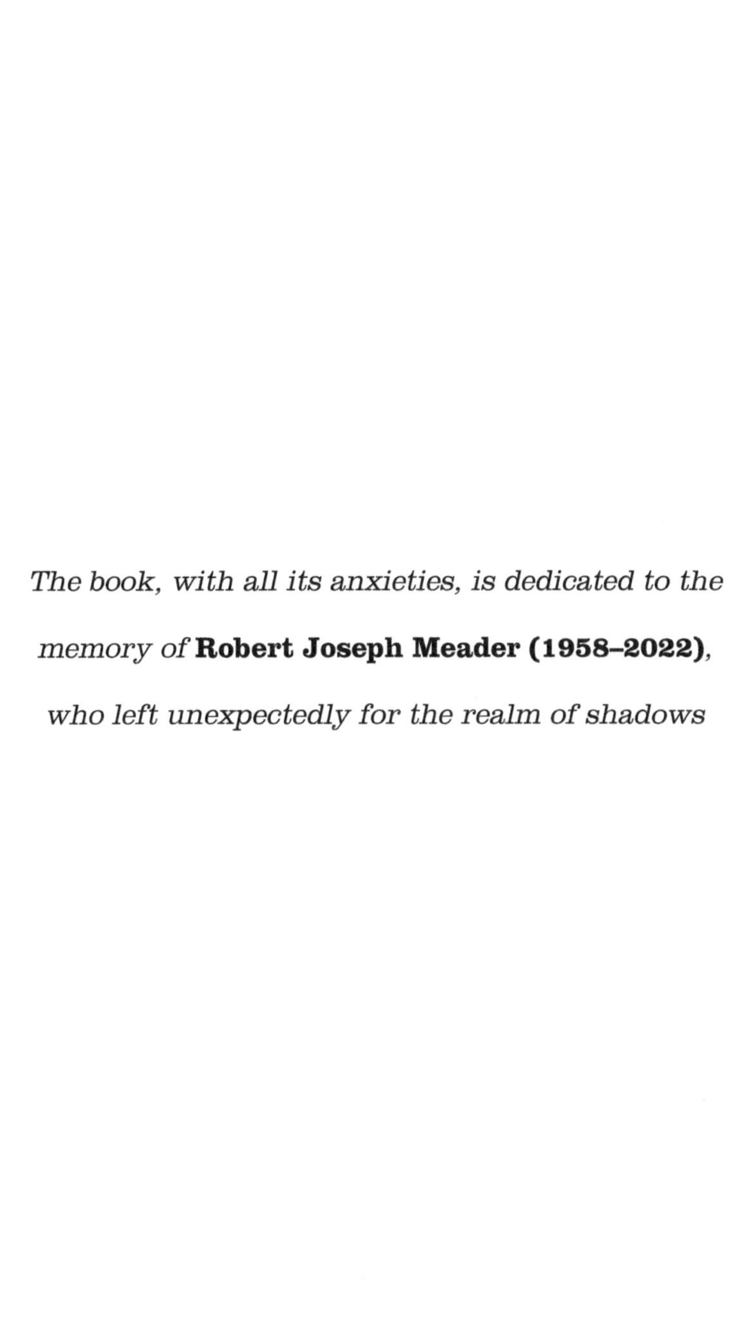

The book, with all its anxieties, is dedicated to the

memory of **Robert Joseph Meader (1958–2022)**,

who left unexpectedly for the realm of shadows

Contents

Illustrations

Visual Essay: The Discovery of the Psyche

1 & 2 From Metaphysics to Physics. *Landscape in the Mist* (1988) directed and written by © Theo Angelopoulos. All rights reserved. Produced by Greek Film Centre, Greek Television (ERT-1), Paradis Films (Paris), Basicinematografica (Rome), and Theo Angelopoulos Productions.

3   The Challenge of Modernity. *Megalexandros* (1980), directed and written by © Theo Angelopoulos. All rights reserved. Produced by: R.A.I., Z.D.F., Greek Film Centre, and Theo Angelopoulos Productions.

4   The Call of Secular Mystery. *Landscape in the Mist* (1988) directed and written by © Theo Angelopoulos. All rights reserved. Produced by Greek Film Centre, Greek Television (ERT-1), Paradis Films (Paris), Basicinematografica (Rome), and Theo Angelopoulos Productions.

5   Out of Plato's Cave. *Eternity and a Day* (1998) directed and written by © Theo Angelopoulos. All rights reserved. Produced by Theo Angelopoulos Productions, Greek Film Centre, Greek Television ERT-1, Paradis Films, Intermedia S.A, and La Sept Cinema.

6   The Question of Suicide. *The Beekeeper* (1986) directed and written by © Theo Angelopoulos. All rights reserved. Produced by Greek Film Centre, ERT-1 TV (Greece), Paradis Films (Paris), Basicinematografica (Rome), and Theo Angelopoulos Productions.

7   The Reality of Death. *Megalexandros* (1980), directed and written by © Theo Angelopoulos. All rights reserved. Produced by: R.A.I., Z.D.F., Greek Film Centre, and Theo Angelopoulos Productions.

8   The Redemption of Poetry. *Eternity and a Day* (1998) directed and written by © Theo Angelopoulos. All rights reserved. Produced by Theo Angelopoulos Productions, Greek Film Centre, Greek Television ERT-1, Paradis Films, Intermedia S.A, and La Sept Cinema.

9   At the Still Point. *The Weeping Meadow* (2004) directed and written by © Theo Angelopoulos. All rights reserved. Produced by Theo Angelopoulos, Greek Film Center, Hellenic Broadcasting Corporation ERT S.A., Attica Art Productions (Athens), BAC Films S.A, Intermedia S.A, and Arte France.

10 The Gathering Gaze. *Ulysses' Gaze* (1995) directed and written by © Theo Angelopoulos. All rights reserved. Produced by Theo Angelopoulos Productions, Greek Film Centre, MEGA Channel, Paradis Film, La Generale d'Images, La Sept Cinema, with the participation of Canal+, Basicinematografica, Istituto Luce, RAI, Tele-Muenchen, Concorde Films, Herbert Kloider, and in association with Channel 4.

Preface

Or Against the Historicist Imprisonment of Art

The present book constitutes a philosophical engagement with Theo Angelopoulos's ideas on the nature and function of cinematic images. It is not an analytic presentation of their cohesion, logic or fidelity to a certain school. It addresses the nature of images as *thought-pictures* and explores Angelopoulos's attempt to construct a visual language about human experience.

The central argument of the study is that in Angelopoulos philosophical thinking can be found in what is seen and not in what is implied, or in what could be translated into words. In his most significant films, Angelopoulos creates moving images that *think* beyond linguistic articulation or conceptual abstraction. Angelopoulos didn't leave behind a theoretical text, or a book of reflections, like Sergei Eisenstein and Andrei Tarkovsky; and whatever he said in various interviews changed considerably from 1970 till the end of his life in 2012. My task was to extrapolate from his actual images their own philosophical inferences and explore their transformations over a period of forty-five years. His interviews offer the landscape in which he was operating for each one of his images and, by studying them, we can detect the specific visual concerns in each point of his evolution.

Visual thinking is an enigma in many scientific and cultural fields. The visual unconscious is structured like an icon: a Byzantine icon in which all naturalistic and realistic elements are extended to their most abstract and *aniconic* manifestation. Angelopoulos's cinematic imagery is constructed out of intense abstraction and geometric linearity. In his images we see a Platonic world formed out of the rhizomatic matrices of archetypal shapes. They tend towards the elimination of all naturalism. What matters is the geometry of the underlying pattern—and as such they visualize the aniconic. It is true that his political involvement overshadowed the extremely complex *ocular* theory that defined the structure of his works. In an uneasy way, they both coexist in his films: the ontology of image as *urgrund* of being and the ideological faith in social change.

Angelopoulos made the human eye the central axis of all perceptual and conceptual reality. I mean the human eye *in* the camera recalibrating temporality, action, and language. The *ocularocentrism* of his iconological thinking is expressed through silence, long takes, and dead time. The loss of language, due to abuse and misuse, created an absence of critical exploration of the real, and the radical potential it entailed. Angelopoulos felt that language had lost its ancient provenance of offering a home to our being. According to him, only cinematic images could play that role even today, the era of the spectacular and the specular.

Throughout his century, language became the *topos* of false perception and falsifying certainties. Only images, cinematic images, could remedy the loss with a new language of visual morphemes. His films are invocations to the power of images to un-conceal the real, make it visible, and render it comprehensible in all its prismatic complexity. Focusing on his most important films, this study aspires to reveal the deep structure of his cinematography, what I call his *iconosophy*.

The ontology of cinematic images redefines our relationship with the world: this is the conclusion we can find in Angelopoulos's cinematography which still unfortunately remains hermeneutically imprisoned by historicism and by sociopolitical interpretations of its structure. My approach here simultaneously ambiguates and disambiguates his visual forms, foregrounding the ontological dimensions of his ocular poetics.

I would like to thank Eleni Angelopoulos for the permission to use stills from Angelopoulos's films, and for providing me with the unpublished scripts of his later films. Also, for her enthusiasm and encouragement during the process of writing the book.

I would like to express my deepest gratitude to my sister Aimilia Karali as her own engagement with Angelopoulos's films has been a constant source of inspiration in my work.

My heartfelt gratitude also to Dr. Achilleas Dellis not only for providing me with material hard to find but also for his own essays on Angelopoulos in Greek, full of brilliant originality and profound intuition.

My thanks also to Dr. Costica Bratadan for accepting the proposal to include Angelopoulos in the series. And to the reviewers of the proposal, as both their positive and negative comments were instrumental for clarifying, in my mind, concepts, methodologies, and perspectives in the emerging realm of film-philosophy.

Finally, my gratitude to Liza Thomson, Bloomsbury senior philosophy editor, for her attention and trust in the project; also, to Lucy Russell for her constructive approach and encouragement during the whole process. The Covid lockdown and the imposed restrictions seriously delayed the completion of the project; I thank Costica, Liza, and Lucy for their patience and understanding.

Chapter 1
The Quest for Existential Poesis

Or Prelude to Theo Angelopoulos's Iconosophy

Preliminary Notions

The present study of Theo Angelopoulos as a philosophical filmmaker marks a long history in my engagement with his work. I have already dedicated a lengthy monograph, several book chapters, and a number of articles to his cinema from the perspective of film studies, auteur theory, and finally history of cinema. I was always interested in his *mise-en-scène*, the specific arrangement of spatial continuities and discontinuities that made his images simultaneously polysemic and problematic, beyond and despite any formalist analysis of their structure. In all my efforts, I tried to avoid repeating observations about the political aspects of his films which are monotonous and platitudinal, especially in the Greek bibliography. In the present study, I intend to approach his works from the perspective of their engagement with philosophical questions or, more specifically, to explore the construction of his cinematic images as embodiments of specific *diachronic* questions of thinking and philosophizing.

Theo Angelopoulos (1935–2012) made thirteen movies, one short film, two docufictions for television, and left incomplete his fourteenth film. He was awarded the Palme d'Or at Cannes Festival in 1998 and became one of the most recognizable figures in world art-house cinema, ostensibly representing the *auteur* tradition of the 1960s and 1970s worldwide, even when this way of filmmaking and film-interpreting became rather obsolete. My perception is that Angelopoulos was a chameleon director, changing his visual mythography over time and experimenting with different fields of visuality, especially in the last period of his life. These are the essential elements to know about him and his work.

His films were not commercial successes, and never caused any considerable stir that could lead to a recognizable and classifiable movement, or any cinematic "wave." He is quite a lonely director cinematographer who fiercely protected his independence until the end of his life, without making any concessions to dominant practices or expectations, especially to demands by producers or the implicit expectations of his audience. Hence, his unique and uncanny cinematic vision is Articulated in an uncompromised and undiluted form. He stated:

> I don't make films to please anyone. For people like me, films are simply a way of life. When I talk about my life, I have to talk about my life "in film." That is, filmmaking is my second life, a parallel life. I like Faulkner's words that the world was created to become a novel. So, in my case, I like to believe that the world was created to become a film.
>
> In WADE 2021: 8

It is not strange therefore that, every time we watch his films today, we discover new points of entry and latent subtexts which make them rich in references and complex in connotations. We know that what is found in them epitomizes and embodies his ideas, perceptions, and finally his own existential *presence*. There is an undefinable *dimension* in all his works which goes beyond the historical particulars of their origins, the genres he worked in, their reception by critics and audiences, or even the cultural milieu that produced them. Their scope goes beyond their contextual connections and conditions. "The purpose of my films," he stated, "is to find a reason to exist" (Fainaru, 2001: 69).

Keeping such highly theoretical and almost abstract perspectives in mind in the present exploration of his films, I have foregrounded the "deep structures" of signification which are not reducible to the ideas that he advocated in his life or deducible from the overt meaning of the filmic scripts, which were all inspired, written, and edited predominantly by him personally. The writing of the scripts, in collaboration with other professional screenwriters add another dimension that is completely personal and self-reflexive to the philosophical ideas embodied by the films.

Following Noam Chomsky's linguistic dichotomy between "deep grammar" versus "surface grammar" and the foundational interplay of asymmetries that creates new meanings, I argue that in Angelopoulos there is a constant attempt to create new structural grammars for the syntax of his cinematic images. It is their structure itself that defines their meaning. The dialectical interplay between underlying forms and implied representations leads, in his best films, to an astounding expansion of philosophical significations that ultimately transform them into theoretical statements about the nature and the "essence" of cinematic images—and ultimately about human creativity. To the duality of deep versus surface structure, I would like to I add another dichotomy, borrowed this time from Ferdinand de Saussure, between *synchronic* and *diachronic* structures—linguistic in Saussure's analysis, formal and philosophical in the case of Angelopoulos.

Saussure stated that "synchronic linguistics is concerned with the logical and psychological relations that bind together coexisting terms and form a system in the collective mind of speakers. Diachronic linguistics on the contrary studies relations that bind together successive terms not perceived by the collective mind but substituted for each other without forming a system" (Saussure 2011: 99–100). Given the impact that Saussure's ideas had on Jacques Lacan, Roland Barthes, Jacques Derrida, Michel Foucault, and the analysis or reception of films in general over the last fifty years, we understand that this conceptual dualism is extremely important and necessary for studying what changed and what remained the same in Angelopoulos's aesthetic and philosophical evolution, the continuities and discontinuities of his work. Angelopoulos, like Roberto Rossellini, Federico Fellini, and Pier Paolo Pasolini but also Jean-Luc Godard and François Truffaut, searched for new signifying imaginaries throughout his career. For all of them, cinema was a way of living, a visual proposition about "the purpose of life." The scope and the perspective of filmmaking was too broad and complex to be interpreted or understood from a singular angle or theoretical principle. A synchronic reading of his films embeds each one of them within their specific contextual, mainly sociopolitical, web of meanings whereas a diachronic reading, which I am attempting here, investigates the subtle or obvious transformations and extrapolations that can be detected in his thought and approach to cinematic praxis.

Angelopoulos's filmmaking has been "imprisoned" within specific frameworks of interpretation or horizons of expectation. For many, he was a uniquely *Greek* director whose work can be understood in his quest for Greek identity and the visualization of an iconography for the representation of the elusive concept of "Greekness," a quest that has bedeviled all cultural and philosophical approaches to the wider questions of identity. For other scholars, he was predominantly, or even exclusively, a political filmmaker, a left-wing ideologue or a melancholic socialist, full of nostalgia for the grand and betrayed visions of universal brotherhood and working-class solidarity as embodied by an idealized Soviet Union and by Lenin's romanticized revolutionary activism. To this day, (I avoid referencing here for reasons of readability) the political background of his work is dominant whether one reads David Thomson, Andrew Horton, Dan Georgakas, Fredric Jameson, Sergio Arecco, or Christian Zimmer. Even David Bordwell's neo-formalist analysis is tinged with such residual ideological reading of his work; not to mention his recent elevation by Enzo Traverso to one of the dominant figures of "left-wing Melancholia," whose work revolves around "the adoption of the memory of the defeated" (Traverso 2017: 24).

In a way, only Yvette Bíró and, occasionally, Vasilis Rafailidis have tried to establish a different framework for the interpretation of his work, with varying and uneven results. Bíró explored "rhythms of slowness" in the visual temporality of Angelopoulos's images, suggesting a Bergsonian philosophy of temporal duration unfolding in the films, whereas Rafailidis foregrounded contested and contradictory cultural agendas in their architectural masterplan; both scholars suggested a renewed epistemological scrutiny of his works based on temporality, mood, and "openness." Recent scholars like Thilo Rising in Germany (Rising 2008) or Manuel Vidal Estévez in Spain (Estévez 2015) have started exploring the underlying *mythopoetic* philosophical ideas of his films, like facticity and everydayness, in an attempt to incorporate his work into what could be called a *history of emotions*, or was considered in the recent past as intellectual and conceptual history. The recent short book by Chris Wade (2021) articulates a philosophically inclined analysis of his works, which deserves more attention.

Ultimately, the delineation of his cinematic thinking belong to an overall European *Begriffsgeschichte*, as it visually explores ideas and their contexts and crosses the boundary between various philosophical frameworks. His narrative structures offer what Robert B. Pippin stated about Hitchcock:

> a nondiscursive treatment of aspects of human irrationality [. . .] attempting to show us the "nature" of these phenomena, what we need to understand in order to understand systematic and deep mutual misunderstanding, self-opacity, self-deceit, and other forms of limitations we are subject to when we try to learn what we need to know (but cannot) in cases of trust, love and commitment.
>
> 2017: 11

Pippin's statement applies almost perfectly to Angelopoulos, with a minor reversal in the order of things as they unfolded in his work; in him, it is first commitment, then trust, and ultimately love. If we focus on the deep and diachronic structures of his films, a *new Angelopoulos* emerges, free of any partial ideological denominations and separated from all suffocating political demarcations; a multi-dimensional philosophical thinker, a *problematizer of established visual and conceptual idioms*, dedicated to the investigation not only of social identity but also of human *interiority* and intentionality.

Furthermore, after the collapse of communism and the dissolution of the Soviet Union, most approaches still look at his work as a relic of the history of socialism or as a fossil from the glorious era of the revolution betrayed. Especially in his native country, the main way of looking at the central structure of his Angelopoulos's works seems to be based on Che Guevara's famous proclamation just before his assassination: "We have lost, but the revolution is immortal." Strangely enough, this approach is coupled with worship of the *auteur* ideology, emphasizing the genius of his work, relegating him back to the period when the director was the centripetal axis of value in the cinematic endeavor, especially through the conceptual appropriation of the director as the sole center of significations by *Cahiers du cinéma*. The glaring contradiction in this approach of making movies for the masses (with the masses as the central protagonist in the action) by an exceptionally creative and superior genius who could see above and beyond the masses became a point of discussion and reflection only peripherally and infrequently.

The mélange of such incongruous approaches is indeed strange and somehow self-defeating. If anyone today wants to study or even enjoy his Angelopoulos's films they must find an Archimedean point outside the existing frameworks of interpretation, or, if possible, totally ignore them. The best analysis of his films was always given by him in the successive interviews collected and edited by Dan Fainaru (2001); at the same time, some of his most problematic ideas came up in interviews, especially in the collection by Yorgos Archimandritis (2013). However, as a highly self-conscious and self-reflexive director, Angelopoulos knew what to eliminate from the horizon of meaning he constructed for his films, inviting viewers to themselves complete the gaps emerging from the constitutive elements which he left deliberately inconclusive. Angelopoulos had a *synergistic model* for the act of seeing: the viewers complete the image constructed by the director, in the way that various conductors reinterpret the same musical scores differently.

In my recent book *The Cinematic Language of Theo Angelopoulos* (Karalis 2021), I tried to implicitly dissociate the director from many dominant assumptions. I present Angelopoulos as a collaborative, multilayered, and reflexive filmmaker. I focused on his constant attempt to be the *visionary demiurge* of various contributions unified through his personal aesthetic and *ascetic* vision of cinematic art in search of the *cinematic sublime*. His personal approach was constantly morphing through different (re)articulations, incorporating diverse philosophical subscripts while at the same time forming a unique theoretical framework for a philosophical understanding of cinematic images.

The haunting and popular soundscapes composed by Eleni Karaindrou for the films are important and significant; however, they rarely rise up to the deeply ontological and existential concerns that permeate his films. They enhance a romanticized mood and hyper-emotionalize the representation. The central suggestion in my recent monograph was that, between 1970 and 2012, we can detect four different periods or phases of development, mostly in stylistic and what I termed *morphoplastic* terms, in the construction of his cinematic language. In this study I will try to foreground the philosophical concerns that underpin and determine the construction of meaning in his films in their diachronic succession.

The four periods are obvious to anyone who carefully watches his films: they consist of the early period of political commitment, followed by an ensuing period of existential questioning, which changed to the third period of cultural ontology, and finally the period that remained incomplete, the phase of exploring emotional historicity. The transitions in form and style from one period to another were subtle and somehow well disguised. The philosophical subscripts, however, became rather obvious, especially after 1980, in the most important film of his maturity, *Landscape in the Mist* (1988), and were sealed by the most accomplished and "sublime" *ontologization of his images* in his multi-award-winning film *Eternity and a Day* (1998).

Leaving the filmic and formal transmutations aside, the philosophical and conceptual theorizations underlying his evolution are equally significant, underscoring a constant exploration of existential questions through a profound investigation into the ontological foundations of cinematic thinking. André Bazin had pointed out the paradox of cinema that

> the photographic image is the object itself, the object freed from the conditions of time and space that govern it. No matter how fuzzy, distorted, or discoloured, no matter how lacking in documentary value the image may be, it shares, by virtue of the very process of its becoming, the being of the model of which it is the reproduction; it *is* the model.
>
> 2005: 14

The paradox of being both an original and a copy, something primary and secondary, can be found in Angelopoulos's profound problematization of cinema in its reproduction of "a greater degree of realism [. . .] [with] more means at its disposal to inflect and modify reality from within" (Bazin 2005: 105).

Angelopoulos the thinker who *problematized images* is much more challenging and interesting than Angelopoulos the "poet of images" or Angelopoulos the ideologue. In a previous study I explored his "ocular poetics" (Karalis 2017: 157); that analysis must be completed with the exploration of his *ocular ontology*: how the eye in the act of seeing encodes the real and contributes to the *emergence* of meaning from within the *morphoplastic* materiality of images as experienced in cinema. Images embody in themselves philosophical concepts or questions because of their very construction and formal manifestation. The structure of visual images corresponds to a specific conception of the world, in the way that Erwin Panofsky indicated the "intrinsic analogies" or "parallelism" between Gothic architecture and scholasticism (1951:

1–3), or, as we can argue, between apophatic theology and Byzantine style.

Panofsky himself transported the analogy from the Middle Ages to the twentieth century and used cinema as the ultimate contemporary example in technological invention of "what might be termed *the principle of coexpressibility*" (1997: 101). According to him,

> a film, called into being by a cooperative effort in which contributions have the same degree of permanence, is the nearest modern equivalent of a medieval cathedral; the role of the producer corresponding, more or less, to that of the bishop or archbishop; that of the director to that of the architect or chief; that of the scenario writers to that of the scholastic advisers establishing the iconographic program . . .
>
> PANOFSKY 1997: 119

What unites them all, however, is the common belief in the construction of a conceptual and a material artefact which presents a specific ordering of the world and consequently a specific understanding of human nature in its various manifestations. Angelopoulos is one of these chief *architects* in contemporary cinema who organized their films with the intention of articulating a specific understanding, structuring, and interpretation of shared experiential reality.

In the following exploration, I will try to extrapolate some of the principles that overarch the architectural formations in the philosophical structuration of his films. I will delineate his full trajectory, exploring identity and difference, continuity and discontinuity, albeit in a selective way; movies like *The Travelling Players* (1975), *The Hunters* (1977), and *O Megalexandros* (1980) deserve full-length monograph studies of their own. Furthermore, in my research, I usually follow the line of chronological sequence, since the films unfold patterns, themes, or styles which either are elaborated or disappear for certain reasons and at certain moments of the artist's development. In this reading of philosophical and theoretical motifs, I will move anarchically from one film to another without chronological fidelity, and focus on specific films and their visual specificities.

For example, the question of time which is usually dominant in all his films can be seen as divided between filmic temporality and historical linearity: in his major films, Angelopoulos elongated filmic time (*The Travelling Players*), but in others like *O Megalexandros* condensed it in a way that de-historicized it, transporting it to an almost fabulist universe of legends. In other films, like *Voyage to Cythera*, *Landscape in the Mist*, *The Beekeeper*, and *The Suspended Step of the Stork*, he followed a linear evolution of temporality in an almost Aristotelian sense; in these films time has a purpose and directionality. (As I have argued elsewhere, the conflict between Aristotle's *Poetics* and Bertolt Brecht's theatrical stylization remained dominant in his works.) In his monumental *Ulysses' Gaze*, time is in and out of joint, circular and most interestingly *spiral*, as it is in *The Weeping Meadow* and ultimately in the wild experimentation with *parallel* temporalities in his last released film *The Dust of Time*. Temporality as felt and imagined existence in *Eternity and a Day* is something unique and extremely complex to which I will dedicate more attention and discussion in the final chapter. The central philosophical question about *time and temporality* permeates his films but receives different articulation in different periods of his historical development.

From the early dilemma of freedom and determinism, Angelopoulos moved to the question of chance and possibility, and finally to that of consciousness and memory, while in the last decade of his life he was moving towards something more fundamental, which remained incomplete because of his sudden death. In a way his diachronic evolution reminds us of Henri Bergson's philosophy, as Angelopoulos intuitively perceived the heterogeneity of duration in terms of space since

> The truth is we change without ceasing . . . there is no essential difference between passing from one state to another and persisting in the same state. If the state which "remains the same" is more varied than we think, [then] on the other hand the passing of one state to another resembles—more than we imagine—a single state being prolonged: the transition is continuous.
>
> BERGSON 1911: 23

This continuous transition, called *duration* by Bergson, provides the philosophical justification in Angelopoulos's work for the exploration of the inner life, of the psyche as he called it, where there "is neither unity not qualitative multiplicity" (Bergson 1946: 14). Through the experiential reality of duration, Angelopoulos went back to the philosophical ancestor of fluidity and impermanence in antiquity, Heraclitus. It is interesting to remember that his seminal film *Eternity and a Day* begins and ends with adapted fragments about time by this obscure Ephesian thinker.

Because of these transitions I will focus on certain films, especially *Landscape in the Mist* and *Eternity and a Day*, since they represent the peak moments in his ontological investigation in the realm of visuality. His other films look like *propaedeutic* exercises, preparing the viewer for the synthesis of image and meaning, of concept and inception, something, which I call his iconosophy. In the images themselves lies the meaning of the story, in the way that Marcel Proust indicated that colors and forms tell different yet complementary stories. As Proust stated, "An image's beauty does not depend on the things portrayed in it" (1987: 57). If we take beauty here to mean structural unity, this is exactly what the images in Angelopoulos's films want to achieve. He wants to break down singular interpretations and infuse the story with emotional significations beyond the ones we usually invest it with as merely cinematic: the meaning of his colors and images points towards an *ethical* valuation of emotions with a profoundly existential conceptualization of history always lurking in the background. The philosophical argument which comes out of the images is about what constitutes human interiority and not simply about the pragmatic (historical) details of human actions. In literature, the parallels would be the *Diaries* of Soren Kierkegaard but also Jean-Paul Sartre's *Nausea* (1938) and Albert Camus's *The Stranger* (1942), where, in the form of the novel, we essentially encounter treatises about the formation of human consciousness as it emerges out of life's obvious contingency and randomness.

From Liberation to Self-transcendence

There were many reasons for this—social and personal. Progressively, in his attempt to address both philosophical and political issues, Angelopoulos created a "thick" imagery, consisting of his emblematic visual strategies, the slow movement, the depth of field and the long take, which both reveal and conceal. For example, the emblematic image of the broken statue of Lenin in *Ulysses' Gaze* is not simply a symbolic depiction of the failed god of socialism (in his last film the broken statues of Stalin have a similar function), but also an indirect statement that the past is going to fertilize the vision of a new revolution from within the center of a new order in history. History has not been fragmented into small and quotidian individual episodes, but the argument of an all-encompassing historical project of emancipation and liberation is lurking to emerge *suddenly and spontaneously* out of the new factories of knowledge in the contemporary capitalist world.

For Angelopoulos, after the collapse of all projects of social liberation and the demise of existing socialism, the social world had entered a prolonged period of loss, lack, and disintegration. It lost the ability to enunciate projects of critical valorization of its own historical experience. There is no negative culture anymore: political discourses do not possess the strength and the courage to question their own foundational principles. The only projects that could inspire individuals and rejuvenate societies are the memories of the rebellious spirits of the past. Remembering, however, is not nostalgia or melancholia but a rebellious act of self-transcendence, beyond the confines of the everyday occlusion of horizons. Remembering creates moments of rupture and interruption as the canonized and normalized continuum of existence determines the pressure of intense emotions, or forces individuals to choose their sacrificial demise.

In his epic *Ulysses' Gaze* and to a degree in *The Weeping Meadow*, memory is not simply remembrance of things past, but a constant *re-membering* of past experiences in order to restore the lost plenitude of those liminal realities for new generations. History, however, has its own *cunning*, as Hegel predicted, and despite the re-membering, new generations are not able to discern the closing horizons of meaning, the introverted form of social existence and the occluded reality of their being, the rising tide of irrationalism that takes over their existence. In his last film, the young have fallen into the dark labyrinth of drugs and self-destruction while the memory of the lost revolution drowns itself in the murky canals of industrial urban waste.

In all Angelopoulos's films, there is an elemental *ambiguation* towards their own material both in its semantics and its imaginal patterns. In this tension between image, signification, and perception, we can locate his cinematic iconosophy; not only because Angelopoulos originates from the Byzantine iconographical tradition, although this is part of *his* story, but also because he consciously attempted to incorporate themes in his films that indicated an abstracted reflexivity beyond any idealization and romanticization. In a sense, Angelopoulos's iconosophy aspires to un-frame his cinematic forms from any hermeneutical homogenization and free their significations from all ideological constraints. In Platonic terms, his films want to establish an "*eikos mythos*" for an "*eikos logos*," a likely image for a likely argument, knowing of course that we "must be satisfied if our account is as likely as any, remembering that both I and you who are sitting in judgement on it are merely human" (Plato 1977: 42). Because he understood the lack of shared *mythoi* in contemporary society, Angelopoulos problematized his own patterns of cinematic articulation and infused their structural formation with philosophical questions *seen and not verbalized.* He expanded the cinematic form, aspiring to simultaneously expand the argument. Details, incidents, episodes, or words function almost unconsciously and gradually find their appropriate configuration in his best films—something about which he talks in one of his few texts explaining his poetics, the introduction to the edition of the script of *Eternity and a Day*. A film, he stressed, is the final outcome of "underground processes" that suddenly come together to the concrete moment, "the moment in which an unexpected, privileged encounter with the ineffable took place" (Angelopoulos 1998: 7).

By studying such "underground processes," we have the opportunity to address the specificities of his work so that we can detect the philosophical complexities encoded by his images. In Angelopoulos's films we see the same process that we also find in the interpretation of Eisenstein's works, especially *Ivan the Terrible*. Some scholars keep emphasizing its political critique of Stalinism but, in reality, especially in Part II, we detect strong psychoanalytic subtexts of childhood trauma, religious awe, and homosexual desire, which are visible but not clearly articulated. *Desire is present but not represented* in the film although it infuses the actual structure and colors each scene. The viewers sense the presence of invisible undercurrents in the narrative but cannot clearly conceptualize them. (The question of whether Eisenstein projected them deliberately or involuntarily requires another form of analysis.)

The complex structure of the aesthetic artefact does not disclose but mostly *alludes* and *evokes*. It cannot be restricted by a demonstrative statement or specified by any positivist proposition about singular meaning. The dance scene of the Oprichniks in *Ivan the Terrible* Part II is the most unexpected homoerotic orgy that neither Kenneth Anger nor Rainer Werner Fassbinder ever managed to emulate: the drunken frenzy of the banquet indicates powerful libidinal conflicts within the structure of the film that go beyond the surface denunciation of the claustrophobic secrecy of a political regime. Eisenstein understood that the calibration, through his own homoerotic gaze, of the hyper-masculine army of the Tsar's bodyguards simply challenged their mythology of power and domination—and he left it at that. In the past critics insisted on the political dimension; but today we can clearly *see* that there is much more in his images, something more fundamentally anthropological.

Angelopoulos's works are replete with such philosophical subtexts which need critical elaboration both in their artistic intention and philosophical coherence. They are constituted of images with an underlying and implied meaning that evokes significations beyond the semantic fields of its constitutive parts. Iconosophy implies the *ontological* and *ontopoetic* structures that make his films semantically polyvalent and hermeneutically appropriable by various regimes of truthfulness. Through such an approach we can ask the extremely important question: what does it mean to understand a film, especially a film by Angelopoulos? Is there a fixed and singular understanding so that we can claim that the works of Angelopoulos formulate political statements mainly and principally, and therefore they must be considered as political films? Certainly, the question of what a political movie is must be raised here.

Angelopoulos understood the concept of politics in its most radical and originary meaning as defined by Aristotle: *bios politikos* is what makes societies exist, what keeps them together, and what gives purpose to social life. Aristotle stated:

Since we see that every city-state is a sort of community and that every community is established for the sake of some good (for everyone does everything for the sake of what they believe to be good), it is clear that every community aims at some good, and the community which has the most authority of all and includes all the others aims highest, that is, at the good with the most authority. This is what is called the city-state or political community.

[1998:1.1252a1–7]

Angelopoulos is interested in the presence (or absence) of such an *organic civic community* which exists solely for the good, the *eudaimonia*, of its members. Civic eudaimonia is the raison d'être of human society and is the goal of all interpersonal activity in history. Yet in all his films, political societies oppress people and deprive them of self-sufficient autonomy. In a *religious* sense (although Angelopoulos would have objected to the term), the fallen state of human nature in history is also a fall into unfreedom, self-oblivion, and heteronomy. In his films of the early period, the lack of political community is implicitly stated by depicting his characters as existing in alienation and false consciousness.

These films come out of the conceptual frameworks of the young Karl Marx who foregrounded alienation as the most pernicious and ubiquitous strategy of ruling elites to annul human will for creative labor, cancel freedom of choice, transform humans into abstractions, and abort the desire for change. For Marx, "alienated man is an abstraction because he has lost touch with all human specificity" (Ollman, 1977: 134). As Ollman explained, "if alienation is the splintering of human nature into a number of misbegotten parts, we would expect communism to be presented as a kind of reunification" (1977: 135). What happens, however, when the perspective of reunification of the broken humanity through communism does not seem possible anymore? The profound skepticism that we find in late Angelopoulos refers exactly to a life without perspective and scope. Erich Fromm further explained that

> alienation (or "estrangement") means, for Marx, that man does not experience himself as the acting agent in his grasp of the world, but that the world (nature, others and he himself) remain alien to him. They stand above and against him, as objects, even though they may be objects of his own creation. Alienation is essentially experiencing the world and oneself passively, receptively, as the subject separated from the object.
>
> 1966: 44

Almost all characters in *Reconstruction*, *Days of '36*, *The Travelling Players*, and *The Hunters* define themselves through mechanisms of identification with something outside themselves, through their very estrangement from themselves. In a sense they lack self-knowledge since they lack interiority. The character of Voula in *Reconstruction* presents no individuality, no moral dilemmas, or indeed no moral conscience. Marginalized by history, she experiences herself in a vacuum of values. She cannot evaluate her own actions or exhibit critical judgment or manifest personal autonomy. In Immanuel Kant's terms she cannot escape voluntarily her own ethical and existential "immaturity." The image of her existence never appears completed in her own conscience; it is centerless, mediated by mirrors, and obfuscated by un-thinking. Society conditioned her not to be herself, but to become her anti-self, unable to have any rational or cognitive understanding of who she is and what she is doing—unable, in platonic terms, to look into her own soul. The clinical way that the murder of her husband is reconstructed for the police is the most obvious philosophical subscript of self-alienation and, in Jean-Paul Sartre's terms, "bad faith."

The same can be seen in *The Hunters*, a film whose characters belong predominantly to the upper class and define themselves through the institutions of power they control. The dialectic between alienation and disconnection within the whole of the body politic raises some of the most pertinent questions about the *psychopathology of power* that we we find in these films (and sometimes in his later films). How can we define ourselves in conditions of existential heteronomy and social dislocation? What kind of selfhood do we form under conditions of unfreedom and authoritarianism? Can subjects of totalitarian power ever become free or authentic to themselves? Or indeed can they ever *be* themselves? Do they have a *theory* of what free life in a free society would look like? Ultimately, in our self-alienation do we ever think of what is history and to what degree it determines our human consciousness?

In his later films the concept of alienation is replaced by the existentialist concept of *inauthenticity*. Through memory his heroes struggle to retrieve the lost authentic existence their childhood embodied in privileged moments of self-transcendence or when they were in love or participated in collective social projects. Ultimately, as he moved towards his last films, all projects of self-definition are pushed aside by the effects of *spectrality*, of the domination of an illusory self, as the ultimate form of de-historicization of individual identity under the conditions of corporate capitalism. In Angelopoulos's films inauthenticity is not a fixed existential reality; in privileged, rare, and difficult moments, human conscience becomes empowered to experience the political *communitas* emerging out of mutuality, solidarity, and convergence, or indeed out of the Aristotelian *philia*, friendship.

Authenticity implies the emergence of deep *ontopoetic structures* of existence in history and their rational elucidation through reason and imagination; in such moments of privileged intensity, the individual reclaims its own *being* from the dark abyss of its own unconscious. Natural existence then becomes presence, which means its essence, *ουσία*, is disclosed and is transformed, as Heidegger claimed, into *παρουσία*, through the intensification of its self-thinking. "Thinking is thinking only when it recalls the ἐόν, that which this word indicates properly and truly, that is, unspoken, tacitly. And that is the duality of being and what-is" (Heidegger, 1968: 244). Only then presence becomes actively present and, according to Heidegger, following Parmenides, "being and thinking are one."

For Angelopoulos, however, the identification of being and thinking left out the creative and unexpected *rupture* that all beings can experience and manifest. Individuality means rupture and fissure: something collapses so that the authentic being may emerge. Consequently, he introduces the concept of psyche as the ultimate space where thinking may become *presencing*. In a way, Sigmund Freud's psychoanalytic postulate about the human ego infuses some of his late characters. By elucidating the unconscious, Freud wrote: "[the] intention is, indeed, to strengthen the ego, to make it more independent of the super-ego, to widen its field of perception and enlarge its organization, so that it can appropriate fresh portions of the id. *Where id was, there ego shall be* [*Wo Es war, soll Ich Werden*]" (2001: 80). Freud's revolutionary statement seems to frame the conceptual strain that we find in Angelopoulos's works after 1980. How this happens, if at all, was one of the dominant concerns of his scripts. How does the dark and unknowable unconscious become a lucid and cognizable mental structure? Language is his answer to the question: "I wanted to do something about a poet, and language, reflecting Heidegger's idea that our identity is inextricably tied up with our mother tongue" (Fainaru, 2001: 114).

Furthermore, in *Landscape in the Mist*, *The Beekeeper*, and *The Suspended Step of the Stork*, authentic *presencing* is manifested through strange miracles, symbols, and wonders, like snow, a broken marble hand, an avenging angel, a broken film negative, fragments of forgotten centers of existence, and finally through the quest for a missing father. *Ulysses' Gaze*, the first major film produced in the Balkans after the collapse of communism and during the Yugoslav Civil Wars, explores the ultimate disclosure of authenticity as the pristine gaze in history: the exact moment when the object (the cinematic apparatus) looked back to its own creator and transformed him into an object. In his most complex film, *Eternity and a Day*, authenticity emerges through an enhanced presentation of mortality, or the imminent experiencing of death, which, in the long final magical scene, is also a rebirth and transfiguration. This film, the most eloquent and most silent of his works, is constructed around the central concern that keeps everything together in his late work, the language of life and death. How do we think and talk about death and dying as events of an active conscious existence? What language do we have for our humanity when we have forgotten the words that make it communicable?

In his last film, identity becomes a ghost of itself mediated through machines and its instrumentalization in a post-human world of utilitarian reductionism. Technological apparatuses annihilate existence and make it present itself as occlusion and self-oblivion. *The Dust of Time* replaces the human body and visual presence with photographs, X-rays, and digital imaging by surveillance mechanisms and invisible cameras. As indicated by Guy Debord in his *Society of the Spectacle*, the self becomes the performance of a missing I, of a recollected immaterial self and ultimately of a self without selfhood. With his later works, philosophically, Angelopoulos moves from self-criticism to introspection, from contemplation to skepticism and finally from emotionalism to near nihilism. I don't suggest that he was a nihilist, the same way that Terrence Malick also is not, or even Ingmar Bergman was not; but a profound disbelief in all projects of renewal and politicization colors the images of his last film, replete as it is with the illusionist and impressionistic techniques of Hollywood.

Nihilism is manifested through solipsism: his late characters cannot and do not relate to each other; their stories are so fragmented, although intertwined, that they cannot be linked. The parallel lives of self-imprisonment and mutual exclusion are delineated by the parallel lines of narrative temporality. In the end, the *absurd* emerges as the only possible condition of self-definition. The suicide of one of the main characters is a strange omen: does it end something that had to end or indicate that it is the only solution to a community without horizons? This is the ultimate political question in Angelopoulos's films. Certainly there is no specific or definitive answer to it because Angelopoulos structured his films as open-ended questions, as unresolved dilemmas.

Since the time of Immanuel Kant, the scandal of philosophy is that it cannot even provide a solid and demonstrable proof for the reality of the world. A certain agnosticism appears in some of Angelopoulos's films but it is an agnosticism of means, not of ends. Some of his most demanding works articulate stories without end or conclusion, or indeed closure: they indicate continuity and perpetuity. The cinematic screen inaugurates a new field of thinking, a new method of self-articulation. The real essence of cinematic images is to carry on the latent and ongoing conversations even between people who do not know each other. The lack of closure becomes an incentive to keep searching. The real drama happens around the screen; and cinema points out, as he stated, "The search is not over, the film is not over. In the words of Lars Gustafsson, probably the best contemporary Swedish novelist, 'we never capitulate, we have to go on'" (Fainaru, 2001: 100).

About This Book

The present monograph is divided into five main chapters, each one with its own thematic and methodological approach.

Chapter 2 can be read as an experiential essay that situates my own discovery of Angelopoulos's work. More precisely, following Montaigne's style, the chapter records how I encountered his films, the contextual psychodynamics that defined their reception, and finally the gradual understanding of the *othering subtexts* within his films. The first chapter belongs to the genre of writing which Phillip Lopate calls "personal essay" and aims to foreground a distinct and personalized perception of its topic. In an era of isolating and inflexible orthodoxies, I thought that I had to warn the readers that they encounter an attempt to enter the symbolic universe of an artist by a specific individual whose process of watching movies and thinking about them and through them was defined by Angelopoulos's films in their order of appearance. I grew up with Angelopoulos's films and through them: the chapters that follow also constitute my own intellectual autobiography, as they explore the intellectual biography of Angelopoulos himself.

Chapter 3 frames a discussion of the relationship between film and philosophy, and tries to locate the position of Angelopoulos in the general dialogues about philosophy and cinema while exploring his own contribution to them. Here I focus on his early films, from the so-called "Trilogy of History," and examine some of these preoccupations. Some of them were silently abandoned by Angelopoulos in his late films, others were overtly rejected, while others resurfaced as gestures of reconciliation with his own past.

Chapter 4 focuses on the existential questions of being and dying in the films after his turn (his own Heideggerian *Kehre*) around 1980. First his *Voyage to Cythera* and *The Beekeeper* become the focus of analysis with the uncanny visualization of being and dying they present. Furthermore, the identity, or indeed the subjectivity, of the characters that Angelopoulos presents in these films is also problematized: the transition we see here from Claude Lévi-Strauss and Louis Althusser to Martin Heidegger and Jean-Paul Sartre is discussed as the background philosophical vocabulary to address the new form of historicity and temporality emerging through the re-orientation and re-calibration of his mythopoetics. I also discuss the other films of the same decade, *Landscape in the Mist* and *The Suspended Step of the Stork*, linked through the thematic threads of loss and memory. We cannot really understand what philosophical theory comes out of his engagement with cinematic images, and define his iconosophy, without reference to these simplest and at the same time most existentially problematic films. Both address the most important question of modernity, the absence and silence of the father, and what happens psychologically when the lost father-figure becomes a pointless self-destructive quest or a perpetual deferral of fulfilment.

The chapter also briefly discusses Angelopoulos's epic masterwork *Ulysses' Gaze* and addresses the latent aestheticism that we detect in its structure. In his previous films, Angelopoulos veered off towards intense skepticism and disbelief since it was obvious to him that there were no projects of renewal and emancipation in the European imaginary after 1989. In *Ulysses' Gaze*, a film about the philosophy of political decline, close to Oswald Spengler's *Der Untergang des Abendlandes*, Angelopoulos flirts with the idea of cultural perenniality and an aestheticized justification of existence going back to Friedrich Nietzsche's famous statement. Some of the impasses of this period resurfaced in his later films *The Weeping Meadow* and *The Dust of Time*, fused with new questions and dilemmas that emerged with the new millennium and the gradual transformation of cinema into commodified entertainment. Angelopoulos employed his cinematic philosophy of constant reinvention to oppose the decline of cinema. He did so by foregrounding a renewed historicization of emotions and by exploring, especially in his last film, the inner reality of lonely and broken individuals in a world without redemptive horizons.

Chapter 5 explores his masterpiece *Eternity and a Day* and addresses the most pertinent question of Angelopoulos's ontological thinking: *what kind of redemption can we find in a historical reality without transcendental horizons?* The fusion of Marxist and Heideggerian questions, as delineated by Lucien Goldmann and Kostas Axelos, become the background texts for the exploration of this numinous visual diatribe on dying and the ritual of rebirth, through language and "transfiguration." We detect that in this film Angelopoulos reached a fascinating reconciliation of two totally inimical philosophies and the film is a visual space full of erasures, incongruities, and evasions.

What makes it ontologically relevant is the idea, drawn from ancient Greek philosophy, that the purpose of all creative activity is to "save the phenomena" from obliteration or oblivion. The death of a poet is the emblem of this struggle to salvage the phenomena from their own entropic forces, the self-destructive elements in them, the Freudian Thanatos instinct. It is not simply about the inevitability of death and of Being-towards-Death; more than that the film is about the will to die, the volition to abandon power and rediscover mortality and vulnerability in an almost Homeric fashion. Eros, the other pole in Freud's scheme, appears in his ensuing films, although it is the desire of the powerless to redefine their subjectivity in a world of closed horizons which ultimately remains unfilled or unreciprocated.

In a strange way, the film converses with Simone Weil's interpretation of the *Iliad* as the poem of *force*, in which Homer, through the ravages of war, makes us see people as objects and inanimate realities. *Eternity and a Day* is a counter-cultural film, which deepens our understanding of the Platonic dictum that inaugurates the previous film: *if we want to know about our psyche we must look into someone else's psyche*—a statement that culminates the ethics of visuality in Angelopoulos's whole oeuvre and defines the idea of *bios politikos* that he struggled to visualize in his films. It is on this Platonic statement that I anchor my interpretation of the overall ontology of his films and explore his political anthropology.

In Chapter 6, I examine the concept of the *ontological sublime* which I suggest Angelopoulos articulated in his effort to give a concrete answer to multiple questions about living in a secularized world which does not have any place for the sacred or the numinous. The overwhelming disenchantment with politics today, with what Cornelius Castoriadis called "the era of generalized conformism," which Angelopoulos observed around him with the arrival of the new millennium, aroused a new conceptual problematization about his own previous work. Castoriadis pointed out that this prevailing "kind of generalized conformism" is associated with "the disappearance of true individuals" (Castoriadis 2011: 27), an idea implicitly adopted by Angelopoulos, who constantly envisions the individuated but not the privatized modern citizen. What separates and distinguishes these two social types and mentalities is their own *psyche*, their creative imaginary and the significations it constructs in order to talk about its own topography in history.

The "Visual Essay" at the end of the book foregrounds Angelopoulos's central visual strategy of framing history and historicity through the concept of the gaze. The images culminate in the eyes of the young child in *Ulysses' Gaze* before its expulsion from history. The camera frames the gaze which looks back at us, inviting the viewer into a triangular relationship with the director and the story. The cinematic gaze transforms history into a relationship of emotional experiences, extracting it from the mere knowledge of past events.

What is the value of the work of art in a world without values, in a world that, following Oscar Wilde's truth, knows the price of everything but the value of nothing? If we want to go beyond such cynicism we must problematize not simply the art of making films but also the manner of watching them; as Robert B. Pippin indicated,

> our attention [must be] also drawn in these films, more prominently than in many others, to *the way* that world is cinematically depicted;

what is cinematically highlighted, ignored; why the camera moves and frames events one way rather than another; to what end a musical score signals something sad or ominous; and above all, in many of the films discussed, various figurative and expressionistic means are invoked to suggest that everything we see depicted is not as it seems, must be interrogated, thought about.

2020:11

In a precarious balance between, philosophy, ethics, and aesthetics, the present monograph is both a theoretical synthesis of the ontopoetics of Angelopoulos and an evaluation of his iconosophy. Through the new medium of technological modernity, Angelopoulos explores "the more basic connection [. . .] to be found in a common source of philosophical engagement, life as it is lived, and particularly in film's engagement with the stories we tell ourselves by way of seeking to understand, explain, justify, excuse, and guide ourselves" (Cox & Levine 2012: 18). I wouldn't like to suggest interpretations of the philosophical preoccupations of world cinema in general; the cinema of Kim Ki-duk and Apichatpong Weerasethakul, even the works of Hayao Miyazaki, record a different temporality, which means a different relationship with mortality and finitude. I am specifically interested in the visual engagement of Angelopoulos with the philosophical dimensions of the cinematograph as circumscribed by Robert Bresson's monumental dictum: "The true is inimitable, the false untransformable" (1986: 50).

A *filmmaker*, in Bresson's perception, knows that we cannot quite capture the real and cannot avoid the false altogether. There will always be something absent in all representation which we either project or totally ignore as viewers or thinkers. This glaring absence in the foundational structure of the work of art is disguised under ideological pretensions, religious doctrines, or gratuitous explosions of violence and instinctive sexuality. As Bresson said: "The cinematograph's field is incommensurable. It gives you an unlimited power of creating" (1986: 38).

The changing character of Angelopoulos's philosophical engagements encapsulates the intellectual adventure of many European thinkers, artists, and theorists after the end of World War II who tried to avoid the facile escapism into sensationalism or visual impressionism, making films of "gritty realism." My central point is that

Angelopoulos's cinematic images deprive all visual representations of their rhetorical power, their romantic exaltation of emotions, or the expressionistic magnification of their affect. Angelopoulos is one of the most anti-rhetorical directors. He avoided all forms of montage, especially of Soviet montage, because of its rhetorical illusionism: the gripping rhetoric of Eisenstein's *The Battleship Potemkin* was the exact opposite of Dreyer's *Ordet* and Mizoguchi's *Ugetsu*. Angelopoulos is not alone in denouncing the commodification of the cinematic imaginary; that is to say, the intention to produce a sellable and consumable *objet d' art*. Alexander Sokurov, Terrence Malick, Béla Tarr, Wim Wenders, Werner Herzog, the late Agnès Varda, Nuri Bilge Ceylan try, with differing degrees of success, to address questions about the nature of time, consciousness, death, identity, reality, and ultimately of human nature without succumbing to the impressionistic and distracting techniques that ultimately alienate viewers from their own emotions.

Angelopoulos's evolution from the primary, militant ideas of his political youth to the ultimate concerns of his late maturity indicates the symbolic trajectory of two or probably three European generations' engagement with similar questions. From Marx and Lenin to Jürgen Habermas and Jacques Derrida there exists a long and critical transition mediated by Jean-Paul Sartre, Hannah Arendt, and Cornelius Castoriadis. However, Angelopoulos's medium was not verbal or discursive but visual and iconoplastic: the structure of the film itself becomes the philosophical argument. As Rachel Eisendrath pointed out about the books of the Renaissance, "the structure of a book [. . .] offers a kind of implicit theory of subjectivity" (2021: 4). Angelopoulos's philosophical point of view can be found in the structure of his images, not in the declarations of his characters.

Drawing from Bresson's minimalistic Spartan cinema, Angelopoulos's gaze does not beautify the ugliness of human actions, mythologize the individual, give false coherence to the chaos of history, or mystify the barbarism hiding under every work of art. It does not make universalistic claims or try to serve a purpose beyond the one defined by the cinematic artefact itself and only *indirectly* suggests a universal human essence. But, through its visualizations, it frames the parameters for the emergence, in the intellect and sensitivity of viewers, what he called "the essence of its own being, the autonomy of existence" (Fainaru, 2001: 37); or more precisely the need and the will to become autonomous, the desire to comprehend and unfold their own human essence in their quest for autonomy. Being close to Jean-Paul like Sartre, Angelopoulos explores "the nature of consciousness, to preserve the sovereignty of the individual psyche as a source of meaning. For him, the psyche is coextensive with consciousness," as Iris Murdoch observed about Sartre (1987: 124). Despite a strong anti-didacticism, in the final analysis Angelopoulos's iconosophy has a profound ethical and almost *moralistic* message as given once and for all by R.G. Collingwood's statement: "Art is the community's medicine for the worst disease of mind, the corruption of consciousness" (1958: 336).

Angelopoulos's ontopoetics frame a radical and rhizomatic ethical *theoria* against such corruption of consciousness with profound moral, aesthetic and certainly political implications. As he stated, "you make a film in order to perceive with greater clarity what it is that is not clear in your consciousness" (Fainaru 2001: 109). Filmmaking as the elucidation of the unconscious is the core argument of his *cinephilosophy*—and his films can be adopted to explore and explain many parallel efforts in world cinema. In the way that Daniel Shaw has suggested, "the point of philosophizing about movies should be to enhance our understanding and appreciation of the moving image by thinking through particular films and film genres, and the nature of the filmic experience" (2008: 114).

Angelopoulos's films indicate an indirect form of philosophical engagement which avoids both didacticism and abstract theorization. They "bring philosophy down to earth, [. . .] and show how philosophical issues and concerns enter deeply into our everyday experience" (Falzon 2002: 5). If there is a space for cinematic self-reflexivity that fuses Chris Marker and Jean-Luc Godard with Ingmar Bergman and Andrei Tarkovsky, this is the space for "thinking and poetizing" (Heidegger, 2011: 41) established by Angelopoulos's iconosophy, the space where the osmosis between philosophy and poetry, between σοφία and ποιείν, finds its most problematic and problematized rendering through cinematic images.

Chapter 2

On First Encountering Theo Angelopoulos

Or on the Existential Grounding
of Films

Situating the Writer and the Subject

1974 was a tremendous and wonderful year in recent Greek history. After the July tragedy in Cyprus and the collapse of the Colonels' dictatorship, the Republic was restored in one fatal night and, for the first time in seven years, people could express their views freely and without fear in public. There was enormous passion in the atmosphere, which was a mixture of rage, resentment, and enthusiasm. Everything seemed possible and within our reach. Everything could be demolished and rebuilt anew. Democracy was not only the regime of political freedom and human rights; it also entailed the absolute liberation of the senses, by expanding the limits of the mind and opening the doors of imagination, after many years of oppression and repression. We all believed, especially us, the impressionable and idealistic youth, that a new, fair, and egalitarian society was about to emerge out of the ruins of the military junta and the demise of totalitarianism. Imagination was in power, and we all celebrated its shining path towards the red horizons of the future.

In less than a month, a veritable intellectual explosion began. All banned books, movies, and music became suddenly available. In cheap, and until then illegal, editions we bought the first volume of Karl Marx's *Capital*, Lenin's *The State and Revolution*, Mao Tse Tung's *The Little Red Book*, and Wilhelm Reich's *Listen, Little Man!* Erich Fromm's *The Fear of Freedom*, and Herbert Marcuse's *One-Dimensional Man*, even Marquis de Sade's *Philosophy in the Bedroom* and David Reuben's *Everything You Always Wanted to Know About Sex* (*But Were Afraid to Ask)*. The revolutionary fever spread around the country like wildfire and people who until yesterday were passive spectators of the grand patriotic shows of the dictators about the belligerent bravery of the Greeks took over, literally occupied the streets, with immense energy, creativity, and defiance.

For months, the city of Athens was in an intellectual and political whirlwind which can be seen in Nikos Koundouros's documentary *The Songs of Fire* (1974), filmed during those days of rebellion and civil disobedience, in mass protest rallies, mass-therapy concerts by Mikis Theodorakis, and numerous happenings in the anarchist piazzas of the city. At the same time, the screening of forbidden films, like *Battleship Potemkin*, *The Strawberry Statement*, *The Communist*, and *Pink Flamingos*, all attended eagerly and with the same political passion, was an act of rebellious rejection of the past and its obscurantist legacies. There was a certain euphoric absurdity and political surrealism in the atmosphere, as no one understood or paid any attention to the glaring incommensurability between Sergei Eisenstein and John Waters.

To make things more exciting and confusing, for about two years between 1975 and 1977, when the political system gradually regained its authority and control, the intellectuals who were appointed at the national broadcasting corporation, almost every night after 9.30, screened films that we (especially the younger generations) didn't know existed. German expressionism, Italian neorealism, Vsevolod Pudovkin, Sergei Eisenstein, Alexander Dovzhenko, Youssef Chahine, Satyajit Ray, Glauber Rocha, Vulo Radev, Jean-Luc Godard, Orson Welles, Elia Kazan, Rainer Werner Fassbinder, and at the same time Carl Dreyer, Robert Bresson, Ingmar Bergman, Roberto Rossellini, John Cassavetes, and Andrei Tarkovsky—they were all screened within less than a year and us, the fresh viewers, had to cover the gap between the multicolor musicals that nurtured our youth during the dictatorship and migrate to the critical problematization of reality, especially political reality, through a visual language that we could not yet appreciate. I still remember the night when experimental films by Stan Brakhage and Maya Deren were screened and the consternation they provoked (especially Deren's *Meshes of the Afternoon*) or the moral uproar waged by conservatives the day after Kenneth Anger's *Scoprio Rising* and Andy Warhol's *Lonesome Cowboys* were shown after midnight.

Then suddenly, amid such confusing expansion of our real and imaginative worlds, a new Greek film appeared which caused quite a stir, as the democratically elected conservative government didn't allow it to represent the country at the Cannes Festival in 1975. It was entitled *The Travelling Players*, *O Thiasos* in Greek (maybe the best translation in English would have been *The Thespians*). The title *thiasos* linked the movie to the ancient Greek theatrical tradition while focusing on the modern traveling performers in the countryside. We were told that it was a modern rendering of Aeschylus' *Oresteia*, something that took me some time to understand or even detect when I watched the film. There were no kings or queens, no royal grandeur or aristocratic loftiness. The dialogue was minimal, the acting stylized, almost artificial acting, all wrapped together in a and there was no end or beginning. The only things I could clearly see were low-class squalor, atrocious political violence, and a flat sense of space with muffled colors and stylized almost artificial acting, all wrapped together through a circular sense of time. Watching this film left you in a state of bewilderment. The beginning was also the end and vice versa: time and temporality were the real protagonists in this strangely cold and undramatic presentation of one of the most turbulent and tragic periods of Greek history.

Furthermore, it was almost four hours' long and was made by a certain, rather obscure director named Theodoros Angelopoulos. It was like watching the theater of Bertolt Brecht on screen, only more boring and exasperating, as a famous film critic stated dismissively. However, even the idea that the newly elected democratic government banned a film was enough to make us, still high school students, eager to watch it, even though, according to a famous right-wing actor, it was following the dogmas on art of the Greek Communist Party, which had been legalized only a few months earlier, twenty-five years after the end of the Greek Civil War in 1949.

This was only the beginning of a long and rather convoluted relationship I had with Angelopoulos and his films. Initially, not much was known about him or his work. He had already directed two films between 1970 and 1975, and a short one in 1968 which had won many prizes; but very few people had seen them. It seemed that *The Travelling Players*, his third film, was recognized by everyone as a grand masterwork of political cinema, a genre that was extremely popular in the 1970s especially in countries with political instability. The context of its production, distribution, and screening was also an incentive and an inspiration to watch it, even though we felt that we could not really follow its "message," understand its "meaning," or even explain its style. The glorious linearity in the plots of most of the films we had seen was radically challenged by a completely different way of structuring stories and unfolding their episodes. The famous "unities" from Aristotle's *Poetics* were totally absent and invalidated. Instead, Brecht's theatrical distancing and Russian formalist "defamiliarization" seemed to calibrate its visuality and determine its perception.

As a young man with many intellectual pretensions while involved in chaotic, and always failed, political activism, I watched Angelopoulos's film with intense curiosity, enthusiasm, and bewilderment. Having been formed and conditioned by Hollywood and Greek *vernacular auteurs*, like Yannis Dalianidis, Michael Cacoyannis, Douglas Sirk, and Frank Capra, I found Angelopoulos's films hypnotic and somehow *transcendental*, a feeling that his works of the next decade confirmed. Sometimes, the circumstances in which I watched them were, in my youthful mind, more important than the films themselves, as the density of vision and the complexity of visual language made them somehow impenetrable and incomprehensible. However, it was the first time that I could feel that a film presented something more than what I could see on the screen.

Indeed, it gradually became obvious that something more abstract and quite *theoretical* was imperceptibly expressed through and under the imagery of this film: the elliptical dialogue, the verses of famous poets, the philosophical allusions, the unexpected symbols from arcane rituals, the references to rural realities within we the urban generations had never experienced, all created the suspicion that there was a second plot as a hyper-narrative overarching the obvious ideological statements that dominated the surface structure of the storyline. Indeed, such intriguing signs and wonders which referred to the human condition, the meaning of history, and the nature of human psyche gradually became more obvious and took over Angelopoulos's cinematic *mythopoeia*, constructing an expansive realm of visuality totally unknown and peripheral (or inimical) to the dominant regimes of seeing in his native country.

Furthermore, the context of the film was crucial to accounting for its appeal. All young people of my generation watched *The Travelling Players* mostly because it was an act of resistance against the policing of culture, after the fall of the Dictatorship. Escorted by my father, who started snoring half-way through, I watched it only because I wanted to provoke the police officers who were taking photographs of the people who entered the cinema, and to challenge our teachers at school who warned us against its "anti-national and pro-communist" propaganda.

The same was repeated in 1977 with *The Hunters*, the film, which according to a popular songwriter, "led a whole generation to its deepest yawnings . . ."[1] Certainly, I did yawn profusely as a seventeen-year-old student, who was enthralled by the visual exuberance of *¡Que Viva Mexico!* and at the same time challenged by the bleak pessimism of the Taviani brothers' *Padre Padrone*, while in a feverish mood for rebellion and agitation. I watched *The Hunters* at the grand cinema Capitol, one of the oldest movie theatres of Piraeus; the box-office failure of the film paved the way for the gradual demise of art-house cinemas in Greece. (As the owner of the cinema told me later, the film ruined his finances and he had to transform the cinema into screening exclusively porn films: "Blame it on Angelopoulos," he repeated in despair.) But, at that time, you had to be seen watching an Angelopoulos movie to be regarded as serious, *engaged*, and intelligent. Aside from the theatricality of the gesture, our attendance constituted, as we thought, a bold ideological statement and even a direct form of political activism. His films were the catalysts for changing political interactions and redefining the role of cinema in social relations during the final years of the rebellious 1970s.

Furthermore, his films were rites of passage to political and personal adulthood, leaving behind the infantilizing images of the colorful commercial films that defined our adolescence. They coincided with the collapse of the omnipotent studio system that dominated the post-war decades and the rise of television as the most popular form of family entertainment. For a long period of time, Angelopoulos's "slow" films not only maintained but enhanced the idea of cinematic experience as both a socializing ritual and a visual problematization of the intellectual, or indeed existential, questions of the day. Cinema was not only entertainment and escapism but active questioning of the current political realities and a profound meditation on human existence. It was also a self-reflection on the psychological interiority and the moral conscience of our generation: through images, Angelopoulos's films were problematizing the "psyche" in our self-consciousness, as he himself stated later in his creative trajectory by reference to Plato.

In the 1970s, no other Greek or foreign director's films enjoyed such anticipation and hype. We all thought that they were in themselves something special, almost social and cultural *events* that transcended their cinematic function. Even if we didn't like them, and the next day we watched *Jaws* or *Star Wars* to feel again the magic and escapism that the world of filmic shadows secures for two hours, we did feel compelled to attend Angelopoulos's films simply to reaffirm that there was another dimension in our mind and in our everydayness which his films made us conscious of in constructing a myth about it which linked us to the past while memorializing our present.

Soon, before the end of the decade, as the post-dictatorship state regained its authority, Angelopoulos's films were both the excuse and the alibi for the conformists and petit-bourgeois careerists who took over the institutions of power. They assured the new parasitic class of professional ideologues who took power after the collapse of the dictatorial regime (being a socialist in Greece was not an ideological commitment but an investment strategy) that somewhere in Greek society, someone retained intact their disinterested idealism and romantic innocence, at the very moment when most professed members of the resistance were transformed into ruthless opportunists reaping the benefits of their elevation to power (from both Left and Right). Under these circumstances Angelopoulos's films retained a profound utopian otherworldliness untouched by the cynicism, adventurism, and opportunism that were to envelop the country and its cultural imaginary in the years to come.

On Visual Problematology

Predominantly, Angelopoulos's films problematized our habitual visual temporality, questioning the theoretical and philosophical foundations underpinning their societal structure. Such radical problematization was extremely significant as it happened at a moment when the society of the spectacle took over the cultural and political imaginary in the late 1970s with the gradual domination of television. In the 1980s, Angelopoulos's cinema exited the narrow confines of his own country and conversed with the dominant European cultural imaginary, while later engaging with the global cinematic continuum. His films after 1980 explored the new projects of emancipation that were coming out of the ruins of the Enlightenment and the gradual collapse of communism in Eastern Europe. Indirectly, his cinematic language criticized all forms of technologized mytho-utopias that became dominant in world cinema with the rise of the new studio system of blockbusters from Hollywood or the melodramatic genre that impressed philosophers like Stanley Cavell.

Angelopoulos's slow cinema reflected visually *the crisis of images* that was taking place implicitly around Europe. He was one of the first filmmakers to offer a coherent philosophical system of visuality which I have called elsewhere his "ocular poetics" (Karalis 2017). Indeed, piece by piece, and from one film to the next, he constructed a novel theory of seeing and cinematic perception, going beyond the theories of André Bazin or the formalist aesthetics of Eisenstein. His cinematic language articulated a critical approach towards the various dominant regimes of visuality which were already theoretically problematized by John Berger's *Ways of Seeing* (1972) from a sociological perspective and to a certain degree by Peter Wollen (1969) from the point of structuralist poetics.

However, both Berger and Wollen focused on epistemic meta-structural significations of cinematic images or explored their contextual co-evolution with trends and fashions manufactured by the cultural industry and imposed by hegemonic ideologies. For Angelopoulos, the response to the crisis of images could be made through other images, if the *cinematograph*, in Bresson's sense, wanted to reaffirm the liberating and integrating function of cinema. As filmmaker, Angelopoulos was principally interested in the compositional structure of images presenting a direct *theoretical* critique of dominant visual fields, their mystifying message, and their implied ideological subscripts. As image-maker, an *iconographer* in his own language, he wanted to construct a new visual vocabulary, a radical cinematic language, with many references to the visual systems of perception, but also in a constant and sometimes agonistic dialogue, with the *cinécriture* of directors like

Orson Welles, Yasujiro Ozu, Michelangelo Antonioni, Robert Bresson, Carl Dreyer, and Andrei Tarkovsky, to name a few with whom he remained constantly engaged and sometimes both enraged and enraptured by. His anti-montage and anti-illusionist visual forms are not simple devices to frame another way of telling a story in cinema; they are complex philosophical statements about the power of image-making in an era saturated by mechanically reproduced and commodified images. Given Angelopoulos's origins in the Hellenic tradition, we can point out a semantic differentiation between icons and images; the former foregrounds presentations of the *essence* of the represented and the latter temporalizes *circumscriptions* of their material historicity.

Gradually, his images came to be recognized as converging spaces of contested visualities which he struggled hard to synchronize and, in a classical style, to harmonize: the symmetry and ordered depiction in all Angelopoulos's films characterize the profound *neoclassicism* of his work, especially in what we call his early epic cinema. The contested visual components and their philosophical underpinnings give his films an endless energy for the critical theorization of reality which emerges from within the static *mise-en-scène*, off-camera action, and minimalistic dialogue. In both his political and post-political stages, Angelopoulos wanted to construct critical *existential projects* first for collective and individual emancipation through the de-mystification of the coercive politics of submission that he observed taking over capitalist societies, after the collapse of all projects of social renewal and the rise of nihilism as the central horizon of meaning for self-definition. In a way, his existentialist films constitute Platonic *dialogues*, indeed *visual heterologies*, with the camera being the innocent bystander of unprecedented events and whose discreet presence is only felt indirectly. Settings, colors, and movement bespeak the implied interrogation of themes like memory, mortality, meaning, life, death, and redemption, unexpected questions for a political activist.

As such, his cinema articulates a visual problematics for the ontological grounding of social reality in which individuals try to deal with their own alienation and objectification in history. His visual philosophy came out of a wider context and many frameworks of reference. The "great backlash" happened when a long-term change took place in 1979 as a new world order emerged, with its "strange rebels" (Caryl

2013), the rise of neoliberalism, the triumph of Islamism in Iran, the gradual implosion of the Soviet bloc, and the domination of postmodernist subjectivism as the hegemonic practice in philosophical and intellectual discourse. The gradual disenchantment with politics became dominant also during the late eighties with the grand failure of European socialist parties in France with François Mitterrand, Spain with Felipe Gonzáles, Italy with Bettino Craxi, and Greece with Andreas Papandreou.

Angelopoulos had to grapple with the new realities characterized by "the rise of hypermodernity" according to Gilles Lipovetsky (2005), or "the rise of insignificance" according to Cornelius Castoriadis (1996), the creation of a "burnt-out society," according to Byung-Chul Han (2015). Within the changing context of cultural and conceptual relativism that dominated an expanding globalized world, which accepted the neoliberal ideas while ceasing to believe in "political society," Angelopoulos's films visualized a humanistic vision of lonely individuals who still nurtured the project of social liberation or at least cherished the memory of it as a forgotten, suppressed, or rejected collective dream. After 1980, his cinema took on all lost causes of the European revolutionary movement and tried to explore what led to its demise or what lived on from the failed collective dreaming for truly political societies.

Inevitably, there was a strong *utopian* element in his best films, an imaginary moment in history, which didn't last for long but was achieved in certain short-lived episodes of revolutionary eruption. This brought him close to the early György Lukács and the liberationist aesthetics of Herbert Marcuse, a strange synergy that inaugurated an ambivalent, and inconclusive, dialogue between Karl Marx and Martin Heidegger, between dialectical historicity and fundamental ontology. Traces of such ambivalence can be sensed in his films especially after 1980 and offer the opportunity to explore the dilemmas of left-wing intellectuals and the Left in general in the era of generalized conformism and commodity capitalism. Krishna Kumar called the persistent expansion of human imagination as the "utopian principle," stating that utopia "is about inventing and imagining worlds for our contemplation and delight. It opens up our minds to the possibilities of the human condition" (Kumar 1987: 219). Indeed, this is what the utopian dimension stands for in Angelopoulos's visual universe. Ultimately political activism, experimental art-house films, revolutionary memories were all synthesized within an anthropocentric visuality focused on the axis of the forgotten center, presumably demolished by contemporary posthumanism: the human psyche.

The Dialectics of Context

In the 1970s, the last decade of radical projects and visionary rebellions, a whole new generation thought that they found in Angelopoulos's subversive gaze a new resistance fighter, indeed a cultural hero to be identified with, even though Greek Communist Party officials expressed privately and sometimes in print, under pseudonyms, their pronounced criticism and implicit rejection of his "revisionist, anarchist-leaning, defeatist" art. In a sense, Angelopoulos brought to Greek culture the "lost spring" of the 1960s, as experienced in the rest of the Western world, but gave it a specific orientation which was not libidinal, spasmodic, or indeed destructive, but a recapitulation of what was achieved before. After Angelopoulos's return from Paris, in 1964, Greece had entered a prolonged political and social crisis that led to the Dictatorship of 1967–1974. For almost two decades, Angelopoulos remained an icon of the Left who made the "Party" proud through his international recognition – but it always cautioned viewers about his "unorthodox" ideological proclivities.

But even for the Right, especially the Right in government, his success "proved" beyond reasonable doubt that Greek culture was not provincial, peripheral, or deprived of contemporary relevance. The alternative was a "touristy" image of the country, full of sunshine, sexuality, and carelessness, with exciting landscapes and erotic islands for northern European and American holidaymakers. The alternative to Angelopoulos was *Zorba the Greek* (1965) by Michael Cacoyannis or *The Hook/To Aggistri* (1975) by Errikos Andreou, or indeed Nico Mastorakis's *The Island of Death/Ta Paidia tou Diavolou* (1976), films that presented the strange amalgam that Greek culture was then, and probably still is to this day, of pre-modern, modernist, and post-modernist tendencies all at once and in the same frame.

Meanwhile, as Angelopoulos's filmmaking changed, the country experienced the first peaceful political change of government with the Socialist Party winning the October 1981 elections. The Socialists in power appointed Melina Mercouri, the famous actress of *Stella* and *Never on Sunday*, as the minister for culture who decided to reorganize the Greek Film Center, with ample funding and support, so, as she said, "filmmakers won't have to mortgage their home just to make films." However, it took her almost eight years to bring the new legal framework to the Parliament and when the law passed it was already obsolete; meanwhile, new patterns of production emerged, new technologies were invented, and new cinematic practices were introduced worldwide. Furthermore, the young audiences, formed by reality shows, television films, and video clips, were demanding escapism and entertainment, asking for more comedies or American blockbusters, centered around celebrities and stereotypical plots. When Greek cinema became institutionally strong to confront changing modes of production and dissemination, its films were already antiquated and parochial. Angelopoulos was the only one who understood this cultural asymmetry and tried to address it by incorporating in his work universal or universalizable problematics about time, emotions, and representation, in a way that was truly remarkable as an achievement and, at the same time, provocatively conceptualizable and amenable to philosophical theorization.

During this period Angelopoulos articulated a challenge that confronted the very political conscience and activism of his own fellow-fighters. Suddenly, they were all bewildered when he started his forays into existentialist psychologism. From revolutionary anti-capitalism to surrender to the historic defeat of the Left—that was shocking. In the most opulent cinema of Athens, most viewers thought that they were watching a silent film from another era when his evocative *Voyage to Cythera* (1984) was screened. The questioning had started with *O Megalexandros* (1980) with its quasi-demotic folklorism and its nineteenth-century naïve vernacular narrative of bandits and social outcasts. The jokes about his "silent" films proliferated over time. Angelopoulos's attempt to incorporate silence in his visual narratives as part of the story went totally unappreciated and angered the up-and-coming careerists who were to come to power in the new decade; their minds were full of noise and clatter. Even the appearance of famous actors of the commercial cinema in his films caused considerable tension, as they couldn't fit into the existing pattern of his filmic experience or be connected to their own cinematic past. There was a profound cognitive and aesthetic *dissonance* between what was happening on screen and the way that viewers were used to responding when seeing the spectral bodies of these superstars.

It took the next generation a prolonged, conscious effort to attune themselves to the new temporality of his images and his films after 1984. The serene pace of the narrative looked obtuse, and the sparse dialogue was rather disorientating. Against the background of the *Star Wars* and *Indiana Jones* sagas, and even the provocative films by Luchino Visconti, Rainer Werner Fassbinder and Pier Paolo Pasolini, which employed sexuality and marginality as visual strategies for challenging dominant orthodoxies, Angelopoulos's films were considered dull, prudish, and elitist, at the very moment they were articulating profound existential meditations on the human predicament and radical criticisms of the political and intellectual (or should we say, anthropological?) vacuum that took hold of contemporary European societies.

No explicit sexuality, or sexualization of the body, no drug use or prostitution—not even gender issues, or patriarchal abuse. All his characters are the outcasts of history, outsiders without home and exiles without motherland. Some critics protested about such puritanical and anti-feminist, almost reactionary, cinema. In *Ulysses' Gaze*, six female characters are performed by the same person, representing something more like a male fantasy than fully formed imaginary female characters. The fact that Angelopoulos's cinema presented *all* its characters as sacrificial victims to invisible and incomprehensible political structures simply evaded the attention of his critics.

Yet, whoever watched his films in good faith understood the philosophical and anthropological subtexts informing their visual architecture. When, later in the 1990s, postmodernism prevailed in the academic sphere, the films were ruthlessly criticized and rejected, ignoring the fact that Angelopoulos was one of the first directors who dared to cannibalize his own films and reassemble his images through self-irony and self-subversion. His sublime *Landscape in the Mist* presents one of the most scathing criticisms of his own earlier films together with their ideology and aesthetics, as if the thinker in him was revising his own previous ideas, advocating for their negation and implicit rejection. In this analysis, I refer to this as his own *Kehre*, "turn" in the Heideggerian sense, but could also be the same break as between the early and late Ludwig Wittgenstein, a topic that needs further discussion.

As with the films of most great directors of the previous decades, like Antonioni, Bergman, Fellini, and Kurosawa, Angelopoulos's films suddenly became strange oddities from a forgotten past as the esteemed tradition of the *auteur*, or the director as celebrity, was replaced by a new star system of young, sexy, and seductive actors or opportunistic, amoral, and ultimately nihilistic directors, like Lars von Trier or Luc Besson. Furthermore, while the socialists in power behaved in the same way as the conservatives, providing funds to their party members and producing some of the most forgettable films ever made, Angelopoulos's films were at odds with their very own ideological and philosophical presuppositions. When the Soviet Bloc collapsed between 1989 and 1991, viewers could sense the existential *aporia* and emotional numbness permeating the storylines of his films, challenging the positive and optimistic project of social liberation that the Left supposedly advocated.

Even reviews by certain "fellow travelers" and friends in the mainstream media, newspapers, and magazines started becoming blatantly critical and, some of them, quite dismissive. Angelopoulos responded infrequently but the famous film critic Vasilis Rafailidis went full steam against his "jealous colleagues who struggle in vain to blackmail History," (2003: 11) with their ignorance and stupidity. Rafailidis, who was a close friend and associate of Angelopoulos, went even further and in his many books on Greek history considered him as one of the very few genuine creators of culture, a Homeric mythmaker, as he called him, a unique thinker through images unparalleled in the country's history over the past three hundred years (although Rafailidis died in 2000 and never saw the reorientations of Angelopoulos's late art). Rafailidis was one of the few film critics who understood the *transcultural* significance of Angelopoulos's films and the universalistic philosophical agendas that underpinned their structure.

Through his analysis, despite its stylistic excesses which included heavy cultural theorizing and occasional conspiracy theories, we can situate Angelopoulos in the context of radical theoretical visions about identity, memory, and ultimately image-making. Angelopoulos went further and infused his materialistic perception of image-making with a profound problematization of existence and mortality, love and loss, trauma and redemption. From his early idea of film "not as a surrogate but as a vehicle" (Fainaru, 2001: 28), he moved to the idea of the film as the recapturing of "the dreamlike state it was conceived in" (Fainaru 2001:

39). From the reality of history as lived experience to the representation of reality as dreaming and imagining, Angelopoulos's cinema expresses a radical *turn* in his filmmaking, marking a shift in the representational codes in the cultural imaginary of the European Left.

This highly challenging osmosis of ontological and political concerns is at the heart of Angelopoulos's work, especially after 1980, which is punctured by continuity and discontinuity at the same time. The political projects of social revolution became interiorized and internalized: they expressed "the conflict between memory and non-memory" (Fainaru 2001: 53) and the struggle with his personal unconscious to "imagine" a new symbol for the never-ending human adventure, as Harvey Keitel declares in the end of *Ulysses' Gaze*. As Herbert Marcuse observed, "the authentic utopia is grounded in recollection" (Marcuse 1979: 49). The recollection of imagined homelands became gradually the paradise lost of his stories and characters, framing the utopian vision of a *topos* of existential communion, and indicating a dramatic disenchantment and disillusionment with dominant projects of self-definition and self-articulation.

However, it would be simplistic to juxtapose an early anti-humanist Angelopoulos to a later humanist one; there is a distinct transmutation of style, psychology, and philosophy in his work which needs more exploration and informed discussion. There is certainly a 'later' Angelopoulos marked by a specific paradigmatic shift from the *political homing* of people through historical action to the *ontological homelessness* of individuals through traveling. The quest for or the *nostos* to an originary home in the early films becomes an endless existential journey through the upheavals of history and the gradual loss of horizons *away* from home. Homer's *Odysseus* is transformed into Dante's *Ulysses*. The Homeric desire for *nostimon hemar* (the day of homecoming) mutated into the Dantean *"l'ardore"* (ardor) to explore the ends of history.

After *The Suspended Step of the Stork* (1991), all his films are about perpetual journeys through the ruins of history and the demise of cultures. This caused Angelopoulos himself a certain existential numbness, an *amechania* as it is called in Greek, and his last films were anxiously struggling with the questions of homelessness, deterritorialization, and exile. However, his unexpected and tragic death in 2012, when he was working on his film *The Other Sea*, indicates that the answer to this question – which might have envisaged something like a post-historical utopia focused on transient existential synergies and unpredictable randomness – was left inconclusive.

Note on Philosophical Subscripts

Angelopoulos as philosophical filmmaker embodied a transition from the dominant French structuralist Marxism in the 1960s and 1970s, to Kierkegaardian and Sartrean themes in the 1980s, followed by Heideggerian and Marcusean ontological questions in the 1990s, and culminating with Arendt's *vita contemplativa* in his last films. The continuous philosophical engagement of his films with certain persistent questions of post-Enlightenment modernity makes his work the symbolic space for the gradual reinterpretation of all projects of social renewal within the context of the privatized society of consumer capitalism in what Guy Debord called "the society of the total spectacle" (1995).

The initial optimism and confidence that politics could change the world and consequently the human condition was gradually transformed into a certain pessimism and "dread" (in Kierkegaard's sense) in his later films. The emergence of existential loss and melancholia, fused with poignant reflections on mortality and death, was also connected with a profound meditation on the ability of human creativity to transform reality into the space of positive un-concealment of genuine and authentic *inner* existence—an idea that brings him close to an almost Platonic vision of beauty as recollection, even when Angelopoulos constructs numinous images of old age, suicide, and death.

On the other hand, these were, and still are, universal questions, that can be found in Kurosawa as well as Ozu, Chahine, Kiarostami, Ousmane Sembène, Glauber Rocha, or Ababacar Samb-Makharam, to name just a few directors from global cinemas. Rafailidis responded to the accusation that his cinema was not national cinema that didn't exhibit the characteristics of "Greekness" by declaring that Angelopoulos's films "made us understand that you are not Greek if you are not European" (2003: 65). He also pointed out that Angelopoulos constructed a new perception of what it means to create Greek art, "based on history and not myths," and more importantly beyond any religious understanding of culture which advocates for "a pseudo Greekness which is nothing else but Christianity deceitfully called Greekness" (Rafailidis 2003: 67).

A distinct characteristic of Angelopoulos's work is the glaring absence of religious awe and mystery—but the absence of all religion doesn't really mean absence of religiosity. Three of his films, *O Megalexandros*, *Landscape in the Mist* and *Ulysses' Gaze*, are structured around religious mythographies and evangelical references. In its philosophical *presuppositions* Angelopoulos's project was not religious but political; yet its *consequences* are philosophical and anthropological, as we will analyze here. However, in order to achieve this, he consciously employs religious imagery and even liturgical numinosity (*O Megalexandros*), indicating that there is something deeper happening in the story: the sociopathic character of the film is at the same time the catalyst for a radical transformation of the social and the political. Yet the idea that an individual can bridge the realm of the numinous with the realm of the profane leads to the fracture of the political as the space of political community based on free will and the inevitable fallibility of the human mind.

In a sense, Angelopoulos was pointing to what Eric Voegelin called the "political religions of modernity" and the idea that the realm of history cannot be confused with the realm of the sacred. The extreme secularization in the West and the attempt to experience a post-Christian world led to "the basic emotion of natural abandonment (*kreatürlichen Verlassenheit*) as a state of dreamlike unreality, of coldness, of sealed-off loneliness, the soul breaks out of this state with a burning fervour to be united with the sacred whole" (Voegelin 2000: 67). From this state of abandonment, the modern subject struggles to retrieve a sense of unity through unconscious rituals and an opaque symbolic language that form a substitute religion creating an illusion of an imaginary community. Angelopoulos insists on "the autonomy of existence" and therefore avoids following any path towards transcendentalism or spiritualism, which sometimes bedevil the work of Tarkovsky, for example. Following Voegelin again we can find in Angelopoulos's films "Schelling's fundamental question—Why is there something; why is there not nothing?" followed by the other question, "Why is it the way it is?"—the question of theodicy" (2000: 71). Angelopoulos keeps posing this question of why things are the way they are and therefore transports the question from a form of theodicy that Voegelin would have preferred to a new way of understanding *anthropodicy*: why humans act the way they act and how they understand their own actions.

Angelopoulos's films engaged with or indeed articulated philosophical questions but gave them cinematic answers, not only through the medium of images but through the semantic surplus of images which is not translatable into words. His images expanded the limits of visual comprehension and turned interpretation towards post-verbal and post-lingual forms of conceptualization. This can be seen in the irruptions of otherworldly omens in his brilliant *Landscape in the Mist* and the mysterious and transformative being-with-death in his *Eternity and a Day*. Philosophically, these two films frame his most important contribution to the exploration of the theme of historical anthropodicy, which unfolded in his work after 1984, exploring the question of human suffering in a world without belief in metaphysical redemption.

Certainly, these are not questions unique to Angelopoulos; Bresson, for example, addressed parallel questions in a distinctly Catholic way, in his most misunderstood movies *Le Diable probablement* (1977) and *L'Argent* (1983). In Angelopoulos, the absence of religion creates contested spaces between signs and signifiers. The aesthetic and the political, *theoria* and *aufheben*, seem to intersect but without really fusing in his films. The humanist in him could not tolerate the subjection of human autonomy to any transcendental order. Hence, he didn't try to subsume the aesthetic dimension of his films into any pre-existing philosophical axioms or principles about representation. As Robert Sinnerbrink pointed out, "the 'film as philosophy' debate is an aesthetic as well as a meta-philosophical dispute: one that challenges us not only to think through the philosophical significance of cinema but also to entertain the possibility that cinema might expand our conception of philosophy" (2019: 7).

The deep changes that Angelopoulos was constantly introducing to his own filmic practice are complex and multi-layered. He struggled to universalize the Greek visual experience by establishing a language based on what J.J. Gibson called "formless invariants" (in Gordon 2004: 143–82) and David Bordwell termed "planimetric shots" (2005: 173). In the beginning, the visual experience of his films is puzzling and confusing, almost awkward. Static shots in horizonless depth of field circumscribing forms re-enacting history. The early films, despite their radical iconography, are cold and detached formalist architectures emptied deliberately of all psychological depth. The de-psychologization of characters led to geometric abstractions, indeed to visual symbolism without inner life. Hence, the near perfection of formal arrangements lacked atmosphere and mood: no human warmth infuses the images of *The Travelling Players* and especially of *The Hunters*, the coldest masterwork of European cinema.

Ultimately, such self-conscious style became somehow alienating: sometimes, Angelopoulos pretends, or at least tries hard, to be Angelopoulos. His early films, as we will see, become a constant *reductio ad absurdum*: can we have history without historical consciousness, without historicity? Can we talk about the human condition without exploring the actual experience and individual ethos of those who embody it? How can we know that the other is like us if we have no conceptual equivalent of our common predicament as humans? These meta-philosophical questions started becoming dominant with *Voyage to Cythera*, culminating with the grand Balkan epic *Ulysses' Gaze* and finding their most "sublime" expression in *Eternity and a Day*.

It was as if in this period Angelopoulos discovered the early humanistic Karl Marx of the *Philosophic Manuscripts of 1844* and abandoned the Althusserian and Lévi-Straussian epistemologies of ahistorical and suprahistorical structures and overdetermined identities. In this film, and we must also add *The Weeping Meadow* (2004), *The Dust of Time* (2009), and his last short film *Mundo Invisível* (2012), Angelopoulos revisited Marx's liberating realization:

> Every one of your relations to man and to nature must be a *specific expression*, corresponding to the object of your will, of your *real individual* life. If you love without evoking love in return—that is, if your loving as loving does not produce reciprocal love; if through a *living expression* of yourself as a loving person you do not make yourself *a loved person*, then your love is impotent—a misfortune.
>
> MARX 1988: 140

This foundational statement must be supplanted by Marx's eighth "Thesis on Feuerbach" stating that: "Social life is essentially *practical*. All mysteries which mislead theory into mysticism find their rational solution in human practice and in the comprehension of this practice" (Marx 1988: 143). Class consciousness or even political engagement is not enough to redeem the creative anxiety and the longing for fulfilment.

Although already delineated in films like *Voyage to Cythera*, the impossibility of love becomes the critical element of his cinema, although there remains in his dealing with this emotion a sense of awkwardness and distance. It is interesting that the very charged Greek word *agape* is never uttered in most of his films. In a sense Angelopoulos was close to T.S. Eliot's perception of love as distancing unfamiliarity: "Who then devised the torment? Love. / Love is the unfamiliar Name . . ." (Eliot 1970: 207). In the implicit dialogue between Marx and Eliot, it is the emotion of Love that renders itself unable to be shared and give people a common destiny. In the malaise of the late twentieth century, feelings themselves create the inability of reciprocity and mutuality: in Angelopoulos, the more his characters feel, the lonelier they become. The force of their emotions makes them feel abandoned and forgotten, as love is not the Christian centripetal force of the universe, "the Love that moves the Sun and other stars," but the feeling that shows social dissociation and therefore the inability to build a new *polis* based on the bonds of friendship, reciprocity, and mutuality.

Nevertheless, Marx and Eliot frame Angelopoulos's metaphysics of social and existential experience focused on a person in the pursuit of reciprocity within the de-humanizing realities of contemporary social life, like war, alienation, exile, and despair. With this premise, there was no place for metaphysics, mysticism, or religion in Angelopoulos's ocular ontology. His anthropodicy could not presuppose or lead to any form of transcendental order that would justify in any way the human phenomenon. The real implies the actual presence, or the imagined absence, of the concrete and specific. There is *the* specific other but not some form of abstract Otherness. His last films precisely explore the chaotic labyrinth of history in which the only threads for orientation and closure are given by the corporeal existence of specific individuals in luminous and numinous encounters.

In *The Weeping Meadow*, reality becomes eschatological only after being created by the individuals and their community. The refugees create a new life in a new community which is soon dissolved and vanishes. The utopian project of building a new city is constantly imploding. Power relations, social hierarchies, but most importantly the confusion and chaos of human emotions undermine and ultimately destroy the city as the topos of restoration and healing. The central characters in *The Weeping Meadow* are entangled in a web of emotions without fulfilment and redemption: the stepfather becomes the lover and the stepdaughter falls in love with her stepbrother and both elope, with their children separated and ultimately fighting against each other in the Civil War.

The old tragic theme from the Theban myth of Oedipus and his destiny indicates that Angelopoulos wanted also to revive the feeling of the *tragic* as the ancients understood it. In a way, it is Sophocles' perception of hereditary sin, a *hamartia* that is transmitted unconsciously through generations and leaves everything human under an imminent danger. Historical experience remains existentially voiceless because it is unpredicted and undetermined; as Wittgenstein stated: "Not how the world *is*, is the mystical but that *it is*" (1958: 187). Within such dialectics of necessity and contingency, in some of his films, Angelopoulos constructed a concrete vision of the miraculous as epiphany in everyday life. In other films, Angelopoulos depicted a vague vision of the numinous as the approaching sense of an end. This oscillation between the miraculous and the numinous constitutes one of the thematic threads informing the understanding of his work throughout its development.

It is obvious that Angelopoulos could never compromise and never became complacent with his achievement; he knew that every work of art is never finished and was therefore open-ended and re-signifiable. "I am satisfied with the music," he said in a moment of self-criticism about *The Beekeeper*. "However, I wonder whether there weren't other solutions, for still there is something that bothers me, the *feeling* that at times, the music is not sufficiently integrated in the picture' (Fainaru, 2001: 140). The shifts in epistemological frameworks became also shifts in the visual articulation of meaning. Angelopoulos understood that the structured circularity of his early films was not sufficient or commensurable to the visual fecundity of his later dramas of interiority and inwardness.

Yet he never felt strong, or certain, enough to denounce the ideological orientations of his early years. His films are *flawed* masterworks because they struggle to fuse elements of disparate political temporalities and dissonant theoretical connotations. There are indeed many stylistic elements in his films that feel "not sufficiently integrated" because of the scope of his efforts and the fusion of genres he attempted. In that sense, Angelopoulos not only undermined and de-structured hegemonic genres but made his films spaces of colliding signifiers, rendering them unplaceable and unclassifiable. Until the end, he remained *un homme à part*, an isolated case, whose cinematic affinities could be traced beyond the borders of his native tradition.

There is also an element we must discuss before investigating his ocular ontopoetics. There are no real characters in his films because he wanted to avoid the romantic mythologies of individualism that dominate contemporary (especially American) cinema. What is important in his dramaturgy is how the plot is structured, and the ancient mythos under the plot, which makes the story not an individual case or even a personal incident but the dramatic re-enactment of various aspects of a *diachronic* question. The director is diffused equally among the forms that shape his narrative, but you cannot really claim that a specific character speaks the mind, or the ideas, of Angelopoulos himself.

The strong presence of music, sometimes more imposing than the images, made some of his films quasi-operas closer to his negative other Eisenstein than to the silent psychodramas of Antonioni or Bergman. There are some sublime moments of poetry, the visualized poetry of the ineffable, which we encounter even in his least successful movies. Yet in most of them you feel that Angelopoulos, *the last auteur of post-war political modernism*, was grappling with difficult and challenging questions of cinematic visuality in his philosophical conceptualization. The personal and the collective seem both at odds and at peace with each other. Angelopoulos stressed the strong autobiographical background of his films: the idea that he was simply political is quite erroneous and misleading. As Plato's dialogues record and express the changing philosophical views of Plato based on his own life experience, so Angelooulos's films anchor themselves to different philosophical questions and give his own answers.

Because of them, we can situate Angelopoulos amongst philosophers and philosophical filmmakers, such Martin Heidegger, Herbert Marcuse, Hannah Arendt, Terrence Malick, Terence Davies and Andrei Tarkovsky. As stated at the outset, the purpose is to broaden the field of the interpretation of his work and not simply repeat what has been stated by other scholars who focus on the political ideas of his films but not on their philosophical structure. In his pioneering study on Angelopoulos, Andrew Horton listed 'Twelve Characteristics of Angelopoulos' Cinema' circumscribed by what he called 'the *experience* of watching his movies' (1999: 5–17). Horton analyzed with clarity and succinctness certain aspects of his filmmaking and offers a comprehensive view about the *contemplative* character of his films and the implied aesthetical and political micro-texts in their structure. Here I am not interested in the structure of his films from the point of film studies, or even from that of cinema history; on the contrary, I attempt to explore the philosophical implications (intended or unintended) of Angelopoulos's *theoria* of cinematic images and the ways they have reformed and recalibrated our ability to look at reality and make us aware of our *presence* in society.

I suggest that Angelopoulos's films constitute contemporary Platonic dialogues, *heterological visualizations*, which dramatize human reflexivity and interiority through various iconographic idioms. In a sense, his films can be seen mainly as epistemological treatises around the question of human nature as historical creation and cultural praxis. The grim natural background of his films, in the mountainous areas of the Balkans under dark skies, foregrounds the separation between nature and humanity. Nature, as we see in the preserved corpse of the partisan in *The Hunters*, or the archetypal silence of the mountains in the *The Reconstruction*, remains unfriendly and unwelcoming to the events of human history. Avoiding any biological determinism, Angelopoulos presents human activity as the result of absolute freedom, drawing from Sartre's famous statement: "Man is condemned to be free. Condemned, because he did not create himself, in all other respect; because, once thrown into the world, he is responsible for everything he does" (1985: 23). In his late films Angelopoulos examines the consequences of such a statement and the various ways that the event of our freedom empowers us to envision our finitude and mortality, in a world which has denounced the possibility of any metaphysical redemption or psychological closure.

Freedom for Angelopoulos is the ability to create and re-create the real and therefore change it. In his philosophical ontology, we can change things because of our birth: we can be political because of this primary and unique event of our natality. Natality saves humans from the horizonless and claustrophobic world of Heidegger's being-towards-death. As Hannah Arendt stressed, after the rejection of all faith and eschatology, "Modern man was thrown into the inwardness of introspection where the highest he could experience were the empty processes of reckoning of the mind, its play with itself" (1958: 320). Work, the idea of *animal laborans*, is Arendt's response to the loss of faith and therefore of the shared world of classical polis. This is what

Angelopoulos's ultimate exploration frames in films like *Ulysses' Gaze* and *Eternity and a Day*. As Arendt stated, "the only thing that could be now potentially immortal, [. . .] was life itself, that is the possibly ever-lasting life process of the species mankind" (1958: 321).

Beyond our work, between our birth and our death, there also exist the countless human beings we encounter, starting with our parents, which impact on our directions, inclinations, and desires, or indeed define the images we construct to talk about us and them. The lost father, the absent mother, the missing siblings, and the void they left behind are from the beginning some of the most pertinent philosophical questions about origins, belonging, and identity that we find in Angelopoulos's films. In most of them, the absent father remained always the centripetal axis of orientation. The scripts frame this quest in various ways, trying to find images of the paternal origins that cannot be found anywhere today but in the remote past. The script of *The Beekeeper* ends with a strange and somehow anti-Angelopoulos note, which didn't find its translation into images: "The rain glides over his distorted face. His right-hand knocks on the ground with the old language of his comrades in prison, as an invocation to an unknown God". (Angelopoulos, 1986: 63). It is strange to find in Angelopoulos the idea of an unknown God, with its biblical references and immense metaphysical consequences. Who is this unknown God of history whose language is secret and was invented by persecuted comrades in prison? Furthermore, his father was the projectionist of the cinema which screened Hitchcock's *I Confess* and the only thing that the son can find in the ruins of the abandoned temple of art is "the old mask of my father" (Angelopoulos 1986: 58).

There is an unexpected and strange gesture on behalf of Angelopoulos's symbolic language towards one of the most profound and popular philosophical treatises in contemporary Greek, *The Saviors of God* (1927) by Nikos Kazantzakis. In one of the grand statements of the final Creed we read: "I Believe in the Innumerable, the Ephemeral Masks which God has Assumed throughout the Centuries, and behind his Ceaseless Flux I Discern an Indestructible Unity" (Kazantzakis 1960: 130). The idea of the masks of God was later popularized by the great books of Joseph Campbell; however, the mystical concept of the real as the mask of God is given by Angelopoulos the strange semantic twist that the cinema itself is a form of epiphany in history, or at least a ritual that leads to an epiphany, which means to the realization and understanding that there is something uncanny (*unheimlich*) in everyday experience which remains beyond definition and beyond visualization. Such hyper-reality becomes Angelopoulos's philosophical attentiveness over the visible and its various forms. However, between sounds and forms there are two dimensions of being that Angelopoulos struggled hard to incorporate, as we constantly find in the diegetic evolution of his films: silence and the void.

Angelopoulos is the master-worker of icon-images which attempt to frame the invisibility of the uncanny in history; and for him, all historical action is ultimately a mask of the *unheimlich*. He never stated this explicitly but, in his most crucial films, historical materiality and objective space are ruptured by uncanny signs and wonders, which come out of nowhere and disappear back into nowhere. In a way, he stands next to El Greco in his understanding of how images transfigure the real and the concrete into mysterious openings through which a transcendental order enters history, as we see in *View of Toledo* (1596–1600), for example. This is not a romantic quest for the absolute or for the disclosure of Being; it indicates, however, the Platonic perception that prevailed during the Byzantine and the Renaissance art, according to which the artist was "bathing his canvases in *lumen*—that inner, incorporeal light which flows everywhere inexhaustibly and is the manifestation of that vital energy which lies at the origin of life and movement—and eliminating mere *lux*, the light we perceive, which illuminates earthly bodies" (Guinard 1956: 111).

Angelopoulos's iconosophy occupies the tense visual space of such essential luminosity, of *transcendental immanence*, when the boundaries of the real break down and the *kenotic* emptiness of existence takes hold of the cinematic screen. (It is important to remember that in none of his films does the word "end" appear that we usually see at the end of each film.) The end of *Ulysses' Gaze* is precisely about the unrepresentable void: the origin of being that transcends all potential manifestations in history. The screen is blank like Kazimir Malevich's supremacist composition "White on White" depicting *pure space* before the birth of forms. In the pure space of the cinematic screen which we see at the end, an infinity of potential icons can be envisioned and projected. Pure space is pure because it makes time for the emergence of the unseen and the unrepresented. In such moments, Angelopoulos points towards the experience of pre-rational thinking, of the work of art as emerging out the aniconic, tracking down, its existence as flux and movement. The white screen illuminates the tragedy of history: "an empty luminous frame flows on the walls of the destroyed Cinematheque and the music of the orchestra and the night" (Angelopoulos 1995: 112), writes Angelopoulos on the final page of *Ulysses' Gaze*. The "empty luminous frame" is the fecund void, the being in time and being made of time. Linked to such formal luminosity are the images of his first films, so concrete, material, and solid, where the presence of a transcendent lumen defines their essential historicity and temporality.

Aesthetically, however, instead of dividing and separating the formal unity of his films, we can detect their figurative complementarity and formal correlations, linked together in an organic way, through the transition from the iconic to the exploration of the aniconic. Angelopoulos's empty spaces, especially the sky, the sea and the vast expanses of his late films, situate the human drama in its proper cosmological reality of the unrepresentable, and the un-visualized. In the absence of images, the filmmaker must struggle to indicate the traces of lost unities or imagine the elements of new configurations. It is this effort which entails, or even presupposes, a moral valuation of human finitude, fully explored in *Eternity and a Day*. Human life is primarily a natural phenomenon; but is it also a moral one? Is there a moral center within the universe, or the pluriverse, of physical reality? Can we extract a pattern of ethical choices out of the historical experience of humanity? Angelopoulos grapples and struggles with these questions in his late films, both obsessively and inconclusively.

Chapter 3

On Seeing Films Philosophically

Or From Politics to Existence

Can Filmmakers See Philosophically?

The present chapter is an investigation of Angelopoulos's "iconosophy" in its theoretical and conceptual dimensions, addressing both its presuppositions and consequences. It explores his attempt to make the cinematic screen the *topos* for the articulation of an *existential phenomenology* circumscribing a certain mythopoetics of everyday life as eruption and emergence within the visuality of cinema. His filmic territory is inhabited by complex theoretical dilemmas which are presented in the form of images, while being enwrapped by the aural evocations and narrative markers appropriate to the cinematic medium. In a way, and this point will appear on many occasions throughout the philosophical investigation of his films, the whole approach here starts with Plato's famous yet deceptively innocent remark in the *Republic*: "The question you are asking needs an answer given through an image" (Plato 2000: 191).

There are various translations of the Greek word *eikon*, as parable, analogy, fable, or even myth; yet all of them are defined by the verbal framework of the dialogue and their conceptual in-framing through various philosophical ideas in juxtaposition or complementarity. Plato's question is extremely prescient, elaborated mostly through poetic imagery and pictorial representation, but cinema framed the best answer to the Platonic quest for an ultimate *eikon*. Cinematic "kinetic" images depicted the symbolic disclosure of objective forms through their material presence on film while at the same time foregrounding the ontological foundations of their existence. There is a profound ambiguity in our approach to images, especially cinematic images. In a lecture aptly called *The Evil Demon of Images*, Jean Baudrillard analyzed the paradox of cinematic images as "sites of the *disappearance* of meaning and representation, sites in which we are caught quite apart from any judgement of reality, thus sites of a fatal strategy of denegation of the real and of the reality principle" (1984: 27). Angelopoulos knows all too well about the constitutive ambiguity in the construction of images: "The cinema is a disease," he stated. "But the cinema is very strong—one cannot live without it. It's not just a medium of expression, it's a form of life" (Fainaru 2001: 35).

Drawing from Plato, the present chapter suggests that we can *see* his films not simply as ideological texts, aesthetic statements, psychoanalytic symptoms, or technological artefacts but as visual forms of conscious life and therefore as embodying a symbolic reflexivity on the human phenomenon. The Parthenon, Hagia Sophia, and Notre Dame are not simply marvels of architecture and engineering. They presuppose and embody different foundational elements — not always visible yet actively present: a theology, a cosmology, and an anthropology. Even works of secular modernity, like the Statue of Liberty, the Eiffel Tower, the Sydney Opera House, or the Golden Gate Bridge, embody similar foundational and elemental structures, probably in a reverse order from those of religious buildings, embodying the values and the ideals of an anthropocentric cosmology. They are indeed visual depictions putting forward a specific structuring of the world and therefore a specific encoding of its meaning in their own terms specific.

There are analogous claims to be made about filmmaking that move beyond a reductionist psychoanalytic, sociological, aesthetic, or formalist understanding of films' existence as human artefacts (especially in complex works like those by Angelopoulos, but also Tarkovsky,

Malick, Bresson, Ozu, to name just the most prominent). Each film embodies a specific encoding of the visible world *intentionally* and as such it emerges out of a specific ontological grounding while pointing towards a specific historical milieu. Philosophical filmmakers emphasize such grounding as the dominant axis of their work: their films do not include or imply a philosophical or a theoretical system. They *are* themselves philosophical textualizations and can be read as a series of propositions expressed visually.

Usually, we presume or indeed expect that a movie be informed by, contain, or propagate a specific point of view, political, aesthetic, or philosophical. For example, when we watch Eisenstein's *Battleship Potemkin*, Bresson's *Diary of a Country Priest*, Bernardo Bertolucci's *1900* or Malick's *The Thin Red Line*, we immediately sense that their storyline is almost independent, a mythopoetic narrative to which philosophical references are added *a posteriori* borrowed from Marxism, Catholicism, psychoanalysis, or other speculative thinking. There are some notable exceptions in this great canon of filmmakers who make cinema *ancilla philosophiae*. I would point out especially a number of Japanese directors from Ozu to Kurosawa, even Nagisa Oshima, with their "virtual elimination of plot" (Mars-Jones 2011: 6) and their "sublime indirectness" leaving ample space "for some Zen vagueness" (Mars-Jones 2011: 238). However, there are others in whose works anthropology, philosophy, and ontology are so intricately interwoven in their filmmaking that they define the specific experience of viewers and the ways that the cinematic images are interpreted. Or as Donald Richie observed about Japanese aesthetics, they are "more concerned with process than with product, with the actual construction of a self than with self-expression" (2007: 15) which is precisely the case with Angelopoulos's sense of personal and collective self: it is a process and a project but not a product or an end in itself.

I would mention here three directors whose films embody complex philosophical perspectives: Dreyer, Kubrick, and Tarkovsky. Each one of them used the cinematic inventory of camera, mise-en-scène, lighting, acting, narrative, music, and so on, as specific approaches to the foundational ontological axis of each of their films. What makes meaningful the sequence of images, words, and formations that constitute the "deep structure" and the "architectural skeleton" of the film. Dreyer's *Ordet*, for example, is a passionate treatise on the possibility of miracles in an unbelieving world, Kubrick's *2001: A Space Odyssey* an elucidation of evolutionary randomness, and Tarkovsky's *Stalker* a probing into the experience of nothingness. They invite different readings, indeed different justifications of their very conceptual structuration. Geoff Dyer went far when he wrote: "*Stalker* has always invited allegorical readings, and since the film has something of the quality of a prophecy, these readings are not confined to events that had occurred by the time the film was made" (2013: 40).

Considering a film as a prophecy is a far-fetched analogy, especially for Tarkovsky. As Maya Turovskaya observed: "*Stalker* seems a more 'theoretical' film, and perhaps for that reason it has a quality of lassitude, as though the artist now pausing to take breath before the next step" (1989: 109). In a strange way, Angelopoulos's *O Megalexandros* or *Voyage to Cythera* can be read as prophecies about the historical circumstances that followed: the demise of the personality cult, the collapse of socialism, and the redefinition of borders through the mass waves of refugees that started arriving in Europe. But they were also historically accurate diagnoses of what was to come and eventuate.

There are many more sub-texts in these films, but what holds them together as unities is the ontological axis they try to exemplify through cinematic means. We must also add another dimension: the philosophical axis is not always present or indeed visible in many films by the directors named we just mentioned. Cinema is the art of the spectacle and the specular; on many occasions, the need to produce something acceptable to audiences in advanced capitalist societies, in which consumerism has taken dimensions of a secular religion, is de facto imposed by the demands of the industry. However, even within structures – such as the melodramas, we can simply mention here the hyper-realistic melodramas of Douglas Sirk, the tragicomedies of Charlie Chaplin, the ritualistic films of Martin Scorsese, or indeed Paul Schrader's Protestant cinema of protestation – there always exists a second narrative voice articulating an ongoing commentary of what is depicted. The film does not simply record action but provides a *theoria*, a critical commentary on its own composition. As Robert P. Pippin asked: "it has been said from Socrates to Wittgenstein that philosophy does not produce new results, new knowledge, but helps us see what we already knew and did not know we did. If that is a task of philosophy, why should film not be a major means for doing so?" (2020: 28).

Angelopoulos is one of the most ambitious visual philosophers in recent cinematic history who addressed major questions from the history of philosophical thinking, elucidated them visually, and translated them into cinematic morphemes. Certainly, in order to transform effectively the filmmaking process into a philosophical *topos* he evolved as a filmmaker and a thinker, and changed over time not simply the questions he addressed but also the methods he employed to conceptualize them. Not all his films entail philosophical problematization in an ontological sense. His first films are mostly essays on political thinking and, to a degree, political activism. They are films of critical exposition and "demystification" of existing institutional realities. They presuppose a political philosophy, that of Marx, Lenin, or Louis Althusser, which is at odds with their own material.

The philosophy of history, for example, that we encounter in *Days of '36* and *The Travelling Players*, with its circularity and closed self-referentiality, is, deep down, a manifestation of the idealistic optimism and utopian sublimation, strangely enough coupled with defeatism and pessimism, that characterized post-war revolutionary political thinking. For Angelopoulos the case was both personal and cultural. The defeat of the Left in the Greek Civil War (1944–1949) was not simply a political event; it was also an existential statement about the failure of the emancipation struggle within the European Enlightenment project. The recent, unfair, criticism of the Enlightenment tends to forget the guiding principles of the movement that redefined the political philosophy of democracy. The expulsion of the defeated communists after the Civil War was also an existential break, as Angelopoulos started delving into the undefinable identity of displaced and exiled individuals, a concern that will take monumental dimensions in his later films. However, as Andrew Horton observed: "Angelopoulos's films are not historical documentaries. They are clearly fictions, but fictional narratives that reflect his perspective on the complex web of Greek history" (1999: 57).

The same can be said about his most cryptic and enigmatic work, *The Hunters*, which foregrounds the active reaction of the Freudian unconscious; the presence of the undefinable *das Es* undermines and practically rejects the class-consciousness depicted in the film, as the unconscious and the ego merge, and the individual is completely subsumed under the desires of *das Es*. His film *O Megalexandros* is also a strange and self-contradictory visual space, in which Angelopoulos tries to explore the depths of human political conscience, especially of how power affects civic and individual subjectivity. Against his own intentions, the complexity and the internal contradictions of the material in the film framed a cryptic visual parable, a political fable, on the reality of de-historicized subjectivity.

> Megalexandros disappears in the mass, which suddenly push towards the centre, as if they were undoing him, or devouring him, howling in an outburst of rage. Then silence. The mass calms down and opens up slowly. When it opens completely, Megalexandros is not there anymore. At the place where his body should have been found, there is nothing, as if they have swallowed him.
>
> ANGELOPOULOS 1997: 326

In the script, the act of god-eating, of *theophagia*, even of a failed god, takes on dimensions of an anthropological ritual about regeneration beyond that of the usual deposition of a political leader. The leader was devoured by those who entrusted him with power: power returned to those who gave it to him in the first place. The mass, a typical Marxist notion of the body politic, becomes the giver and the taker of authority.

A similar ritual of death in *Eternity and a Day*, the liturgical burial of a murdered child, is similarly interesting, as it indicates that in liminal moments the archetypal rituals of human existence bring out the realities of "deep time" which in itself leads to the emergence of "deep history": in these films Angelopoulos explores the diachronic persistence of the desire for redemption, in a secular or a post-secular world, as unconscious rituals offer the ultimate psychological atonement, which in the past only religious practices could achieve. In the last scene of *O Megalexandros*, the stage is extremely uncanny: "the shepherd of the beginning enters slowly, sits on a rock. Looks at the direction where the child disappeared in the donkey. The city at dusk, fumes from the factories, that inexplicable constant whisper. Then his voice is heard, soft. – *This is how Alexander entered the cities*" (Angelopoulos 1997: 327). The uncanny setting prepares the transition to the actual reality of modernity with its stupor, chaos, and incoherence but maintaining the subliminal expectation of a redeemer. Megalexandros (Alexander the

Great) becomes simply Alexandros and later is transformed into a Kafkaesque mask named simply with the initial A: he becomes a mood and an atmosphere, a self in the process in gaining selfhood, and ultimately a secular expectation within the political formations of contemporary urban culture.

This happens as Angelopoulos's voice reads the final lines at the end of the film: the director is the "shepherd of being" pointing out to the audience the new stage of self-understanding. History becomes the active reality that forms and conditions human conscience. However, it is another kind of history: self-conscious, self-critical, and self-questioning. It abides in the urban spaces where conflicts and atrocities are committed and uses the past only as an exemplary story and a cautionary tale.

In his films after 1980, Angelopoulos struggled to achieve his iconosophy of which we find fragments even in his early works. In these films, he had to face and confront the dilemmas of cinematic representation that Dreyer, Kubrick, Tarkovsky, but also Bresson, Ozu, Mizoguchi, and Rossellini struggled with in order to achieve the holistic purity of their best films. Rossellini offers a good parallel case, since he achieved his cinematic dream not with the gripping melodramas of his early career but in the profoundly "educational films for television" of his late period. Behind films like *Descartes*, *Socrates*, *Augustine*, or especially *The Taking of Power by Louis XIV* loomed a deep philosophical project to defend the cultural values of the West in an era in which they were challenged by totalitarianism. As Colin MacCabe pointed out: "It is not impossible, indeed, that for future generations they may rank as even more important than his earlier films."[1]

Rossellini, despite being the father of neorealism, knew that cinema is a play of shadows and illusions; it misleads and carries away. It transports and misguides as well. His self-conscious, stylized, and undramatic *mise-en-scène* wanted to create a critical distance between the audience and the story. The film *Blaise Pascal* (1972) examines the critical conscience that was developing in the seventeenth century in the process of turning against its own constitutive realities. Pascal the mathematician struggles with Pascal the theologian, the scientist with the metaphysician. Rossellini de-dramatized the conflict because he was interested in its philosophical outcome; not the romanticized struggle of the individual, as in Carol Reed's *The Agony and the Ecstasy*

(1965) presenting in hyper-plethoric pictorialism the tormented personality of Michelangelo. Angelopoulos's de-dramatization of action and de-individualization of character that we see in his early films foreground the profound question of contemporary political subjectivity, its genealogy and its implosion.

The American cinema was, and still is, full of the seduction of illusions, enhanced and multiplied lately by digital technology and special effects employed for the sake of impression and excitability. Great directors from D.W. Griffith to Francis Ford Coppola were enmeshed in badly digested or uncooked philosophical ideas which they tried to incorporate in their work to the detriment of their overall achievement. Griffith's *The Birth of a Nation*, for example, revolves around a half-baked and completely simplistic, Manichean historicism based on racialism. Coppola's *Bram Stoker's Dracula* and especially his most philosophical attempt *Youth without Youth* (2007) show that he uses philosophical thinking, or in this case the life of philosopher and anthropologist Mircea Eliade, as the background to articulate something which he himself is not fully aware of: the continuity or discontinuity between life and ideas, the connection between the philosopher and his philosophy, if there is any or if it can be detected *a posteriori*.

On the other hand, Dreyer in the miracle of the bodily resurrection in *Ordet* knows deeply the significance of what he was trying to do: presenting a miracle cinematically might look in bad taste or simply ridiculous. However, it makes the cinematic screen the locus of an eruption of the unexpected, of what all miracles were, the suspension of the natural order. The miracle in Tarkovsky's is *The Sacrifice* is also another case at hand: how can the extraordinary and anti-natural become visible without sensationalism and hyperbole? The presentation of the miracle in Tarkovsky is much more ambiguous: the viewer cannot distinguish if it is a dream or an actual experience. Tarkovsky knew that people have ceased to believe in miracles but in a strange, anti-modernist way still believed in dreams, or indeed in *oneiromancy*. So, he adopted the oneiric mode of representation, the derealization of the material and finally the actual enhancement of disbelief to present the unrepresentable and the un-visualized.

In his post-1980 works, Angelopoulos psychologized these dilemmas and extracted from them a specific temporality of images encoding a distinct *theoria* about what is most central in contemporary thinking;

namely, history, being, loss, and redemption. His images are intentionally constructed to explore these liminal questions, especially at specific historical moments, when it was becoming increasingly obvious that the last remnants of the projects of the Enlightenment were gradually fading away or were self-imploding. As a child of post-war liberalism and revolutionary spirit, he was shaken to the core when he witnessed the political corruption and disintegration of socialism, which, for him, represented the last echo of the radical movements that wanted to redefine history, society and self-perception after the French Revolution. There is a very clear philosophy of history in *The Travelling Players*, which is not indicated by the circular temporality of the film but by the long poem of Michalis Katsaros (1919–88) that his exiled poet recites towards the end of the film:

> The intervention of events of sounds of parties / the intervention of boats from the wild sea / the people orators my chest the voices / the factories / the October of 17 / the year 1936 / the December of 44 . . . / For this I will remain in my rags / as the French Revolution gave me birth / as my mother Spain gave me birth / a dark conspirator . . .
>
> ANGELOPOULOS 1997: 194–5

There is an implied and hidden historical order in the narrative of dialectical continuity between past and present. From the French to the Soviet and then to the Spanish Revolutions, and to the Greek Civil War, which he sees as another revolution, we can detect almost an inevitable and deterministic historical unfolding. It is a historical order based neither on economic power nor on relations of subjection but on the human will to reassert and affirm the self from the conditions that determined it. In the beginning, as he says, the trauma of history leads to identity crisis. Both, however, contribute to the emergence of something more important: "now he has to find the solutions for his problems on his own. That's his only choice. Nothing and nobody can help with that. Not love, or anything else on the outside. It's the essence of his own being, the autonomy of existence" (Fainaru 2001: 37).

The films of the early period are based on such linear historicism, even if their mode of representation is circular. Yet the poet's monologue, after a delirium of utopian projects about the abolition of power and authority, culminates with a cry of despair and hopelessness: "They promise you again a mutilated freedom" (Angelopoulos, 1997: 195). Implicitly there is an element of *voluntarism* under the idea of collective history: ultimately individuals attempt to take their destiny in their hands, but they fail and are annihilated. In an indirect way, Angelopoulos dealt with history in Heideggerian terms, as "Geschichte des Seyns" (history of being), laying the foundations for his later thinking on the meaning of history. In this early history of being there is no psychology and interiority: the subject is de-subjectified because something larger than the self intervenes—the collective ideology of a society which restricts the exercise of individual freedom and agency. The super-ego annuls the ability of the individual to develop an ego, to recognize its own biography to articulate the expression that dominates his *Voyage to Cythera*: "Ego Eimai / I am."

For some Marxists, like Louis Althusser, echoed by the early Angelopoulos, social ideology takes over the individual and even erases, or supplants, its consciousness. Althusser writes:

> Ideology is indeed a system of representations, but in the majority of cases these representations have nothing to do with "consciousness"; they are usually images and occasionally concepts, but it is above all as structures that they impose on the vast majority of men, not via their "consciousness". They are perceived-accepted-suffered cultural objects and they act functionally on men via a process that escapes them.
>
> ALTHUSSER, 1969: 233

The idea that history is a shadow theater of superhuman forces within the mind of individuals who nevertheless are unable to understand, elucidate, or control them was one of the main tenets of French structuralism. Many Greek intellectuals who had found refuge in France, like Nikos Poulantzas, had wholeheartedly espoused them.

However, as it was obvious from Althusser's own intellectual trajectory, as we see in his autobiography *The Future Lasts a Long Time* (1993), something was missing in the process; the human interiority, the introspective conscience, the need for self-criticism, which means self-reflexivity, which Althusser reserved for himself but gave no right to others. The events of December 44 and Greek Civil War (1947–9) whose memories and consequences permeate Angelopoulos's films, more than the German Occupation, or the 1967 Dictatorship, were symptoms of that profound crisis within the revolutionary tradition and the gradual degeneration of socialism into another totalitarian mechanism of ideological control and political coercion. The romantic revolutionism and abstract political philosophy of his early films was transformed into a theoretical re-evaluation of principles and experiences. Despite the defeat, in his mind the revolutionary project remained alive and galvanized, especially for the youth, because we cannot experience history without direction and purpose.

Angelopoulos remained until the end fascinated by the heroic and relentless human resistance against collective oppression and voluntary submission. At the same time, he was fascinated by the persistence of heteronomy and authoritarianism: his political thinking questioned the structure of contemporary subjectivity and the forces that make people desire and pursue their own subjugation. "Freedom itself," writes Byung-Chul Han, "is bringing forth compulsion and constraint" (2017: 2). Contemporary capitalism together with a class of new masters develops the strange desire for self-enslavement. As we move towards the velvet authoritarianism of "digital psychopolitics" (Han's term), the old active citizen vanishes and enters the Lacanian sphere of *aphanisis*; it becomes a technologized self without self-awareness. The spectator democracy, the society of the spectacle as Guy Debord called it, creates a sense of everyday discontinuity. Every experience is an eternal now, a moment unconnected and disconnected from the next, creating what Michel Foucault termed "experience which has the function of wrenching the subject from itself, of seeing to it that the subject is no longer itself and that it is brought to its annihilation or its dissolution" (2001: 241).

However, Angelopoulos wanted to explore the ontological and anthropological foundations of historical states of mind, of both freedom and subjugation as experienced in the contemporary world even with its reverential memorialization of the past. In his early films, he posed the question of "what is history", and in his attempt to answer he moved towards different directions redefining human activity and what can be considered a historical event from the point of human agency. He investigated the structure of political subjectivities like master and slave and the dialectical co-dependency between them. *The Hunters* is the most obvious example of the master–slave dialectic as expressed by

Hegel and theoretically elaborated later by Alexander Kojève. Under this dialectical connection between master and slave, freedom itself is existential and social anomie: we cannot be free in a society based on the psychodynamics of authoritarianism, even when through acts of individual rebellion we believe that we are momentarily free. In a sense, that was Angelopoulos's gesture towards anarchism and political adventurism, which had become dominant in Europe after the insurgencies of 1968 around the world.

Ultimately, Angelopoulos's voluntarism addressed the question of the role of personality in history, a question that had a crucial function in the discussions of the Marxist and post-Marxist Left in the 1970s. His philosophical and political investigations became the basis and the foundation for the great existential quests that we will find later in his work. In a way, he had first to explore history, as a collective activity, in order to delve into the complexities of the human psyche. Historical consciousness can emerge out of social and collective experience, in order to establish the ground out of which human uniqueness and specificity can emerge as an ontological possibility. Despite his reluctance to address existential questions in his early films, the permeating principle of his work is based again on Jean-Paul Sartre's famous statement: "existence precedes essence and we will to exist at the same time as we fashion our image, that image is valid for all and for our whole era. Our responsibility is thus much greater than we might have supposed because it concerns all mankind" (2007: 24).

The idea of an existence which defines independently its own ontological presuppositions and foundations is an extremely provocative subtext of his early films. Even the unself-conscious protagonist of his first film, the woman who kills her husband, in a way, through her crime, wants to make her existence known and active; therefore, she confronts her own ontological determinants, the history of her own being, the restrictions imposed upon her own agency. However, she still remains a "structure," a practice according to Althusser; she is unable to articulate her emotions and explain her actions. In the real story of Althusser's life, we read his own confession as follows: "I have decided to explain my actions . . . I am doing it for my friends and for myself too, if that is possible, to remove the weight of the tombstone which lies over me. I wish . . . to free myself from the circumstances in which I found myself as a result of my extremely serious state of mind" (1993: 27). The philosophical question of the freedom to choose becomes for Althusser the attempt to free himself from the circumstances that created him. The philosophical abstraction needs an experiential framework to explain itself and give an account of its actions. Most characters in Angelopoulos's films deal with this question and try to find an answer that is not autobiographical like Althusser's to solve it. Althusser's erroneous argument that "all ideology hails or *interpellates* concrete individuals as concrete subjects" and that "ideology 'acts' or 'functions' in such a way that it . . . 'transforms' the individual into subjects" (Althusser 1971: 11) was answered in the most tragic way as an *autobiographical* event.

During the same time, the certainties of Angelopoulos's early ideological trajectory were shattered by several successive disillusions. First were the socialists in Greece who, after winning power in 1981, became the corrupt beneficiaries of the bourgeoisie that they have been fighting against for decades, usurping the legacy of the Civil War and introducing a system of nepotism and self-aggrandizement; then came the disillusion from his intellectual motherland, France, with François Mitterrand and his Machiavellian politics; finally, the sudden rise of anti-regime movements in Czechoslovakia, Poland, and Yugoslavia showed that "existing" socialism was moribund and turned against its own citizens.

Before the end of the decade, history gave the answer to a looming philosophical question: how can we start new political projects in an era of lost causes and utopian illusions? Can we trust political ideologies or social systems, or will all civic sociability be based on the hermeneutics of suspicion, disbelief, and negativity? Consequently, the realm of the historical subject as psychical interiority and introspective conscience appeared wide open in Angelopoulos's philosophical and aesthetic horizon. By moving from history to historicity, Angelopoulos confronted some of the most critical questions of contemporary thought and until the end of his life struggled to articulate a formally coherent and mythopoetically solid image about the inner self and its adventures within a reality that negated its active agency. As Horton stated:

The cinema of Theo Angelopoulos is a cinema that crosses the borders of the first two areas of culture – the state and the individual – to explore this third "culture of links." His films show us such a variety of fragments. [. . .] But it is a tribute to his cinematic art that the concept, style, structure, framing, and texture of his films provide

us with the means to transcend the fragmentation and thus enter
into a culture of links.

HORTON 1999: 208

Historical Knowledge in Angelopoulos

After 1980, Angelopoulos's films embody and develop a sustained
exploration of regimes of historicity through their very structure, imagery,
and mythopoetics. It is true that such critical investigation happened
gradually and almost imperceptibly; Angelopoulos was a cinematic
chameleon, who reformed his poetics in at least four crucial moments
of his evolution—something that is usually forgotten by those who see
him as a monolith or judge his late films in the light of his earlier ones.
Furthermore, Angelopoulos struggled, like Dreyer, Bresson, and
Tarkovsky, to transform films into the *topos* of a meta-cognitive method
of experiencing reality, by empowering the viewer to be able to "dream
again," as he repeatedly stated; not simply to make films the place
where unique and extraordinary revelations take place, but specifically
the *topos* where a unique formal articulation about the latent forces that
have created events can be experienced and clarified.

His meta-cognitive epistemological project, his iconosophy, belongs
to a long iconographic tradition that we find in Orthodox Christian art,
starting with the work of Theophanes the Greek, Andrei Rublev, and El
Greco. It belongs to an artistic heritage that goes back to the paintings of
classical Greece, the frescos of Pompeii and the grand static panels of
late Byzantium, enhanced and animated by the Renaissance sense of
perspective and the optics of El Greco's panoramic imagination. His
Angelopoulos's images recapitulate the effort of iconographers to capture
the depth and the complexity of reality and history, although in this case
it does not possess a sacred narrative to underpin its presence in history.
If in Byzantine iconography the gaze of God, or sanctity, looks back upon
human finitude, whose gaze do we sense looking through the cinematic
images at us? The great philosophical project in Angelopoulos's
iconosophy consists of the attempt to construct a visual framework for
the questions of being, memory, and redemption, ultimately about human

nature from the view of its existential history, its lived and imagined reality, fusing the evanescent and the diachronic and forming the ontological foundation of being in time now. The being in Byzantine icons is not the "real" character or the "historical" incident they represent, but the imagined essence or, in other terms, the diachronic presence of such representations in the perception of their viewers, the material trace that their substance impresses upon the viewer's conscience.

Based on this assumption, Angelopoulos's films constitute irregular "events" towards the philosophical re-imagining of the function and nature of cinematic images in contemporary culture. Although his films are mostly appreciated as political treatises, towering amongst them *The Travelling Players*, Angelopoulos went through a profound "turn" in the Heideggerian sense of the word. Thereafter all his films became existentialist *visual essays* about identity, loss, memory, self-consciousness, and ultimately mortality and human nature. From *Voyage to Cythera* (1984) until his last completed film *The Dust of Time*, Angelopoulos produced striking images exploring the predicament of "problematic" heroes in search of meaning and purpose, engaging in continuous dialogues with great philosophical thinkers, like Plato, Marx, Lukács, Heidegger, and Arendt, implicitly or explicitly.

In his evolution as a *filmmaker,* we detect that his cinema engaged, for a long period of time, with the philosophical questions that Herbert Marcuse and Lucien Goldmann termed *Heideggerian Marxism*. Richard Wolin, who analyzed systematically the project, was both positive and negative, as it carried within its structure the "Germanic primordialism" that led to Nazism but also through its heirs, in particular Arendt, "has managed to preserve a distinctive manner of philosophical questioning, one of whose virtues is a willingness to remain out of sync with the predominantly utilitarian orientation of the 'globalised' contemporary life-world" (2001: 235). There are two ways to see the connection: from what Heidegger's philosophy was used for and from what Heidegger's philosophy achieved against Heidegger himself. Marcuse firmly associated Heidegger's Dasein with the need of abstract thinking to become historical in the sense of being concrete reality in society: "Concrete philosophy can thus only approach existence if it seeks out Dasein in the sphere in which its existence is based: as it acts in its world in accordance with its historical situation" (2005: 44).

Such a concrete philosophy may come out of a synthesis between Marx and Heidegger, which was later regretted by Marcuse as "pseudo-concrete" and "pseudo-historical." The truth is that Heidegger had a very specific perception of history which could not be the perception of Marx. Heidegger suggested that "time is Dasein. Dasein is my specificity, and this can be specificity in what is futural by running ahead to the certain yet indeterminate past. Dasein always is in a manner of its possible temporal being. Dasein is time, time is temporal. Dasein is not time, but temporality" (1992: 20). Marx's perception of history is so radically antithetical that there is no common ground for convergence or reconciliation: "History is the history of human industry, which undergoes growth in productive power, the stimulus and vehicle of which is an economic structure, which perishes when it has stimulated more growth than it can contain" (Cohen 2000: 26). The difference between temporality and industry, between active work and abstract contemplation, creates the rather utopian impossibility of merging *vita activa* into *vita contemplativa*. Heidegger's temporality poses the question of a beingness beyond actual beings. Marx's history materializes its own identity as production, as objectification, and material creation.

Goldmann concluded his pioneering study on Lukács and Heidegger in a rather ambiguous paragraph:

That is why all positive reflection on the relationship between man and Being, or even more simply, between man and History, necessarily end up in such ontologically fundamental concepts as: the effort to humanise reality—the necessity of incarnation, the hope of succeeding in this effort, the risk of failure, and—the synthesis of the three—the gambling element which is found at the centre of all thought which is truly and rigorously dialectical.

GOLDMANN 1977: 109

Furthermore, Kostas Axelos observes that "Marx speaks very explicitly about the externalisation, divestiture, objectification, alienation of modern man. Heidegger speaks of the objectification of all things which have being through the will of subjectivity, of the homelessness of humanity in the modern era, of the abandonment of being, of the oblivion of being" (2015: 52–3). Goldmann and Axelos bring together lucidly the main themes that Angelopoulos adopted from Marx and Heidegger. Ultimately the question is not about power structure or institutional domination, but about the *essential presence* of human beings, both in history and nature, about the *presencing* of being as both historical activity and natural phenomenon.

Certainly, the project of Heideggerian Marxism looks like a radical synthesis of colliding conceptual paradigms; in Angelopoulos's films, their tension explores the epistemological *impossibility* in the way they articulate historicity and subjectivity. In his early films a more simple, one-dimensional, Marxist theory of history determined the structure of his images. There was a clear line between the oppressor and the oppressed, between alienation and domination. However, as subjectivity is problematized, the questioning of the domination of structures brought to the fore the actual project of human agency and the possibility of moving from subjectification to human autonomy. His films *Days of '36*, *The Hunters*, and *O Megalexandros* struggle, inconclusively, to fuse the incongruent signifiers of Marx's belief in a social ontology and Heidegger's foundational beingness. Only in *The Hunters* the subject develops or gains a selfhood which can be understood and therefore presented in images. By interrogating the subject of power Angelopoulos had to dive into the complexities of the psychological reality within the oppressors. How can we have history without historicity? Or indeed the exact opposite: can we have historicity without history? Is history a shadow theater of invisible forces beyond the understanding and control of individuals? Heidegger believed that this was possible whereas Marx, especially the young one, thought of it as an absurdity. Can we also articulate a subjectivity when history overdetermines the existence of individuals?

Following Claude Lévi-Strauss and Althusser, Angelopoulos's early films frame subjectivities without psychologies: they are practices or institutions or structures without agency and autonomy. If I may paraphrase Heidegger's poetic dwelling, cinematically man dwells in the liminal space from which

he does not describe the mere appearance of sky and earth. The [cinematograph] calls, in the sights of the sky, that which in its very self-disclosure causes the appearance of that which conceals itself, and indeed as that which conceals itself. In the familiar appearances, the [cinematograph] calls the alien as that to which the invisible imparts itself in order to remain what it is—unknown.

HEIDEGGER 1971: 223

It was impossible to look and present the real without bringing out the unknown presence in the real, the human psyche. The word "psyche" became gradually extremely important for Angelopoulos. He is not talking about the Hegelian spirit, Geist, or the logos, the religious Word; he insists that the *urgrund* of everything can only be the dark unpredictability of the human soul. Psyche is both the creator and the creature of images: it is a mirror that duplicates and perpetuates the longing for communion, therefore the need for the Other. If the potentates of social systems really exist there must be also a historically determined ontology of their existence. *The Hunters* frames the internal structure of a psyche formed by power whereas *O Megalexandros* monumentalizes its demise. Later, the central character of his films will be the everyday and ordinary individual whose psyche is so conspicuous that it becomes unknown.

It was obvious that the symbiosis between Heidegger and Marx constituted a philosophical and cognitive dissonance and finally led to an epistemological implosion. Nevertheless, the effort that Angelopoulos invested in converging the most incompatible epistemologies of being indicates how strongly he believed or hoped that the filmic space could become the most "open" form which would allow their coexistence to produce, through their semantic friction, new networks of communication, new imaginaries about social existence, and ultimately new possibilities for the resignification of the real. Some would claim that, on the contrary, they led to a philosophical and existential *aphasia*, which in his mature work emerges as the legendary "melancholia" that many scholars have talked about as permeating his films.

Angelopoulos experimented with both temporalities as the postulate of convergence between these two paradigms was in the intellectual horizon of his life and work. The synthesizing process had started with György Lukács, the Frankfurt School, Sartrean existentialism, and to a degree with Praxis philosophy in Yugoslavia, and Erich Fromm and his school. Such synthesizing revisionism was both a collective and individual effort, encompassing whole groups of thinkers, like Theodor Adorno and his associates, Heidegger and his followers or Althusser and his fellow travelers, but also isolated individuals like Simone Weil, Arendt, or Cornelius Castoriadis. To the active presence of such thinkers, we must add the philosophical re-invention, or better re-inscription, of cinema from the arts of technological modernism to its role as practical intervention in the political becoming of society by French thinkers, especially around the journal *Cahiers du Cinéma*, in particular Jean-Luc Godard.

Angelopoulos's early ocular philosophy is an amalgam of all such elements, to the degree that his language contradicts the obvious, 'surface-meaning' of his stories. His effort to synthesize through moving images diverse projects of foundational ontology and political emancipation looks like an intellectual, not to say epistemological, titanism. The question was further complicated in its philosophical consequences, as Angelopoulos stated that he was an atheist, although elements of religiosity, through a search for the numinous and the uncanny, can be felt in his best work, like *Landscape in the Mist* and *Eternity and a Day*. However, if the *mysterium tremendum* does not lead to the *mysterium fascinans*, if the terror of existence does not lead to the fascination with the enigma of human mortality, what is the role of artistic creativity and expression? In a world without religion is it possible to achieve redemptive closure though union with the natural continuum, or is human adventure a pointless journey through randomness and mere chance?

Between Physics and Metaphysics

Images however bring in them and within them their own semantic and existential opening. The awkward connection between images and meaning goes back of course to Plato, a philosopher whose visual thinking is at the heart of Angelopoulos's creative imaginary. The usual saying goes that Plato posed many crucial questions as a philosopher but answered them as a poet through myths. By employing images which he expanded and elaborated as myths, Plato introduced a different way of philosophizing: by translating philosophical arguments into myths, the myth itself took the form of a philosophical argument, replacing rationalization and syllogistic argumentation (something that his student Aristotle tried to re-address and indeed avoid in his *Metaphysics*). As he had stated, "a poet, if he is really to be a poet, must compose myths and not speeches" (Plato 2005: 213 §61B); myths are usually translated erroneously as arguments, but the reader must have the appropriate key to decipher the philosophical question embodied in the myth itself. As John Hendrix observed, Plato, in his dialogue with the pre-Socratic philosophers, especially Anaximander, illustrated "how visual forms are related to conceptual structures in philosophical systems" (2004: 1); and through his own work, followed by so many artists and thinkers throughout history, articulated a text as "a product of a belief and an approach to an understanding of the arts based on underlying conceptual frameworks, in that the visual arts act as a form of communication, arts act as a language, which has an architectonic structure; the creation of forms in art and architecture is as essential to communication as language itself" (2004: 2).

Platonic myths in particular, and myths in general, embody philosophical questions, as on many occasions philosophers construct questions that are not necessarily or immediately answerable. Through their dramatic formation and dramaturgic intentionality, they recreate the question without dictating an answer. This can be seen in several filmmakers, like Terrence Malick, or Terence Davies, but also in philosophical directors, like Alexander Kluge, Alain Resnais or Godard and Pasolini. The same can be seen in many Russian filmmakers, not like the staunchly Marxist, but secretly Freudian, Eisenstein or the devout Christian Tarkovsky, but in directors who know the answers to the questions they posit: the question of imagination in Sergei Parajanov, for example, permeates visually the whole of *The Color of Pomegranates* (1969) without ever being analyzed rationally. Another great example of translating notions into images can be found in the rather under-studied Maurice Pialat film *Under the Sun of Satan* (1987). In a unique manner, Pialat depicted the presence of evil in the movie, not in the usual Hollywood spectacular fashion but through the gradual loss of color, the imperceptible shrinking of space and finally the slow disfigurement of human form every time that Satan encounters the main character. Pialat depicts "the powerful supernatural events of Bernanos's novel, like the nature of the saint's apprehension of them, [makes them] remain invisible and incomprehensible to the viewer, manifesting themselves as breaks in the narrative." Furthermore, "the gaps and breaks not only mark the passage of time, but also an essential and unrepresentable change in the nature of reality" (Warehime 2006: 64).

Angelopoulos's attempt to translate evil into images is extremely interesting as we notice in the rape scene in *Landscape in the Mist*: we see and hear nothing. The same happens with all forms of death in his post-1980 films: everything evil remains *unfilmed*. Alexander Kluge wrote in a brief but extremely succinct note that in Angelopoulos's films "the not-filmed criticises that which is filmed" (2015: x), indicating the dialectical tension that we find in his work between the iconic and aniconic tendencies, between what Wilhelm Worringer called "abstraction" and "empathy" as the "psychic dualism" that leads to artistic creation. "Just as the urge to empathy," wrote Worringer, "as a pre-assumption of aesthetic experience finds its gratification in the beauty of the organic, so the urge to abstraction finds its beauty in the life-denying inorganic, in the crystalline or, in general terms, in all abstract law and necessity" (1997: 4). The ultimate product of cognition through abstraction in art, as he wrote, is to detect the understanding that "man is now just as lost and helpless vis-à-vis the world-picture as primitive man" and investigate "the immense dread of space" (Worringer 1997: xi–xii).

The question here as articulated in Angelopoulos is about the limits and limitations of representation: is there any way to (re)present the unrepresentable, the human psyche for example, in both its aspects as good and evil? Or in ontological terms as both *ens* and *esse*? Parajanov constructed images for the enhanced re-living of the imaginative world in the mind of the poet. The platonic flow of associative images in *The Color of Pomegranates* became the method of understanding the poet's mind through unexpected visual architectonics. The same can be claimed for another Russian, Alexander Sokurov, not so much for his hyper-rhetorical epic *Russian Ark* (2002), but in his lesser known, visual film-essays, *Mother and Son* (1997) and *Father and Son* (2003). In the first, collective history is represented as a mass entity of fleeting existential moments, liked together by the poet, but in the other two the question of natality becomes the central question of human existence, filmed in silence. Angelopoulos did the same with the intra-diegetic use of music in his early films. Music defines the social dialogues and conflicts in the story. In his later films the music is extra-diegetic and almost disconnected from action. If someone removes it the image becomes pure cinema because the music is their own structure. For Sokurov we do not exist towards death, but we exist because we reflect on our birth: our parents constitute the ontological grounding of our being. At the moment we think about mother and father, we relive our origins, the source of being, our natality as a gift, indeed as the transition from un-being to being. Cinematically this must be represented as a visual question, not as a realistic episode. Parajanov depicts the event of natality as the founding ground of being in front of the camera but also in holding the camera.

This is predominantly a philosophical question which, because of its nature and its scope, can only have a philosophical answer. Wittgenstein presciently stressed that you must know the answer first before formulating the question. The answer is visualized and through its images we can reconstruct the questions each film answers. In the same way, Angelopoulos's films embody philosophical statements and theoretical propositions: they don't reproduce simply existing topical questions or use them programmatically to clarify their consequences or indoctrinate their viewers. By eliminating the rhetoric from his images he transforms them into specific articulations of epistemological questions.

For this reason, his images do not have a singular interpretation; they are prismatic forms that need specific angles of light to reveal their irreducibility to all forms of structuration. The domination of structures in his early films imploded because they had no space for any form of existential subjectivity. The metaphor of the prism is extremely apt here as it gives us the ability to visually experience the statement as the synthesis of sub-statements of implied subtexts, which the image itself is made of. Furthermore, as Aristotle had suggested, "the whole is not, as it were, a mere heap, but the totality is something besides the parts, there is a cause of unity" (1924: 121), a suggestion that in our case could be reformulated as: each work of art is always something more and beyond its constituent elements.

One could claim further that films do not present a philosophy or elaborate a philosophical point of view. There is nothing more philosophical than cinematic images – moving images as Noël Carroll defined them. They are and they are not at the same time: this paradox is more intriguing than the paradox of photography because cinematic images are in motion and their movement creates illusions, conditioning our mind with the power of illusion.

Each element of film adds a new dimension to its overall architectural form. Ultimately, what the spectator sees is a whole beyond the actual contribution of all participants. Indeed, spectators first see the whole and then fragment it into its constituent parts. Irrespective of what Aristotle was trying to argue for, the idea that the whole is irreducible to its constituent parts can be found in its complete form in cinematic art and the way that the act of seeing film impacts those who see it. Each film is a totalized presentation of the elemental and the partial within a visual space of formal connections: the vision of the director adds an aspect of the creative imaginary which is always present but a functionalist and instrumentalized perception of the work of art does not allow it to become the glue that keeps the architecture of film in its solidity: this is what might be called intentionality.

Intentionality is a rather misconstrued notion, to indicate the element of volition that defines the ultimate completion of the film. Intentionality also means purposefulness: the work of art does not simply exist; it reconfigures the existing perception of the real for a purpose. Aristotle called this purposeful intentionality, *entelechy*: we cannot really appreciate a work of art without investigating or even understanding its raison d'être which in all cases is not circumstantial but anthropological. Films exist synchronically to present the *what of history* but diachronically to articulate the *what for of humans' actions*. The early Angelopoulos films synchronically address the question of historical memory in his country; suppressed, censored, and one-sided. Diachronically they localize the question of being at the nexus of past and future: they reinterpreted the past and prefigured the future. In the privileged moment of confluence, their material and concrete present, they recalibrated historical memory as a phenomenon of consciousness, as a mental event, reconstructed and relived. The privileged moment of confluence creates a sudden illumination: the mind confronts its own limitations and recognizes its own peripeteia. Retaining this idea, we can go back to the entelechy of Angelopoulos's images.

From Home to Homelessness

The analysis of the totality of the filmic text as collective intentionality kept together by acts of voluntary surrender to the unifying vision of the director is the central theoretical subscript in the presentation of Angelopoulos. We all understand the significance that the cultural and social milieu has on individuals; yet Tarkovsky's Christianity, or indeed mysticism, cannot be deduced from the atheistic and irreligious environment of the Soviet Union; it refers to an intellectual and spiritual trend within the actual reality around him. Even Martin Scorsese's well-disguised sacramental Catholicism cannot be attributed to the marginalization of Catholics by the Anglo-Protestant establishment in the American states, or more specifically in Hollywood. We can easily understand that Ingmar Bergman's Protestantism is the ultimate defense against the "empty, cruel skies" of Scandinavian utilitarianism. The absolute connection between the milieu and the individual, however, ignores the possibility of an individuating process that would make someone differentiate themselves from the community and the cultural practices that formed them.

Angelopoulos's films cannot be reduced to the ideas, practices, or technologies that produced them. Angelopoulos was born in a tradition of philosophical pedigree, but which today is totally deprived of any original philosophical engagement with ideas and theories. Modern Greek philosophy, to the extent that it exists, is an academic exercise in exegetical commentary and scholiastic contextualization. It is more *explication de texte* than actual investigation of ideas and engagement with philosophical projects. The only truly significant philosophers, like Cornelius Castoriadis, Kostas Axelos, or the philosophical composer Ianis Xenakis had to write in another language, French, in order to be able to philosophize, whereas others, like Elli Lambridi or Panagiotis Kondylis, remain totally unknown to their own compatriots—and both wrote in other languages. In contemporary Greece, there is a distinct anti-philosophical tendency which is both surprising and astounding for a nation that prides itself for the glories of its ancient philosophical legacy.

Like the anti-intellectualism in American political thinking, modern Greek cinema avoided statements of visions: it focused and still focuses on the peripheral, the local and the appropriable. The only exception was and remains Angelopoulos. Unfortunately, Angelopoulos's reception, especially by American and British film critics, is still restricted to his political films of the 1970s. His films are imprisoned by historicist pretensions of a total interpretation through reconstruction of dominant discourses; yet what such approaches achieve is to make Angelopoulos more of a visual chronographer and less of a thinker of images. Most "historicists" still see his work as recording the political melodramas that have defined Greek historical adventures. They continue to privilege the exotic and the peripheral element in Angelopoulos's origin, without being able to detect or even see the ontological fabric of his images, or moreover the political ontology that emerges out of the films themselves. The interpretation of his work focuses on orientalized Balkanology and not at all on the universal existential projects that permeate his works. In my perception, Angelopoulos's cinematic images continue the philosophical optics of Plato and Plotinus in particular: they embody the challenging *ocularocentrism* of Greek art from the Parthenon sculptures to Byzantine iconography, and struggle to add the new dimension of modernity, the heterogeneity of temporality, the psychological depth of perspective, and the fragmentation of the self.

There is a special element from Plotinus's optics that has a direct correspondence with Angelopoulos's visuality. Plotinus stressed that "actual seeing is double; the eye has one object of sight which is the form of the object perceived by the sense, and one which is the medium through which the form of its object is perceived, which is also itself perceptible to the eye; it is different from the form, but it is the cause of the form's being seen" (Plotinus Enneads V.5.7). Angelopoulos's *doubling* of everything in his films, from *The Travelling Players* to the mesmeric end of *The Suspended Step of the Stork*, does not conflate what is seen with how it is seen, but duplicates the structures of perception in order to point out the underlying subscripts. From a cinematic point of view, it also extends the screen towards the viewer in an attempt to bring down the fourth wall, something that in early films was done by having the actors talking directly to the camera. The *doubling of forms* throughout his films foregrounds the philosophical grounding of his iconosophy about the hidden forces that produce the forms, actions and psychologies of individuals.

From Plotinus to Angelopoulos the distance is considerable both in terms of historical circumstances and philosophical beliefs. But we can draw certain formal and theoretical analogies between them, which do not aim to legitimize or justify the relations between philosophy and filmmaking, which we take as a transcendental given here, but express the ontology of images both moving and still. In his famous essay on the ontology of the photographic image, André Bazin observed that photography and the cinema are discoveries that satisfy, once and for all and in its very essence, our obsession with realism, because "cinema is objectivity in time" (2005: 12, 14).

How can we use these categories introduced by Bazin to philosophically understand the anti-realistic and indeed hyper-realistic Angelopoulos, the liturgical cinema of Tarkovsky, or the ritualistic films of Miklós Jancsó or ultimately the "slow cinema" of Béla Tarr? We need to perceive the phenomenon of their films within the categories that signified their semantics. This stipulates that we must outline the conceptual categories that make these films meaningful today. In other words, we have to search for the philosophical considerations that are not reducible to the particulars or the circumstances of their production.

In order to reach the pure visuality of his late ontology, Angelopoulos had to go through the demonic sirens of contemporary philosophical speculations. Sartre had opined after 1945 that Marxism was the unsurpassable horizon of our time. In peripheral traditions, which wanted to reassert themselves against the big hegemonic centers of power that wished to control them, Marxism was always the starting point of resistance. It was a peculiar kind of Marxism, as most of Marx's own books were not translated into Greek and were studied through their "easy-to-read" summaries issued by the Soviet Communist Party and translated in sloppy and unkempt fashion by notoriously uneducated party hacks.

Marxism's appeal was an emotional reaction towards the abuse and misuse of power that was inflicted upon the Greeks by consecutive conservative governments within the framework of the pseudo-democracy that ruled over the Greeks after the end of a divisive and disastrous Civil War. Angelopoulos grew up with this environment and the question of *power* will become the most important problematic underpinning his early work, until the grand epic of *O Megalexandros*. In his early works, power takes a twofold expression. First, it is depicted as the invisible network of implied assumptions that govern society *unconsciously*; second, it takes the form of a Nietzschean will to power *intentionally*. Both representations exist in all his films in various degrees, permeating the actual and the symbolic world of his stories. What legitimizes power in history is the most crucial question in his early work, which has defined the way that his work has been received and interpreted, as a political commentary on the political misadventures of his native country.

This approach is simplistic and focuses on direct correspondence to external political events, even if colored by political ideology. His trilogy of history, *Days of '36*, *The Travelling Players*, and *The Hunters*, gives only the background, as ancient Athens is the background for the first books of Plato's *Republic* where the question of what legitimizes and justifies power is debated. Even if we haven't read Thucydides and his Peloponnesian War we would be able to understand that there is a historical and social subtext in Euripides' *The Trojan Women*. Angelopoulos's early films problematize the nature of power in terms of *praxial* reality, psychological affect and finally anthropological valorization. When and how the *praxial* becomes *axial* or engenders values is the main question underlying this early period. His later problematrization of power and the moral valorization of acting underlined the question that was going to become the most important postulate of his late work, the question of human subjectivity.

Indeed, the question of the political subject is the most important question in the films that followed. Beyond the immediate particulars, these films are also in direct dialogue with analogous movies made mostly in Italy, Bertolucci's *The Conformist* or Buñuel's *The Discreet Charm of the Bourgeoisie*, but go beyond the question of power as institutional coercion and violence, exploring the subjectivity that is created out of their strictures and practices. *The Hunters* explores the question of power as psychological reality, in an attempt to bring into the field of visual elucidation the irrational forces that define the nature of power. In *The Travelling Players* the central question refers to the defeated and downtrodden individual: the issue is to explore the heteronomy of contemporary humans whose existence is reduced to mere instrumentalized beings, unfit for self-reflection and self-determination. In this film, as also in his earlier one, we watch Heidegger's "they" in their most visible exhibition of their "inauthenticity and failure to stand on one's own" (2010: 127ff.). The presentation of the "they" in the practicing of their own experience of meaninglessness, their own nothingness, foregrounds some of the most important questions of his later work, when the subject of nothingness strives to assert projects of authentic possibilities.

The Hunters is a film precisely of what happens in the mind of individuals in power, of individuals who have internalized the nothingness dwelling in the essence of power. Angelopoulos here deals with the split subject of moral conscience. The film investigates the tendency of the Unconscious, Sigmund Freud's drive, to repress and displace, indeed its tendency to believe its own illusions. It could have been Heidegger's analysis of the Nazi mind, if the hidden king of philosophy could have found time to discuss his *führer* principle that was glorified so much in his

Rectorship speech and in his *Introduction to Metaphysics*. *The Hunters* represents the most ambitious philosophical engagement with Freud's topography of the human mind, depicting the constant conflict between id and super-ego in a way that foregrounds a new perception of the fragile and self-destructive ego. Freudian topography remains broken and incomplete, reflecting the broken and incomplete subjectivities that are absorbed by power and surrender their own autonomy.

Such tendency towards self-unravelling, towards the eclipse of individuality in Hegelian terms, becomes the central space in his monumental *O Megalexandros*. The charismatic individual who starts with a just cause is gradually transformed into the actual tyrant of history: an anarchist, almost Bakunian ontology of power was always a temptation for Angelopoulos. Bakunin's association of state and God lurks behind this film, leading to the absolute dissolution of the individual self as both state and God as the products of moral and natural corruption. The end of the film is probably the most striking representation of the classical theophagy principle. The god that took power was indeed a flawed mortal who was deified through power. The apotheosis of the Roman emperors was in reality an *apocolocynthosis*: Seneca understood that the pernicious narcissism of power can be confronted through satire and a ludic approach. Angelopoulos understood that Stalin and his legacy still remained diffused and defined politics, especially for the Left.

The philosophical substratum of the film is given by Plato's *Gorgias* about the "Great man" and the restrictions imposed by ethical considerations. The ethics of authenticity emerge in his work after the collapse of the grand myths of the Marxist romantic hubris. For him, the demise had already started with the gradual degeneration of socialist republics into tyrannical regimes. Today we tend to believe that the exposé of Soviet atrocities became immediately accepted after the publication of Aleksandr Solzhenitsyn's *Gulag Archipelago*; but that was not the case. The battle between philosophical perspectives was also an inner conflict in the mind and the psyche of individuals who grew up believing in the emancipatory and liberational potential of Marxism. But history took another turn and showed to the Western European ideologues that Jan Patočka and Václav Havel had an experiential connection with the *inauthenticity* foisted by the cult of power that Soviet Marxism had imposed. Even Herbert Marcuse observed that Soviet Marxism used "an Aesopian language which conceals rather than points to the real distinction" (1958: 12). Angelopoulos came out of this atmosphere of disillusionment with this language of fairy tales and fables—and in a way he was always bedeviled by doubts and reservations about the failure of socialism. What is authenticity in human subjectivity will be a central concern from now on.

Ultimately we have to address the ethics of authenticity time and again, yet in a world without metaphysical horizons. In the 1980s, Angelopoulos abandoned Foucault's slogan that "power is everywhere" and rediscovered central questions of existentialism in being, feeling, and dying which later morphed into more specific questions on loss and finally redemption. However, various philosophies and philosophers informed Angelopoulos's iconosophical projects. With his oneiric *Voyage to Cythera*, *The Beekeeper*, and *The Suspended Step of the Stork*, Angelopoulos moves away from the question of history which gradually becomes the contested and somehow "misty" background of profound collective and individual psychodramas. The great existential and ultimately ontological questions of Western metaphysics take precedence in these films which visualize a new perception of the individual psyche.

If the crux of modernity emerged out of the vacuum left by the death of God, in this film the search for origins takes its most awe-inspiring expression. In secular modernity, the Nietzschean declaration that "God is dead" indicated that there is no paternity as an originary source. This is also an indirect reference to both Dostoevsky and Freud concerning the central question of modernity, that of patricide. In the midst of these dilemmas, the film *Landscape in the Mist* appears like an escape to the uncanny and the miraculous. Probably his best film, this "metaphysical road movie" is structured around a vision of reality shaped by the innocence of children, with their search for their lost father incorporating his older revolutionary critical understanding in a rather metaphysical sense of an ending.

The question of lost paternity brought out the experience of loss and memory that we see dominated in his final films, like *Ulysses' Gaze*, *Eternity and a Day*, *The Weeping Meadow*, and *The Dust of Time*. In a world without a father or the maternal consolation of grand myths, Angelopoulos searches for a redemption without eschatological implications or metaphysical presuppositions. Is this possible? Can we experience redemptive closure in history without the presence or the project of transcendence? Is it possible to consider immanence as the only redemptive possibility in a world without metaphysical expectations? These are the questions that we find in his later films, where Marx and Heidegger struggle to coexist within incommensurable structures, until they finally fail to do so in his most philosophically eloquent work, *Eternity and a Day*.

Questions of History and Identity

In his early films, an answer is given in the negative. Angelopoulos maintained a very strong devotion to T.S Eliot's poetry which he quoted constantly, especially regarding time. "Only through time / time is conquered" (Eliot 1970: 145) is probably the most salient background principle of his early films. But ultimately, what is identity and history in Angelopoulos's films, especially the early ones? How do they manifest themselves through the actions of individuals? Is there such a thing as free will in a reality overdetermined in its structural core by ideologies of power and oppression? His first films, from 1970 to 1980, show a reluctance to deal with history as lived or imagined experience. In the later period the concept of *historicity* is more appropriate to investigate the self-reflexive structures employed to talk about the human phenomenon as existential testimony.

However, after watching the Trilogy of History, we still have a question to answer: not only how history is depicted, but what is history? What creates a historical event and makes its participants historical agents? In the films after 1980, Angelopoulos moved on to the living presence of past experience in the everyday life of the people who suffered it or were exposed to it through contact with those who lived through it. The father who comes back from the Soviet Union in *Landscape in the Mist* is not only an individual but the resurfacing of history in the life of people who have lost the connection with the past. They want to forget and yet the past confronts them with its unexpected emergence. If in the previous films, history is above all collective memory, as seen through political movements and common beliefs, now history is a personal immersion into the experiential content of the past. The repatriated refugee is not simply a symbol of a defeated Left or the example of lingering political ideologies; the person returns with another history and another form, with new stories about his existence, wife, children, friends, his new family, his new identity, indeed his new biography.

After thirty-odd years exiled and restrained in another country, he is not the same person who migrated; he has a completely different perception of identity from the one his fellow country people still call him with. Does a sense of belonging to a place also mean a stable identity of the self? Is identity a marker of describing origins or an external ascription for characteristics by others? Angelopoulos explores what happens when the connection between land and individuals is severed and interrupted. A sense of a new ontological identity emerges here which seems to confirm Sartre's pithy statement: "Existence precedes essence" (2007: 27). The existence makes, or produces, as Sartre said, its own essence as conscious identity in history—or even a purposeful self-identification with history. Previously, based on Althusserian ideas, it is the social specificity of the political institutions that create, indeed construct, the foundations of self-consciousness and identity. In the new period, consciousness is formed by society, but reforms it in a reciprocal dialectical sense. Then it turns towards itself and reflects on the potencies and the limitations of its being.

The individual is not a passive reflection of what exists but an active agent of what is not yet. The unpredictable nature of the individual psyche as a philosophical question about human nature, and a persistent problematization of its nature, will be found in Angelopoulos's later films again. However, in this early period there is an ambivalent and somehow contradictory philosophy of history which returns Marxist thinking back to its Hegelian origins. In the next decade he explores both possibilities, attributing to art an existential duality that went beyond ideological or aesthetic lines: Aristotelian catharsis or Brechtian distancing. "My Brechtian period came to an end with *The Travelling Players*," he stated (Fainaru 2001: 132). However, he never defined the nature of Brechtian distancing and stylization which was more than a method of structuring performance and performability.

Aristotle ultimately triumphed, and the discovery of the human psyche also meant the rediscovery of the unpredictability of history. Having stressed many times that what his cinema was looking to construct is a framework for the "autonomy of existence," Angelopoulos proceeded to a new stage of philosophical exploration. "The problem of being," he stated, "must be solved by each person on his own. But in the creative process, 'to be' means 'to understand' before anything else. To understand yourself. In creation, in order for communication to take place, there have to be at least two beings. What happens between people is creation" (in Fainaru 2001: 37). How human beings create, re-create, and de-create each other in their attempt to communicate became the central concern of his iconosophy till the end of his life. "How many borders do we have to cross in order to reach home?" asks one of his characters in *The Suspended Step of the Stork*. And the child in *Landscape in the Mist* whispers: "In the beginning there was Chaos. And then there was light." His characters now explore the existential homelessness in their own body and within their psyche, realizing that there is no home anymore, in a world without redemptive rituals.

Chapter 4
On Being, Loss, and Memory

Or The Social Ontology
of Historicity

Philosophical Entanglements

The 1980s was the most challenging decade of the post-war period. Globalization slowly began to create new forms of artistic dissemination and art production through the new digital technologies, free-market economics, and the philosophical frameworks that articulated their cultural legitimacy. In a way the decade stands next to the post-World War I period in redefining the questions, methods, and ultimately perceptions of how we study the human phenomenon in moments of accelerated and uncontrolled modernization. According to Wolfram Eilenberger, 1919 to 1929 was "the era of the magicians" focusing on the foundational question, debated at Davos between Martin Heidegger and Ernst Cassirer, "What is a human being?" In hindsight, the discussion defined the philosophical history of Europe, as it was based on Immanuel Kant's universalistic statement that "Humans are beings who ask themselves questions that they are ultimately unable to answer" (Eilenberger 2020: 12). In contrast to such fundamental conversation, the 1980s became the era of verbal pyrotechnics by celebrity professors, mostly from France, who took the inability to answer this fundamental question as an invitation for the promotion of solipsism, cynicism, and ultimately nihilism.

Certainly, the question as such is unanswerable, something that Kant already knew. Modern secular hubris, however, led to the conceptual problematization of all human activities, through moral relativism, existential subjectivism, and ontological occlusion. Cinema confronted the nihilistic inability to answer this question when postmodernism started becoming dominant and moved from the grand modernist narratives of the auteurs to episodic and centerless anti-narratives. Cinematic images became fast moving, fading into each other, in a speedy succession that made impossible a *distinct* experience of filmic temporality. Hyper-modernity accelerated perceptual practices by emptying them of any humanistic or integrating content. The critique of humanism by Michel Foucault and his followers legitimized the dominance of the established, the given, and the obvious by removing all forms of self-transcendence and relegating to the realm of numinous, and ominous, the so-called "liminal experiences." The rise of blockbusters in the film industry undermined the ability to construct images about the new era of existential "disappearance of true individuals, given the kind of generalized conformism," as Cornelius Castoriadis observed (1997: 42). The New Philosophers in France declared that "Marx is Dead," Andrei Tarkovsky was expelled from the Soviet Union, while the movement for global cinema started becoming more concrete and influential.

Marxism was also questioned as a philosophical system; Nikos Poulantzas's suicide in 1979 marked the end of structural Marxism, confirmed by the tragic destiny of Louis Althusser, while the death of Sartre in 1980 also marked the end of French existential Marxism. From the beginning of the 1980s a political *interregnum* was inaugurated which soon became an interregnum in philosophical and anthropological thinking. The relativistic subjectivism of postmodernism which undermined all epistemologies of truth and truthfulness established a regime of philosophizing which could not be called properly philosophical. Many thinkers, or indeed mere *commentators*, or *lexicographic scholiasts*, were given the title of philosopher, through an anarchic eclecticism of ideas that pleased and confused everybody at the same time, through its jocular pastiche, recombination, and self-referentiality. The "representation of the self as an autonomous subject," Castoriadis again observed, and "the human capacity for reflectiveness" (1997: 157,

170) were questioned and were replaced by projects of adaptation to the dominant social practices which reaffirmed the existing for-itself and the complacent, through-itself. The instrumentalization of the individual became the main form of self-definition, experiencing a social and moral universe without any horizon for the other. Philosophers without a philosophy became the flavor of the day as the intellectual coalition between psychoanalysis, Marxism, feminism, and structuralism (later of queer, transhumanist, and transgender theories) started disintegrating into absolutist interpretations of the human and ultimately of the cinematic imaginary. The unity "of reflective self-representation and of the deliberate activities one undertakes" to assert its autonomy were lost within the dense opaqueness of existential and political heteronomy (Castoriadis, 1997: 170). The concrete *other* mutated to the abstract *otherness* which included everyone and therefore no one: the end of modernity made "nihilism not only an 'error' of the mind but a destiny of Being itself," as Gianni Vattimo observed (1988: 179).

The end of these philosophical modes of thinking created an intellectual vacuum which was filled by the radical subjectivism of Foucault and textual fantasies of Jacques Derrida. French philosophy of the period philosophies became "an essay on antihumanism," as Luc Ferry and Alain Renaut called it. Through the "deconstruction of modernity" inaugurated by Heidegger, thinking essentially annulled the possibility of a collective movement of emancipation, questioning the subject's capacity to know the truth, or to know itself, or indeed the truth of the self, as such. Indeed, the self became the most acute problematic during the period, through its "heteroclitic submission to multiple logics: the inscription of what was called the "subject" into the multiform register of heteronomy," according to G. Lipovetsky (Ferry-Renaut, 1990: 227)

New frameworks gradually formed around the self which were to dominate Angelopoulos's thinking till the end of his life. A new theory of the self started being formed in this period when Angelopoulos explored the question of subjectivity from an increasingly post-Marxist perspective. In his case, post-Marxism means through Marxism not against Marxism, not. Angelopoulos kept maintaining the humanistic and revolutionary tenets of Marx's early thought but enriched it with the existentialist concerns of the period especially those of Sartre and Camus. The atomized and anomic self-tormented by vague nostalgia or confused *weltschmerz* became the iconic background for his creative imaginary in this period. *Being There* (1979) by Hal Ashby, Louis Malle's *My Dinner with Andre* (1981), and Ridley Scott's *Blade Runner* (1982) frame the post-humanistic and post-social individual defending, through a hermeneutic of hope against all hope, an inner self which vanishes during the process. The dialogue between Angelopoulos's films with such currents of thought is rather underestimated and disregarded.

At the back of these subtexts, György Lukács's idea about the "problematic hero" of the modern novel looms large in the conversations around which Angelopoulos textured the storylines of his films. In Lukács, Angelopoulos he found, especially in the *Theory of the Novel*, a foundational concept which was to become the central organizing principle of his films until the end of his life—something which he couldn't find for example in Lenin's ideas about art. Lukács suggested that after the eighteenth century the problematic hero, as found in Cervantes, Goethe, Gogol, and Dostoevsky amongst others, exists in a radical disharmony with the natural world because of what happens within his inner life. Lukács's concept of "inner life" supported and corroborated the concept of psyche as elaborated by Angelopoulos in his own filmic exploration. Angelopoulos's "turn" indicated that the external realities were at variance or indeed in conflict with the inner life: there was a growing incommensurability between the natural subject and its inner symbolic universe. The conflict itself was part of the so-called "breaking up of personality," leading to the image of a fragmented subjectivity in a world without God, center, or destination.

Angelopoulos's main mythological character, Ulysses, is the eternal wanderer and traveler, but knows that there is a home waiting for him. Upon his return his identity will be found and be consolidated. It is an identity of ritual order, centered attentiveness, and collective validation. Historically, Ulysses' inner life is absent in Homer and the classical epic tradition in general. Deeds are more significant than thoughts and more relevant than the psychological dilemmas of the mind, if any. The ancient melancholy within a closed world is replaced in the modern novel, and in cinema, its successor, with the emergence of a new realm of claustrophobic interiority which delineates the profound separation and distancing from the grand myths that gave unity, solidity, and purpose in the past. Lukács wrote:

The inner form of the novel has been understood as the process of the problematic individual's journeying towards himself, the road from dull captivity within a merely present reality—a reality that is heterogeneous in itself and meaningless to the individual—towards clear self-recognition. After such self-recognition has been attained, the ideal thus formed irradiates the individual's life as its immanent meaning.

1971: 80

A journey towards a vanished or forgotten self is the project in films like *Voyage to Cythera*, *The Beekeeper*, and *the Suspended Step of the Stork*. The journey itself becomes a method of self-recognition and indicates that in its purpose is an unpredictable and singular process of becoming. As Lukács indicates,

the objective structure of the world of the novel shows a heterogeneous totality, regulated only by regulative ideas, whose meaning is prescribed but not given. That is why the unity of the personality and the world—a unity which is dimly sensed through memory, yet which once was part of our lived experience—that is why this unity in its subjectively constitutive, objectively reflexive essence is the most profound and authentic means of accomplishing the totality required by the novel form.

1971: 128

Substituting novel with cinema we will better understand the role of memory and loss in this new period of Angelopoulos's filmmaking. As Lukács concludes:

The subject's return home to itself is to be found in this experience, just as the anticipation of this return and the desire for it lie at the root of the experience of hope. It is this return home that, in retrospect, completes everything that was begun, interrupted, and allowed to fall by the way—completes it and turns it into rounded action.

1971: 128

The return home takes place in *Ulysses' Gaze*, but this is a strange home and a stranger return. The problematic of the self is now articulated in terms of the "tragedy of people who have psychology, who have a past" (Archimandritis 2013: 43). Angelopoulos calls it his "post-Brechtian" period" because now emotions take precedence over situations and a new perception of internalized temporality expresses the trauma of the gradual demise of all collective projects. In Angelopoulos the dialectical tension between emotionality and history (Angelopoulos usually talks about History and not history) contributes to the emerge of a new understanding of the human self as "rounded action." The individual now is free but lonely and abandoned. It has no bonds or roots and looks lost, awkward, and unrelated. At the heart of its existence there is a gaping hole, a lost center of unity and reference, the *arche* and *nostos* at the same time.

Starting with *Voyage to Cythera*, Angelopoulos frames a question about the unknowability of existence: "Don't forget that he is without citizenship, without ethnicity. Without a country. We don't even know who he is, or if he is simply using a name. Are you sure that this is your father? Time changes faces and figures" (Angelopoulos 1984: 89). The Homeric Ulysses is also the Homeric *Outis*, nobody, who abolishes an identity and its destiny. This happens because the bond of mutuality, the I–Thou relationship, is severed and lost. The *Outis* exists in a confusing network of unrecognizable realities, for which he cannot find an image that could objectify them and a symbolic home in which he could dwell. The feeling and the mood of being thrown into the world, of the Heideggerian *Geworfenheit*, raises possibilities both authentic and inauthentic, as it enables and limits existence and freedom. In a world of "facticities" according to Heidegger, the anxiety of being yourself forces existence to confront "the world's nothingness" in an attempt to "be authentically what it already was" (Heidegger 2010: 310, §325).

In Angelopoulos's seminal film, the repatriated refugee keeps repeating only one expression as the ultimate statement of his presence: *Ego Eimai*. The refugee was exiled for over thirty-five years and like Ulysses, when he returns, he tries to find a past that is not there anymore. The only expression that he utters about himself, about his self, is *Ego Eimai*, which can be translated as I am, I exist, or it's me; because of the sentence, the verb to be in the first person singular denotes an existential reality without predication. The verb to be, as in Shakespeare's famous soliloquy by Hamlet, has the connotation of a qualitative being: I am something, I am someone. I don't simply exist. I exist as my specific existence, my history, *I exist as*. The absence of such predication indicates that Angelopoulos used the verb irregularly as a marker of another condition of self-determination. The questioning of being begins with the problematization of its language. In the film, images try to present a centrifugal vision of the self—a self moving away from its own center. Hence, Angelopoulos leaves the question open if the man they follow is their father returning from exile, or the man who comes out of the Soviet vessel is their repatriated father. There are two fathers: a father-desire and a father-memory. However, the desire is misplaced, and the memory is distorted. The ambiguity in presentation points to the fact that Angelopoulos wanted to avoid a conceptualization of truth as correspondence between notions and facts. Indeed, the centrifugal self becomes undefinable and fluid; the quest for the unknown self culminates with *Ulysses' Gaze's* final monologue; it remains always a project and a never-ending process.

The phrase *ego eimai* resurfaces many times as the confrontation between the self and its perception, its own otherness, escalates and the character enters a state of existential decentering and expulsion from the *topos* of his originary authenticity. The father returns to retrieve his family, children, and his own childhood but suddenly realizes that he has lost his own self and therefore he cannot find anything. He is not himself anymore. Language betrays him and he has no physical home to live in: he is expelled from everywhere. If in his previous films, Angelopoulos dealt with the question of history and how we experience it, in this film his whole philosophical anthropology takes a new direction and starts searching into the origins of the self as such, within the circumstances of the period, and delving into the essential core of the human being. But he presents a character with existential amnesia in whose mind "the confrontation is between the real world and the dream world, a world unsullied and still pure which exists only in memory" (Fainaru 2001: 42). The question of history torments the repatriated refugee because now he comes out of history, he becomes history itself. The collective experience is lost when he goes back to his village: only his lethal enemy remembers him. The old selves resurface but within a context that renders them irrelevant and inconsequential. They don't complement each other: they annul their own existence. Instead of re-membering they are dis-membering history.

Friedrich Engels wrote the most ingenious statement about history, which accounts for the situation that the post-metaphysical individual had to deal with:

> History is made in such a way that the final result always arises from conflicts between many individual wills, of which each again has been made what it is by a host of particular conditions of life. Thus, there are innumerable intersecting forces, an infinite series of parallelograms of forces which give rise to one resultant—the historical event. This may again itself be viewed as the product of a power which works as a whole, unconsciously and without volition. For what each individual wills is obstructed by everyone else, and what emerges is something that no one willed.
>
> ENGELS 1972: 761

The reality of living a history that no one ever wanted, under historical circumstances that delegitimize existence, became another salient element of Angelopoulos's philosophical in this period.

Until the end of the film, the memories function as fragments of lost totalities and proofs of "the inner exile, of dispossession" (Fainaru 2001: 44). *Ego eimai* becomes the most ubiquitous thread that links all his films as an affirmation and interrogation of the nature of the self in an era of minimalistic expectations. Nietzsche remarked that "we are unknown to ourselves, we knowers: and with good reason. We have never looked for ourselves – so how are we ever supposed to find ourselves?" (2006: 3). Angelopoulos, overtly metapolitical in *Voyage to Cythera*, frames its semantic space by reference to the famous poem of the same title by Charles Baudelaire (Baudelaire 1993: 255)—as a place of escape and oblivion but also of danger and loss.

The discovery of the fabled island of mythological utopia becomes something completely different, almost a place of exile and punishment instead of the liberation of the senses and of subliminal memories: the political refugee, who returns thirty-five years later, recognizes only ruins and abandoned places, and experiences his own homeland as a hostile place without mercy and mutuality. Certainly, this is not something singular or unique. Lukács has already talked about "transcendental homelessness" (1971: 41) which deprives all problematic heroes from all forms of meaningful communication and indeed from all forms of transcending the limitations of their historical specificity. They will never become the Kantian universal imperative; they will remain peripheral incidents, irregularities, somehow random accidents. A world without opening to the shared values of a cultural community becomes the most pertinent and persistent question in Angelopoulos's film.

However, the "call for silence" permeates the gradual descent to the absurd: the refugee is sent out to the international borders in a no man's land, legally, culturally, and *politically*, as no country wants to accept him. The dialogue denotes that Angelopoulos engages with a new form of post-political selfhood, that of embodied conscience. Not all ideas that we find in the script made it into the actual film. In the script we discover a deep connection between embodied feeling and existential conscience. What links those two "deep structures" of cognition and sentience is the responsiveness of the mind to the challenges around. In the film, what exactly is missing is the responsiveness of the self to the questions and the dilemmas of the historical moment. It seems that an existential numbness takes over the conscious self and causes a personal annulment; later, this human condition in abeyance evolved into a form of proto-nihilism in his late films.

However, the central source of this self-abolishing consciousness is that it has been alienated from its own feelings, "embeddings," and roots. Is this because of exile or maybe because of the new self that emerged through his other life elsewhere? Is there any connection between those lived realities? In a crucial moment, the sister of the director has a casual sexual encounter with a sailor and turns to the camera saying: "There are times when I discover with horror and relief that I believe nothing. Then I return to my body. Only my body reminds me that I am alive" (Angelopoulos 1984: 118). The centrifugal self, which has lost all its responsiveness, ultimately reverts to the physical reality of the mere *bios*, living without predication in order to regain the integrity of its naturality. It is as if Angelopoulos takes the homeless problematic hero back to its origins in Jean-Jacques Rousseau's natural existence and the idea that civilization destroys the innocent self by corrupting its essence and imposing an alienation in its own self-perception. Lack of responsiveness leads to "bare life" according to Giorgio Agamben, the exact opposite of Aristotle's *bios politikos*. Sheer biological facts are given priority over the actual way that life is experienced and also imagined. As Agamben defined it, in opposition to the Aristotelian understanding of *bios*, bare life means "a zone of indistinction and continuous transition between man and beast" (1998: 109). There cannot be any individual projects of liberation and emancipation: the end of the film leaves everything in limbo. The original dream for a new reconnection with the authenticity of his origins is lost. The self vanishes as "it floats away and is lost in the mist" (Angelopoulos 1984: 125).

Mist, Vasilis Rafailidis argued, is the most *political* symbol in Angelopoulos. The natural phenomenon of mist stands for the illusory and mediated perception of reality and by extension for the mystification of existence through inauthenticity and "bare life." It is both the imprisoned mind in Plato's cave and Heidegger's ontological concealment. Angelopoulos wrote:

> The world is a chessboard on which man is just another pawn and his chance of an impact on the proceedings, negligible. Politics is a cynical game that has turned its back on the commitments of the past. This does not necessarily mean we have to go back to the hero in the primitive sense of the word, but at least to a narrative that puts man in the centre.
>
> FAINARU 2001: 49

In the era of Foucauldian anti-humanism or post-humanism, Angelopoulos's anthropocentrism sounds romantic and idealistic, indeed anti-modernist. In his next films he engages with the dominant question of twentieth-century philosophy, according to Camus, the absurdity of existence that frames the possibility of suicide and voluntary death.

How Subjectivity Ends

The Beekeeper and *The Suspended Step of the Stork* are the least commercially successful of Angelopoulos's films. I call them *transitional* films because they indicate the new ground his iconosophy tried to claim, shape, and consolidate. By leaving his Marxist revolutionary past behind, Angelopoulos had to construct new formal *gestalten* in a way that would constitute an actual visual language for his new thinking. Both films are replete with subliminal and libidinal subtexts that indicate that something extremely intimate and personal was announcing its own articulation. How do we understand the self when it dissolves, vanishes, or voluntarily extinguishes its own existence? Death dominates all these films, but voluntary death also makes its dreaded appearance. Between them stands his most successful and finest work, *Landscape in the Mist*, which must be seen as a great Platonic myth or an arcane Sufi parable. The language of images takes on a completely new epistemological articulation: instead of presenting the question as such it translates it to the form of a poetic allegory. It is an allegory both as mimesis of the real and a mimesis of the symbolic. Its mixed character makes this film exceptionally challenging and provocative. The lyrical fable of *Landscape in the Mist* is later monumentalized in the epic and cosmological *Ulysses' Gaze*, a film about the "ultimate concern" of the human presence in history.

In his transitional films, Angelopoulos explored philosophical questions that his previous cinematic constructions simply hinted at or touched upon indirectly. Furthermore, if his previous films were critical of dominant imaginaries, these films move beyond the horizon of expectations to be either negative or cynical or indeed critical. They articulate visual propositions of their own: they have an autotelic character of semantic self-sufficiency and rounded completeness. Nevertheless, they maintain the form of a visual investigation and leave the questions they address unanswered and open. Their central theme is the possible extent of human communication. *The Beekeeper* is a tragedy of errors, full of semantic dissonances. Something goes wrong from the beginning. What happens when the interpersonal context of mutuality that has constituted interpersonal relations is lost, or becomes a phantasma from the past? This lies at the heart of the critical questioning of subjectivity. The main characters try to remember and decode a language which was used in the past when they were prisoners. The coded messages were not about freedom or revolution but the verses of a rather notorious gay poet, Napoleon Lapathiotis (1888–1944). In prison, poetry gave him the language to survive adversity. "First time was a sunny day / blinding us with its endless light. / No desire of ours was hidden / vainly we searched for a distant shadow . . ." (Angelopoulos 1986: 42). The dialectical collision between what is hermeneutically possible and what is impossible to communicate dominate the deep structure of the film. There are conditions about the self that cannot be appropriated and conceptualized by any hermeneutical system.

Because of the unknowability of the other, the question can be defined as the quest for *interpersonality*; indeed, the film heralds the appearance of the most contentious issue of love as a manifestation of essential human subjectivity, which we will find again in his later films. Sartre, in his underrated Rome Lecture of 1961, tried hard to define subjectivity as "our proper being, that is, the obligation on us to have to be our being and not simply passively to be." For Sartre the question is that, within the given circumstances of occlusion and introversion, the knowledge of the self is limited by the constrictions of relativism and solipsism, indeed by the very presence of the other. Sartre declares that "the true problem is, in fact, that of knowing how, through an objective knowledge of the real, we who exist subjectively can transcend ourselves in order to have a relationship with reality" (2016: 37).

The other as the unknown presence in the proximity of the self is expressed with the absolute collapse of communication. The secrets are stronger that the actual truths—and they destroy any attempt to appropriate the real in its multiple manifestations. Moreover, Angelopoulos explores dramatically the question of historical and social amnesia that was becoming dominant with postmodernism all over Europe. The privileging of *now* at the expense of *then* was for Angelopoulos a serious absence in the problematics of contemporary anthropology. The diachronic dimension establishes the individual in a firm and ongoing personal or even interpersonal relationship with the past. If this diachronic dimension is lost, then the individual loses perspective and scope.

Angelopoulos's argument about the lost connection was constructed under the perspective of Francis Fukuyama's "end of history" thesis that was to appear some years later and dominate the cultural and political conversations of the next two decades. By cutting the self away from its history and its foundations, the modern individual is left with digressions and repetitions, in the sense of Kierkegaard. The inauthenticity of motives leads to Kierkegaard's "aesthetic schemer" who admonishes his own self: "Be inconstant, nonsensical; do one thing one day and another the next, but without passion, in an utterly careless way that does not, however, degenerate into inattention, because, on the contrary, the external attentiveness must be just as great as ever but altered to a formal function lacking all inwardness" (1983: 142). Angelopoulos dramatizes this process towards an alienated and deracinated personality, like Kierkegaard's man of fear and dread, employing autobiography and confession, addressing the expanding inner split of the inauthentic subject.

If Sartre suggested that we have a relationship with reality only if we transcend ourselves, Kierkegaard doubts even this possibility—and indeed Angelopoulos seems to condone his doubt with the end of the film and the voluntary death of the central character. The character is called Spyros, which was the name of Angelopoulos's father. However, on a visit to the cinema where the father used to live, he finds the "old mask of my father" (Angelopoulos 1986: 58). The confrontation with the subjectivity of the father is well hidden under the sexual relationship between him and a young girl, as in Bernardo Bertolucci's *Last Tango in Paris* (1972). The loneliness and melancholia of old age cannot be reversed by the brief carnal encounters with youth. Such incidents simply bring out the motif of temptation and confront the self with the limitations of aging—a theme that will become crucial for the "late style" of Angelopoulos.

Old age is tempted by the *will* for self-oblivion, since the center of existence, the past experiences, have been encoded by a language that cannot be deciphered anymore except in moments of mutual cooperation: only when the old friends and revolutionaries are together the sentimental verses regain their authentic, intentional and unmediated meaning. The verses invoke bonds and do not communicate meaning. Here subjectivity ends through historical *aphasia*: we have lost the language of the past. Consequently, the past we cannot connect with Implodes into verbal *kenosis*. Words become meaningless and distort the desire to express the self. The past disappears from conscience and what remains is a nihilistic void where memories exist compartmentalized and unconnected with each other. Subjectivity is thrown into a perpetual limbo between remembering and oblivion, yet in a strange manner waiting for redemption. Spyros embodied the disintegrated self which exists only as lack and loss while still searching for redemption and absolution, or probably for a personal redeemer. The crime is never admitted: we don't really know what happened or indeed if anything happened, or if everything is the idle chatter of the anonymous "they," according to Heidegger.

In *The Suspended Step of the Stork* the longing for redemption ceases to exist and the self is taken over by intense and profound scepticism. The end of the political is one of the most crucial aspects of the film's conceptual and quite likely historical references. Angelopoulos, as we have seen, had a view of politics as found in Aristotle's organic civic *politeia* which, for him, appeared in modern history through revolutionary action, in Paris, Moscow, Madrid, and Athens. But the political system today is probably an ossified formalization of institutions which oppress, coerce, and suppress. Since power is everywhere in the world of everyday reality which exists for its rational mastery, there is a strange *oneiric* element which gives the opportunity to connect social oppression with emotional repression while at the same time multiplying the ways of alienation.

As in *The Hunters*, the principle around which the film organizes its architecture is the debilitating influence of repression. Freud was extremely conscious to stress that the id is the cornerstone of psychoanalysis and of the anthropological model produced in contemporary oppressive societies. According to him, repression is the "force that prevented [patients] from becoming conscious and compelled them to remain unconscious . . . pushed the pathogenetic experiences in question out of consciousness. I gave the name of *repression* to this hypothetical process" (Freud 1995: 25). Repression renders people unconscious of their own circumstances and forces them to forget the truth of their existence: the *aletheia* of their Being.

Repression indicates lack of mutuality and a perception of the self that struggles to evade its own interiority. In *The Suspended Step of the Stork* a young filmmaker searches for a lost politician who disappeared, and nobody can find his whereabouts. The film is based on many non-sequiturs, and its temporality is spasmodic and fragmented, despite the ostensible linear development. Its conceptual argument is about the randomness and contingency of human activity manifesting itself in unexpected twists and turns but ultimately remaining in a total and inexplicable abeyance. We learn nothing about the name and the identity of the man who they think is the lost politician. As in Antonioni's *L'Avventura*, the main female character vanishes, and no one is interested to know what happened to her. She has been forgotten by everybody. The same with the original crime of the father in *The Beekeeper*. They all know that something happened, but nobody reveals anything. The viewers must act hermeneutically, but cognitively the intentions and the motives of the main character remain inscrutable and impregnable.

Strange omens and peculiar events appear and disappear, pointing towards the empty spaces that dominate the skies of the films: the inability of the filmmaker to find a pattern of recognition means that he cannot find ways of connecting his own experiences. Indeed, in the end he is not able to make the movie he wanted to. Unexpectedly another film comes out which is the film of himself trying to make another film. The contingency of human existence extends to the slow realization that we are not in control of our life, but also that the unconscious defines the worlds of imagination. If in his previous films necessity and determinism were the main underlying structural principles, the exploration of interiority foregrounds contingency and chance. The discovery of the *psyche* ambiguates the subjects within themselves. The organizing principles of their interiority now become the only patterns for reconciliation. From the ruins of a lost world, and the vestiges of a lost vision about the world, a new harmony emerges, which transcends the conscious volition of individuals and becomes concrete against their own will.

For this reason, all characters experience the reality of an *elsewhere* in them: "the elsewhere has become a mythical reality" for the refugees, we read in the script (Angelopoulos 1995: 99). They also experience the namelessness of the inner exile: "travel . . . It hurts me . . . Everything I touch hurts me . . . You don't even have a name" (Angelopoulos 1995: 106). However, the central statement of the work is given by the politician before he disappeared: "Somebody must remain silent so that we will be able to listen the music behind the noise of the rain" (Angelopoulos, 1995: 116). The unexpected and the unimagined exist as active principles that define human life in a centerless world.

The discovery of the contingent character of human activity depicted as having both positive and negative consequences. The disintegrating self is "lost and never found' within an unpredictable chain of events. The more they look, they find no real link between reality and perception: the structure is focused on what might be called "non-causal eventuations." Whatever happens could not be predicted: nothing relates to anything. The accidental permeates the action through episodes that happen without any real connection to the story. There is an uncomfortable perception of history delineated in the films—but not clearly articulated. Randomness becomes the only way to experience the world in *The Beekeeper* and *The Suspended Step of the Stork*. All humans move in liminal spaces where communications are precarious and sometimes totally impossible. The hermeneutics of suspicion define the social protocols of behaviour. In the borders between countries, civilization collapses and the primitive instincts of self-destruction emerge.

Paradoxically, the positive disclosure is about the perennial fecundity of existence, its relentless ability to renew itself through creative activities and productive labor. In the middle of a collapsing world, Angelopoulos envisages that human artifacts can bridge the gap between intention and realization and establish new projects of social integration through technology. The film ends like a musical symphony:

> Alexander comes closer.
> The man at the central pole works fast.
> The others work on the final connection. It's over. And then Alexander thinks that he hears a whisper, like music, which in the beginning is hardly heard but slowly grows, gets louder, spreads over the landscape; and it is as if the strings of an enormous harp were made able to produce again musical harmony.
> These are human voices heard in distant phone conversations, thousands of voices in many languages, male, female, happy, angry, erotic, giving farewell or welcoming, laughing and crying: the voice of the world.
> Alexander stops and listens enchanted, like everybody else. A violent emotion runs through him. The music of voices spreads more and more towards the distant horizon.
>
> ANGELOPOULOS, 1994: 190

This is the other side of technology: technophobia is transformed into a cautious celebration of how *episteme* and *techne*, knowledge and craftmanship combined, can essentially assist the fragmented self to retrieve its communicative ability. Contingency is not inaction and sloth: it implies the opening up of the self, not to what is given but to what can be actual. In other words, it establishes a space from which accidental answers can become necessary presuppositions. The optimistic ending of the film points to other existential possibilities that Angelopoulos explored in the films of the period in order to confront the nightmares of an existence steeped in self-alienation and inauthenticity. The self-imprisonment of the human mind to its own inventions becomes another thematic thread. Socialism had just collapsed in Eastern and Central Europe when *The Suspended Step of the Stork* was made. But for Angelopoulos, the project for the abolition of alienation put forward by socialist thinkers is valid and will remain so.

As Marx stated, the abolition of alienation "is the definitive resolution of the antagonism between man and nature, and between man and man. It is the true solution of the conflict between existence and essence, between objectification and self-affirmation, between freedom and necessity, between individual and species. It is a solution of the riddle of history and knows itself to be this solution" (Fromm 1966: 69). Ultimately, together with the disillusionment at the collapse of communism and the critical exposure of contemporary forms of alienation, Angelopoulos seems to enter the realm of an anti-historical utopianism. Even when history takes its revenge against all those who believe that it ended, Angelopoulos's utopia consists in confronting the dystopia of contemporary politics through parables and allegories. Utopia of course is a political concept, and we cannot understand Angelopoulos's political vision about "the autonomy of human existence" if we do not focus on the phenomenology of social experience that he explores unfolding under the most adverse circumstances, during the war in Yugoslavia. With these films Angelopoulos explores how history is defined by utopias and utopias by history: that we cannot disengage the human mind from its quest for impossible ideals even while experiencing the most negative circumstances. Still within a disintegrating subjectivity there is a deep structure that cannot be obliterated by the mere existence of the natural being. Responding to this challenge, Angelopoulos revisited the Platonic idea of the psyche as the ultimate space of convergence between the self and its realities. What he saw in the psyche articulates and gives meaning to the actual visual mythology of his final films.

An Eschatological Parable

Landscape in the Mist "is a kind of fairytale in which I was trying to preserve the delight and wonder of an initial discovery," stated

Angelopoulos. And he added: "A fairytale [. . .] gives you much greater freedom to introduce elements that are outside the logic of the plot" (in Fainaru 2001: 60, 63). Indeed, the central conceptual problem addressed is the refutation of all deterministic action and historical causality. As we have seen in his early films, history and the world, were the sum of sets and sub-sets of institutions determining and overdetermining human agency and activity. In the end, humans were free only when obeying the predetermined action of practices that were beyond their control and understanding. They themselves were the *practices* that dominated them, simultaneously the masters and the slaves of their environment. The fairy-tale form in *Landscape in the Mist* gives absolute freedom to Angelopoulos to construct a story replete with episodes and incidents that are not in any way connected with each other. Angelopoulos here explores the imponderables influencing human actions and impacting collective historical movements, an idea of historical continuity not altogether dependent on the action and the agency of the individuals that produced it.

The story, like Plato's myth of Er in his *Republic* (10.614–10.621), is linear, simple and uncomplicated in its temporal sequence. Two children leave their home and embark on an arduous journey to find their father in Germany. Loosely based on the Hansel and Gretel story by Brothers Grimm (another gesture towards the symbolic imaginary of German romanticism), the film ends with the vague vision of a tree in the borderlands between the real and the unreal, where all human presence is reduced to unseen disembodied voices. The linear narrative indicates that Angelopoulos constructs an allegorical story about the journey towards a destination we don't know really exists. Unlike in the emblematic myth of post-war absurdism, *Waiting for Godot* by Samuel Beckett, the two children wait for their father's return and, since he never responds, they decide to leave and find him. Their journey is a matter of decision and choice: they must start the journey or simply remain inert in a constant limbo within the shadow world of a phantasmic mother. Their mind is focused on a critical decision they must take for themselves: are they going to initiate the encounter or simply reject the possibility of meeting with the origin?

Here, Angelopoulos articulates a new existential anthropology of choice and decision in his attempt to establish the invariants in historical activity and personal continuity. The new anthropology comes out as a negation of what we find in the story. It is organically incorporated in it and presents itself through various episodes, as if all Platonic myths and parables were put together to construct an image about the problem itself. For Angelopoulos in particular the question is extremely important because it is so close to religious and metaphysical problematics which he himself fiercely rejected. For this reason, Angelopoulos chose children as the central characters: because their world is illogical but not irrational. The miraculous does not suspend reality in their mind; but it is part of their reality and reveals without any mediation what the real is about. The children who leave their maternal home, the womb, to find the father who gave them life confront a chaotic and unpredictable world, a world in which questions of good and evil are negotiated instantly, and the inexperienced children must take life-binding decisions. *In the beginning there was chaos*, says the boy: this is Angelopoulos's Hellenic reference to the pre-Socratic philosophers. *And then there was light*: This is Angelopoulos's gesture towards Christianity. The complementarity of the two traditions is elegantly expressed through the most emblematic statements uttered by an inexperienced, innocent child.

In *Landscape in the Mist*, the natural man of Jean-Jacques Rousseau confronts the problematic man of existentialism: history becomes the realm in which they will lose their purity and innocence in order to gain experience and knowledge. It is the only film in which evil makes its appearance in Angelopoulos's universe. It appears as the rapist truck driver, who commits his un-seeable crime, and most significantly with the form of the seductive young man who wants to distract them from their purpose. In a way, the young man on his motorcycle expresses the only theological notion that we find in Angelopoulos's work, that of the tempter, the cunning one, the *Diavolos*, therefore of the fallen dark angel who does the wrong thing out of an immense nostalgia for his lost home. His words are full of constant approval and positive re-enforcement, but his plan is to take them elsewhere, to make that *elsewhere* the place they will call home. At the same time, his words are tinged by a certain melancholy, a sense of bitter regret, of an implied guilt, for something lost and unapproachable.

Like Kierkegaard's corruptor, he wants to make them decide to do evil and "the wrong thing" with their own will. He doesn't try to coerce them or impose upon them anything; but gently and almost intimately he exposes them to forces that they cannot control: pain, desire, sex and pleasure. A similar iconography of evil can be seen in Christopher Nolan's *The Dark Knight* (2008) and its 'schismatic identity' (Goh 2022: 55). It's not simply hedonism that he wants to drive them towards. He exhibits for them, without saying anything, the exchange price of everything. The motorcycle that he loves is exchanged for sex with another man. Everything that he likes, or pretends to, he gives away in front of the children so that a sense of detachment and separation, of a life without attachments, lonely and forlorn, would become part of their experience and therefore of their mind. He seduces them by offering in abundance what he thinks they will like: not by restricting them but by offering pleasures, rewards, and recognition they don't really want or need. The scene in the underground disco in which the lights are dimmed and everything exists as emerging out of darkness is the best depiction of what hell must look like. The human face, which is the luminous revelation of the harmony and beauty of the world, or reflects the image and likeness of God, is simply a flat surface, empty and menacing, without eyes and expression. The *prosopon* in Greek language, which means a face-to-face encounter with the other, is abolished and totally erased. The face becomes a mirror which reflects the other as a fleeting and incommunicable accident, without concreteness and essential being. The other is there to be used and be useful. The children remain in the disco for some time and escape in despair. *Our father is waiting*, the girl says and drags her brother away.

Angelopoulos's anthropology here confronts the uncanny and the *mysterium tremendum* in an almost innocent, indeed pre-modern, fashion. The children cannot be corrupted: the call of the father is stronger than anything else. The quest for the paternal presence takes place through the experience of its absence. Angelopoulos stresses that such absence was a radical paradigm shift in the way we understand sociability and historicity. In order to bring out the changing registers in the language of the conversation, he indicates that he "expanded the dimension of time" (Fainaru 2001: 64). The children experience a condensed sense of the flow of time within them, whereas narratologically time expands and becomes a device that unfolds the various challenges they confront. Meanwhile, at a second *unfilmed* level, a parallel narrative evolves which breaks through the frames of the visible story and infuses them with the distancing effects of the *Unheimliche*: the broken hand of an enormous statue, the sudden snow, the last minutes of a dying white horse, the presence of angels as in Rilke's verse from the *Duino Elegies* is heard to ask for all the angels to be gathered: "Who, if I cried out, would ever hear me among the angel's hierarchies" (Rilke 1995: 331). The two levels of articulation in the film converge when the one breaks into the other in a form of self-transcending projection. "Having its ground in the horizontal unity of ecstatic temporality," writes Heidegger, "the world is transcendent" (2010: 365). The *ecstatic temporality* experienced by the children confronts the everydayness of experience and succeeds in transcending it. "In the beginning was Chaos," says the little boy. "And then, light came to be. And the light was separated form darkness and the earth from the sea, and the rivers were made, and then the lakes and the mountains. And then the flowers and the trees, the animals, the birds" (Angelopoulos 1993: 149). A "never-ending magical fairy tale," a new cosmogony, is actually narrated and enacted in front of the eyes of the spectators throughout the film without ever being seen or being verbalized.

In a sense, the film articulates the moods as found in the literary genre of magical realism: everything is itself and something more. There is a poignant scene in which the children find the actors, the actual actors of Angelopoulos's *The Travelling Players* parodying their own roles, as their "costumes" are for sale. They mimic themselves reciting their roles from that movie and feel ridiculous for what they represent today. The angel that distracts them tries to show some signs and traces of a lost completeness, but nothing is seen: the commercialization of art makes its few surviving traces the last vestiges of the otherworldly and the mysterious. Meanwhile, through their letters, the children try to communicate with the father in a fragmented and confused way: "We only want to know you and then we will go again. Can you reply to us? Reply with the sound of the train . . . pam . . . pam . . . pam . . . here I am. I am waiting for you . . . pam . . . pam . . . pam . . . here I stand and I am waiting for you. . ." (Angelopoulos 1993: 153). This passage, which constitutes an eloquent dialogue with Beckett's nihilistic silence of God, constructs the second level of articulation, the symbolic and the anagogical that appears and disappears spasmodically throughout the film. As they approach closer to Germany, the letters become more expressive:

> Last night we had the idea to resign, what's the use of insisting, we will never come close to you, and Alexander was angry like a grown man and said that I am betraying him. We all write the same things

to you and each one stands silent in front of the other, looking at the same world, the light, the darkness, and you . . .

ANGELOPOULOS 1993: 173

The vestiges of the old grand narratives are gradually erased by the growing presence of a metaphysical darkness. The empty sky, full of black clouds and shrunk horizons, becomes a synonym of the name of the lost father. There is a mystical element in this paternal quest. The apophatic theology of the East identifies God with the dark abyss of the beginning, something that we encounter in great mystics like Meister Eckhardt and Jacob Boehme. Angelopoulos repudiated religion and mysticism and therefore such vestiges represent for him a natural occurrence, something that happens in a specific time and place as the sudden emergence of ontological essence (an experience that I called elsewhere the *ontological sublime*). The disclosure of Being, according to Heidegger, is the ultimate outcome of an ecstatic self-transcendence, or of a Hegelian *aufheben*, of a state of existence in which all contradictions have been synthesized and simultaneously overcome, transformed into a rich unity where contradictions coexist harmoniously as indications of the irresolvable dilemmas of living. The film ends with the eerie image of tree, in the mist: "A meadow and further down a blue tree. Then the children, with the little boy saying the fairy-tale, walk forward and sink into the landscape, which is as bright as the First day of Creation" (Angelopoulos 1993: 186). What is this blue tree about? Angelopoulos gives no answer to this question: but if history has an end, we are not able to predict it—we can only encounter it.

Hence, the whole film is structured around a series of epiphanies which bring to the light of consciousness the anxieties and the panics that were becoming dominant in the late 1980s. The hyper-subjectivism of postmodernity had already raised questions not only about the prevailing order of things in ideological commitment, social affiliation, and spiritual connection. All epiphanic visions foreground the growing disillusion with established practices and ideas, especially within the crumbling edifice of historical consciousness formed through the liberal consensus after World War II. Through the liminal and pre-modern mind of the children, and their determination to find a father they have never met, Angelopoulos raised again the fundamental question in the philosophy of Hegel and Marx: where are we going to, as historical beings? Does history towards an end really exist or is it a fantasy of idealistic political theorists? A year later, Francis Fukuyama published his famous paper entitled "The End of History?" which started a prolonged conversation at a political and philosophical level about one of the most persistent and diachronic philosophical questions.

Fukuyama raised the question on behalf of liberal democracy and its victory over communism, arguing that "liberal democracy may constitute the 'end point of mankind's ideological evolution' and the 'final form of human government,' and as such constituted the 'end of history'" (1991: 1). Leaving the question of liberal democracy's triumph aside, the question about the direction of history is extremely important for the understanding of Angelopoulos's political anthropology, as mapped out in this film but most importantly in his magnum opus of the next decade, *Ulysses' Gaze*. The children in *Landscape in the Mist* are driven towards the border, towards "the long way to Germany," believing that there is an end to their adventure and that when they will encounter it, they will be able to recognize and be part of it. More importantly, that a mythic Germany will accept them and make them members of a totalizing *communitas*. The film is open-ended and left to conjecture: what is the "blue tree" waiting for them? Is this the tree of knowledge in the Garden of Eden or a gesture of connection with Tarkovsky's luminous tree at the end *of The Sacrifice*?

The children approach the tree and embrace it in an act of ritual worship; and then they all vanish in a misty blue colour as bright as on the first day of Creation. The religious reference is too strong to be overlooked. A return to the source provides the ontological consecration of the mundane and the everyday. The symbolism is extremely crucial and can be juxtaposed to the completely different final scene in *Ulysses' Gaze*. If, in this film, history does have an end, an eschatological destination that encompasses the whole of existence, as an objective presence and within the capacity for individual appropriation, *Ulysses' Gaze* ends with a long Homeric prayer "to the whole human adventure, an adventure that never ends" (Angelopoulos 1995: 112). An existence dichotomized between one form of history tending towards the eschaton and another defined by randomness becomes the most important question in the epic and mythological landscapes of *Ulysses' Gaze*. Angelopoulos leaves the question without an answer: he privileges a form of subjectivity that searches for the eschaton while totally immersed in the historical.

As Castoriadis concluded: "We have to understand that being is essentially stratified—and that it is so, not once and for all but 'diachronically': the stratification of being is also an expression of its self-creation, of its essential temporality, or of being as incessant *to-be*" (1997: 373). A *stratified subjectivity* can exist synchronically and diachronically in both realms of history and metaphysics. History cannot have an end because it is not exhausted in the sum of historical actions and events. It is also the urge for self-creation in the human psyche that attributes a metaphysical dimension to human existence because it consists simultaneously of love for being *and* of drive towards death, as a dialectical opposition of impulses. The task for cinema, its little utopia according to Angelopoulos, is like Wilhelm Dilthey's perception of empathic understanding or R.G. Collingwood's re-enactment theory: it wants to transport viewers to another world through their immersion in someone else's symbolic atmosphere of thinking. What happens when we become immersed in the symbolic biosphere of someone else's thinking processes became Angelopoulos's philosophical concern in his next film.

History Without an End

Ulysses' Gaze articulates Angelopoulos's meta-philosophy on the self-creation of individuals under adverse historical circumstances. The film is a modern retelling of the *Odyssey*, set in the post-communist Balkans during the civil wars in Yugoslavia. Its epic scope, and at the same time its reliance on the ancient myth for maintaining its narrative centre, transforms its images into visual testimonies about the tense relationship between History and the historical subject. Macro-history and micro-history are intertwined in peculiar, creative, and dissonant ways. In some respects, the film succeeds in balancing time and duration, but the semantic epistemology of its images remains contradictory and inconclusive. Furthermore, the old modernist tension between myth and history, the symbolic and the real in Lacanian terms, becomes also central and makes each episode a palimpsest of anthropological references.

In the grand History of Angelopoulos, many events happen and at an accelerated pace so that the individual is unable to find meaning, purpose, and orientation in the chaos of modern history, as T.S. Eliot opined about James Joyce's own adaptation of the *Odyssey*. The myth acts as the scaffolding that structures monumental events of both the long duration and the diachronic seriality of history around concrete images of events and actions. The viewer can unpack them and discern the various layers of signification. Nature remains an indifferent bystander to the gradual descent of people into their own catastrophic demise. In one of the most memorable scenes, the broken gigantic statue of Lenin is taken by the real god of Europe, the river Rhine, in a farewell ceremony of the king's burial. This is the funeral of a god that was failed by a society which still believes in some form of redemption, even if it is secular and materialistic. Is there, however, redemption in a society without eschatological horizons?

The duality of the narrative is also important for the understanding of its problematic: there is the actual account of *res gestae* juxtaposed to the other level of articulation, *historia rerum gestarum*. The situation in Yugoslavia evolves at the same time as the reflection on the events and their impact on the human psyche takes place as well. Historicity comes out of the interaction between these two dimensions of thinking recollected through the opening of the actual structure of the event to its own specific and authentic signification. Only when history turns against the individual does the individual gain historicity. Angelopoulos's exploration of a history without horizon and perspective becomes central: what remains after the death of God? E.M. Cioran became the official chronographer of that historical moment with his book *Temptation to Exist*, which confronts us with the innate barbarism and therefore the nothingness of history. How does an artist react to the barbaric regressive drive within political civilisation in post-Enlightenment, post-Christian, and post-democratic societies? "The man who belongs, organically belongs to a civilization cannot identify the nature of the disease which undermines it," wrote Cioran. "Since he knows you cannot *treat* destiny, he does not set himself up as a healer in any case. His sole ambition: to keep abreast of the Incurable" (2012: 48). Angelopoulos wants to sublimate the incurable tendency for destructiveness and self-destructiveness in history through the civilizing effects of art and the cathartic influence of poetry. However, the trauma of history is also the trauma of birth: the anthropology of *Ulysses' Gaze* implies that we are born to perpetuate the trauma of our existence, that the war in Yugoslavia is not simply what happened in the country between 1994 and 1996 but a constant conflict within the human psyche between projects of presumed restorative justice.

The film starts where his previous film ended, at the borders between cultures, states, and systems. It was filmed when the war was happening, and violence represents the real condition during the making of the film. The Greek American director A., an outsider, tries to retrieve certain original reels made in the Balkans around the beginning of the twentieth century after the dawn of modernity and the introduction of the first camera to the region. He travels through almost all of the Balkan countries and ends in Sarajevo during its siege, where he meets the custodian of the cinematic memory of the Balkans, who is killed by militias with all his family. The film culminates with another grand epiphany of the invisible: the reels are finally developed and the originary gaze establishes a connection with the modern eye, which sees nothing but emptiness although everything is there on the cinematic frame. The screen is the answer and the catharsis. The voided frame indicates that history is *elsewhere* because it is unseen and quite likely unseeable. It belongs to the dead. The modern gaze cannot see what is in front of it: the being of the past is not appropriable and cannot become the event that will open up to what Heidegger called, "the appropriated clearing." It remains in obscurity and in a state of numinous otherness. It also stays anonymous and therefore cannot be interpreted. History is the realm of imponderable and imperceptible parameters which have no explanation and no clear causality.

From the beginning of the journey, the main character, played by Harvey Keitel, is constantly overwhelmed by innumerable and incalculable forces that impact his journey. Local reaction, the remnants of the past, the conflicts of the present, an unpredictable meeting with a mysterious woman, the siege of Sarajevo, the destruction of the city, all these events appear suddenly and then vanish, like omens and signs from another *archetypal* realm of existence. His resoluteness to find the beginning of cinema overpowers the pressure of events and imparts a sense of Hegelian ethical recognition to the main character. However, together with his immersion into the events of war and violence. A.'s own personal history emerges from the depths of time. By reliving the traumas of his childhood, he reconstructs the conditions that made them real. Because of such personal trauma emerging from his unconscious, the archetypal myth underlines and foregrounds the interiority of his gaze. History looks back at him and constructs an image that he didn't know existed. His mother appears with his family as they were forty years earlier in Romania before being expelled by the communist regime. As William Faulkner, a writer whom Angelopoulos had read extensively, is known to have declared: "The past is never dead. It's not even past." The past encounters him at the place where it happened. It is his encounter with himself that history, as topographical embodiment of psyche, achieves until the last scene. The past in the film is not linear or even cyclical: it is both concurrent and spiral. It moves backwards and forwards as the present is de-territorialized. The individual falls unawares into the destruction and violence of war and develops Hegel's "unhappy conscience," becoming Lukács' "problematic hero." A sense of malaise and despair forces him to think against himself, as Cioran claimed, and only the narrative substructure of the myth gives his gaze perspective and orientation.

The context is also crucial. Fukuyama's full book title was *The End of History and the Last Man*, and from within the prevailing zeitgeist of the period, the idea of the end of humanism intrigued and frustrated Angelopoulos. In all its complexity, the film is trying to answer the central question of his work, the question of human agency and historical inevitability. The "last man" becomes the lost man, in the sense that the central character does not really know or cannot predict where history will take him. Like the peoples of Yugoslavia who never predicted the war, which, however, was already in them as potentiality, A. cannot perceive where he is and what he is doing there. He is distracted by the sirens of melodrama, Circe, Nausika, Calypso, who offer everything from sexual pleasure to domestic bliss and social prestige. But why is he the last man? Philosophically, the film belongs to the wider debates of the period, after Fukuyama. As David West wrote: "Postmodernism sought to define a space for philosophical thinking apart from the assumptions of Western modernity, in order to think and live without the assurances of any 'grand metanarrative' of progress or dialectical advance" (2010: 243).

Therefore, the film is permeated by a certain *kulturpessimismus* that was engulfing Europe during this period with the collapse of all grand narratives and the undermining of all rational understanding of historical activity. Given the absurdity of the war in Yugoslavia, it was inevitable that many assumptions of the past would be submitted to critical scrutiny and problematisation. It became imperative therefore to reconsider the scope of history and our methods of understanding. "If the future is inevitable," notes West, "then political action is always futile—either superfluous or doomed to fail. A different path is explored, by those recent thinkers what have attempted to 'rethink the political'" (2010: 245).

Vasilis Rafailidis points that that *Ulysses' Gaze* is permeated by only one ideal, "to salvage the primary, the virginal gaze cast by cinema in the beginning of the century, an ideal however marred by *the mal des siècles*" (2003: 120). Angelopoulos's gaze looks through the melancholy of the end of the century, exploring a space that multiplies the unresolved dilemmas of consciousness in their synchronic dimension. The unpredicted collapse of communism and the rise of postmodernist relativism started raising the question "over the foundations of reason or of the political" and the possibility of rational knowledge, a question that goes back to the ancient Greeks with the debate between Socrates and the Sophists. Christian Delacampagne stresses that, after 1989, "all these events are too charged with consequence, in every field of learning, for a great part of contemporary philosophy not to have been affected by them in one manner or another" (1999: xvii). The impact of these historical events on the mind of Angelopoulos's generation was profound and radical. History became an empty space without horizon and perspective. Philosophically, beyond Derrida's *différance* which essentially is not only about the deferral of meaning but also implies its suspension, thinking was taken over by American philosophy which, in all its expressions from John Rawls and Robert Nozick to Stanley Cavell and Hilary Putnam, was based on pragmatism and empiricism. Putnam, for example, declared the possibility of ethics without ontology and that "philosophy is not an empty discourse but a method that has the dual function of helping us live better lives while making society more just" (Delacampagne 1999: 276).

Angelopoulos is coming out of another tradition, attempting to rationally demonstrate and exemplify the "autonomy of existence." Each philosophy has its own concomitant anthropology, with its ethics and politics, but above all its own foundational ontology. His conceptualization of the experience of ideological collapse but also of existential implosion is extremely crucial as an indication of the philosophical trajectory of European cinema after the new millennium. The sense of an ending that we see in films like Lars von Trier's *Melancholia* expressed what Thomas Elsaesser called "thought experiments" which "posit a hypothesis, a principle or a situation, for the purpose of thinking through its ultimate consequences. Thought experiments display a patterned way of thinking, designed to explain, predict or control (possible) events" (2019: 229). On the contrary, Angelopoulos explores the chaos and disorder of history as a constant and inevitable given, which emerges catastrophically if people lose a sense of perspective and orientation, in a sense when they lose the perspective given to them by myth. All historical activity wants to record its own unique and specific *Mythos* and establish its own unique and specific *Mythopoeia* — this is how it gains its diachronic relevance, and this is the only way for the poet to "save the phenomena," as we will explore in the next chapter.

In *Ulysses' Gaze*, history is the realm of absolute and complete *ataxia*; nobody understands what happens and more crucially nobody understands the other. Such total and totalizing incomprehensibility becomes the foundational principle of thinking and the building block of all human activity. In this film, we feel that humans live in a perpetual Tower of Babel unable to establish a common code for communication, a shared language for their existential dwelling. The Homeric myth serves as the subscript that gives meaning to the disorder precisely because of its origin in the realm of symbols. Human experience creates a negative political anthropology very close to the pessimistic and violent theory of "a war of all against all" found in Hobbes. Ulysses looks at humans through the lens of *homo homini lupus* and sees violent society as the proper state of nature, presenting life as an apocalyptic place with no escape. As Hobbes expressed it, "no knowledge of the face of the earth, no account of time, no arts, no letters, no society, and which is worst of all, continual fear and danger of violent death, and the life of man, solitary, poor, nasty, brutish, and short" (2006: XIII.9). This is what A. experiences in the final scenes with a real war raging around the cinematic set.

At this point, Angelopoulos introduces the most Platonic invariable of his late cinema, the concept of psyche. The film, as we have already seen, begins with the famous statement by Plato, that *if we want to know about our psyche we must look into someone else's psyche.* (The second part can also be translated as *we must look into the soul itself.*) The statement indicates the new dimension through which Angelopoulos sees historical activity and human agency. Historians deal with human psyche only peripherally in their investigations and ignore the fact that what matters also is how history is internalized and interiorized, how history is lived and imagined at the same time. Plato hypothesized the existence of a Great Soul outside the individual psyche, a cosmological impersonal principle that permeated the universe. For Angelopoulos, the psyche is the only place where history becomes meaningful through memory, imagination, and "appropriation." In some of the most revealing moments of the film, ordinary people become the conduits for uttering certain exceptional and almost sibylline oracles: "I heard someone saying, a customer, that Greece is dying. We die as a nation. We made our cycle . . . three thousand years amidst broken stones and statues . . . and now we die. [. . .] But if Greece is to die, let her die fast. Because agony lasts long and makes a lot of noise" (Angelopoulos 1995: 31). The idea of historical cycles is rather unusual, especially for an ex-Marxist. In Marxism the idea of stages of development within a form of determinism prevails as the hermeneutical structuring of historical progress. Angelopoulos is dichotomized between two epistemic paradigms: that of a cyclical understanding of history that repeats itself throughout the century and another as found at the end of the film: "I will tell you about the journey all night and all nights to come. Between one embrace and another, between one call and another, I will tell all about human adventure, the adventure that never ends" (Angelopoulos 1995:112).

The two paradigms of interpreting historical experience coexist in an uneasy tension throughout the film. History as the violent explosion of irrational emotions juxtaposed to history as an open-ended process of constant renewal and reinvention. Human agency is a mixture of irrationalism and creativity, because irrationalism, the unpredictable fear of self-extinction, is the *urgrund* of creativity itself. The creative mind must be totally crushed by history in order to see through signs and wonders the grand myth that keeps the journey alive. But there is a purpose in the creative endeavor of the mind: it uses all its resources and potentialities to confront the empty screen and fill it with meaning. The aniconic image at the end of *Ulysses' Gaze* foregrounds the purpose of all creative impulse and activity beyond words and beyond all imagining. With his next film, Angelopoulos constructed his most significant mythopoetic answer to the questions of cinematic visuality.

Chapter 5
On Redemption

Or Saving the Phenomena and the Dread of Shadows in *Eternity and a Day*

Aesthetics and Ethics

Angelopoulos's films instigate some form of "hermeneutics of suspicion." Many leftist thinkers questioned their late "existentialist" concerns while many conservative critics stressed the utopian character of his social imaginary. As I have pointed out, it is obvious that there are many *ideational asymmetries* conceptual, aesthetic, or even philosophical. On some occasions, especially in his transitional films, there exist incongruous and somehow contradictory epistemological paradigms colliding in their structural if Angelopoulos himself was trying to reconcile them by imposing a conceptual unity. In his early films, there is no "freedom" as a conceptual framework: there is a strange form of passivity and surrender, since political structures "overdetermine" individual subjectivity and occlude the inner self. Some of his characters, indeed whole stories, as in *Days of '36* or *The Travelling Players*, seem like lifeless puppets in the shadow theater of history or the plaything of forces which they cannot confront, resist, or even comprehend. Even in his later films, it seems that an epistemic crisis questioning the perception of objective reality and the ability of the mind to rationally understand it becomes problematized and somehow abandoned.

The film that brings these asymmetries to their most intense and accomplished mode of cinematic realisation is his unique *Eternity and a Day*. It received the Palme d'Or at the Cannes Film Festival and can be considered one of the best films of world cinema, even if it is not characterized by the innovative impetus of *The Travelling Players* or the epic scope of *Ulysses' Gaze*. *Eternity and a Day* and *Landscape in the Mist* constitute the two most enduring and most *universal* films made by Angelopoulos dealing with the ultimate questions of mortality and existence, life, and death. Some Greek critics, especially Vasilis Rafailidis, have claimed that this is more Arthur Schopenhauer in the film than Marx, Nietzsche, or Sartre. The theme itself, of the last day in the life of a poet who relives in twenty-four hours his birth, death, and resurrection through art, may justify such an assumption. As Schopenhauer stated, "art lies in setting the inner life into the most violent motion with the smallest possible expenditure of outer life: for it is the inner life which is the real object of our interest" (2004: 150). The deep structure of *Eternity and a Day* is precisely the realm of interiority and inwardness, the realm for which we have no words and concepts. The dying poet "borrows" the poetic fragments of another dead poet and tries to make sense of them and ultimately complete them.

It seems that the model around which he formed his central character and the episodes of his life was the short novel *The Sorrows of Young Werther* by J.W. Goethe, a book that Angelopoulos treasured profoundly and had expressed the intention, around the same period, to make into a film; we can detect its indirect impact in the epistles that are read throughout the work. In these letters the characters reveal what they cannot define in their personal life and interpersonal relationships. Only language creates conscious of them:

> I feel that I have come so close to you that you resist. Do I threaten your world, Alexander? And yet I am only a woman in love. Last night I was watching you. I didn't know if you were asleep or silent. I was afraid of what you might have been thinking. I was afraid that I have entered your own silence.
>
> ANGELOPOULOS 1998: 28

Echoing Burton Pike's observation on Goethe's book, the film recalibrates the cinematic language that Angelopoulos had constructed until then and replaces it "with an impulsive language of subjective feeling" (2004: x). In his previous films, he was piecing together a conceptual language to visualize the structure and the workings of the psyche; but in this, subjective emotions take over and the inner *topos* of the psyche is explored in its own workings, mainly emotions, drives, and feelings, both conscious and unconscious. The film is about what Ulysses' gaze sees when it turns on its own self. In the previous film, the final screen is void while we can hear the mechanical sound of a projector. The empty screen invites viewers to look deeper into themselves; it becomes an opening not only to the next film but also to another perception of the self. Even though *Eternity and a Day* deals with the question of finitude and death, it avoids the ultimate temptation of the religious justification of life that we find in Tarkovsky, for example, or Malick and Sokurov. No religious text is invoked in the film with its metaphysical consolations and promises about life eternal. Angelopoulos firmly insists on the actual, the pragmatic, the material (or even the materialistic). Death magnifies the importance of the mundane and the quotidian; there is no reference to anything that could even seem remotely spiritual or metaphysical. Irregular events take place, omens and signs from another order of things emerge suddenly out of the cracks of everyday experience, but Angelopoulos firmly keeps them within the realm of the visible and the concrete.

The script is full of references to poets and their works, such as like the Greek national poet Dionysios Solomos, who also appears as a character, Odysseas Elytis, Yannis Ritsos, George Seferis, Rainer Maria Rilke, and Paul Celan, together with demotic and popular songs. Some of their verses did not make it into the final cut but the whole mood of the film, because it is predominantly *mood* rather than statement, frames an elegiac farewell to reality in the most affectionate and intimate manner. The verses that define the quest in the film came directly from the poet Solomos: "The late morning fresh star of dawn/ heralded a glorious bright sunshine/ there was no cloud or mist anywhere/ on the sky or the horizon afar. / Then a gentle breeze touched softly on faces / making them exclaim from their heart's depth/ that life is sweet and [darkness is death]."[1]

The poem is about the day of Easter and springtime and the way that death is intimated in the middle of the celebration and renaissance of life. This romantic theme of the drive towards death or the fusion of beauty and Death that permeates Solomos's work becomes the emergence of the *uncanny* in everyday reality. As in most nineteenth-century romantics, in Solomos's poetry, death leads not to mourning and grief but to an enhanced re-discovery of the real. Death makes everything luminous and striking; it discloses uniqueness and singularity. The smallest living form experiences its evanescent beauty as a unique cosmic event juxtaposed to the melancholy of imminent death. As Schopenhauer stated: "The task of the [poet] is not to narrate great events but to make small ones interesting" (2004: 151).

In the film, the signs of the approaching end appear in different forms, as for example with three yellow-vested cyclists following a night ride on the bus which passes through the strangest places of a dematerialized Athens. The journey to the borders between Greece and Albania is also a descent into another world (probably Dante's Hell), with people trying to escape while the elongated figure of a faceless guard controls the passage to the other side. The strange ritual of invoking the dead performed by the young boy is also another sign that anthropological questions are intricately woven into the fabric of the story. Actual death and symbolic resurrection are the two poles that the film itself states in its beginning and completes with its end.

The film monumentalizes the small details of everyday living: the walk with the dog, an unknown person listening to music, the unexpected wedding in the middle of the industrial desert, together with horrible everyday tragedies, like child trafficking, abuse of minors, and police brutality. Being-towards-death does not cause terror of dread but a sense of completion and autarky: the cycle has been completed. The complexity of life is addressed as both grand and miserable, through an anthropology that reminds us of Pascal's reflections on the human condition. The representation of approaching death has inspired many directors to run towards religion for metaphysical consolation and redemption. But the question for such a redemption, as we have seen it throughout Angelopoulos's work, is not religious, metaphysical, or even spiritual. The whole film, if we may refer to the British musician and poet Ivor Gurney, is "the protest of the physical against the exalted spiritual, of the cumulative weight of small facts against the one large" (in J. Stallworthy and J. Potter, 2011: 118). Natural reality reclaims its presence in the face of its extinction, questioning the fear of death and exploring the potential openings in human consciousness when confronted by its own finitude.

Philosophically, the descent into the emotions has deep and long-term consequences, which Angelopoulos tried to further elaborate in his later films. There is somehow a contradictory understanding of individual freedom in them. Coming out of Althusser's structural Marxism, the early Angelopoulos had no place for Sartre's existentialist privileging of freedom. As Jean-Pierre Boulé and Enda McCaffrey observed; 'Freedom, for Sartre, is not a property of our essence. Human existence is synonymous with freedom: we are free because we are. There is, therefore, no distance between our being and our freedom. Human beings are condemned to be free" (2011: 3). This element of absent freedom can be seen in almost all his films, as if humans are trapped within the unexpected consequences of their own creations, or within historical institutions that they cannot comprehend. Even Alexandros in the last day of his life cannot be free: the past will always be within him, something he is reminded of constantly from the moment of birth. Freedom is a condition of being to be discovered and be gained. It is not a given but a project and a postulate. The search for inner and external freedom as experiential reality can be seen in all Angelopoulos's later works.

Eternity and a Day starts with direct reference to the philosopher Heraclitus and implicitly ends with him, as the camera in a famous long and slow shot recapitulates the entire life cycle from amniotic fluids to the eternal mother of all, the sea. Heraclitus's famous proclamation that "everything flows" and that "you cannot enter the same river twice" (1987: 54) gives the viewer the central concern of the film, the concern about temporality. But what is the essence of such temporality? Even though death is the destination of life, it is not the destiny of human existence. Angelopoulos still posits the utopian project of transfiguration of the physical as the philosophical project of his last films. In the Platonic and Christian worlds, physical reality is clearly and inevitably separated from the realm of the spiritual. Angelopoulos wants to fuse these two dimensions of being and orders of experience into concrete images: "Time? What is time? Asks the little boy. My grandfather says that time is a child who plays jacks on the edge of the sea" (Angelopoulos 1998: 12). The philosophical question of how we relate to time in the natural and the symbolic order and how we represent that relationship emerges as the central question. Furthermore, the film encapsulates Angelopoulos's belief that ultimately our sense of lived temporality, as captured in cinematic images, leads to *homochronicity* and *monofocality* that are imperative for a unified vision about the chaos of history. There is the gaze that unifies, integrates, and consolidates a specific image of experience and history. Unlike Alexander Kluge's "poetics of heterochronicity [. . .] consisting of his decidedly asynchronous treatment of image, sound, and lettering panels . . ." (Ekardt 2018: 321), Angelopoulos's films, especially *Eternity and a Day*, synchronize images, sounds, narrative structure, diegetic forms, or non-diegetic elements into a solid mythopoetic unity. The triumph of Aristotle in his last films signifies the anthropocentric vision of the real that he gradually crystallized and condensed, differentiating himself from the illusionist subjectivism and the sentimental individualism that characterizes contemporary cinema.

Ethics for Cinematic Temporality

The question of time and duration in Angelopoulos was addressed by Yvette Bíró, who quotes a letter by Angelopoulos stating: "A film's rhythm is an inner rhythm, therefore a personal sense of time. In my films the rhythm resembles time dilation but in actual fact it is not" (2008: 166). Duration is the structural principle around which the central *ethical* argument of the films is based. Certain conceptual asymmetries indicate some of the most intricate problematics about temporality which Angelopoulos incorporated, leading us to pay more attention to ethics that emerge out of the images. Past and present become contemporaneous for Angelopoulos: they coexist as *visual ideograms*, comprising intentions and actions. The youth and old age of the same person converse with each other, as the passage of time is not suspended but enhanced and intensified. The form of Alexandros when he is old is next to that of his wife as they were fifty years earlier.

From such collision of temporal signifiers, we can extract Angelopoulos's own ethical *theoria*. Ludwig Wittgenstein concluded: "It is clear that ethics cannot be expressed. Ethics is transcendental. Ethics and aesthetics are one" (1958: 183). We will focus on the ethical presuppositions of Angelopoulos's iconosophy especially in this film which deals with finality and finitude; ultimately, his disillusion with ideology never led to the "disenchantment of the world," which Max

Weber predicted already at the very beginning of modernism and was probably at the root of the modernist project. However, it leads to a profound questioning of rational activity and thinking. Are humans able to be rational, or gain their rationality within an irrational world? "The contraction of man's horizons amounts to a denudation," wrote William Barrett, "a stripping down, of this being who has now to confront himself at the center of all horizons. The labor of modern culture, whenever it has been authentic, has been a labor of denudation" (1990: 40–1). How such denudation happens visually and pictorially in film and through film becomes one of the implicit texts in *Eternity and a Day*.

Stanley Cavell called film "the moving image of scepticism" (Cavell 1981: 189), in the sense that we cannot trust images, or even project onto them any philosophical content. For Angelopoulos, on the contrary, cinema is the most important device of contemporary imagination for the re-enchantment of life, for re-dressing the nude mind, and for the resignification of all experience through a critical *theoria* of existence. The suggestion is certainly ambitious as some thinkers, following Nietzsche, have even claimed that aesthetics is the only means of existential justification left for contemporary creative thinking after the death of God, even more than religion, politics, and discursive philosophy itself. The idea was adopted for a while by Angelopoulos and has remained in the background of his fascination with language. However, as Walter Benjamin stated, "it is the function of artistic form . . . to make historical content into a philosophical truth' (1998[1928]: 182).

Beyond being a "political" filmmaker, Angelopoulos constructed visually certain significant existential visual truths about time and mortality as lived and imagined experiences. We usually stress the strange concept of "lived experience" borrowed from French existentialism: however, imagined experiences are equally crucial for the understanding of the human condition, especially in the realm of symbols. Poetry presents the imagined self, one would even say the ideal self which Angelopoulos explores and foregrounds in the mind of his dying poet. Under the eyes of death, the lived and the imagined form a unity of ontological integration. Solomos the dead poet is alive because the poet Alexander relives his existence and anxiety in his work. "Why a writer of your stature abandons suddenly his own work in order to complete an unfinished poem from the nineteenth century?" asks his daughter. The work of art invites the future to its own structures:

it re-writes itself through new and sometimes unknown, or indeed terminal, temporalities.

The temporality of dreams is also important for Angelopoulos: the ethics of cinematic images are structured around the ability we find in our dreams to restore balance between what we desire and what we can achieve, between our history and our psyche. His cinematic visuality entails ethical truth-making claims whose philosophical epistemology embodies a new conceptualization of death as a visual experience. In their diverse ways, Terrence Malick, Apichatpong Weerasethakul, Béla Tarr, and Lav Diaz continue a series of philosophical investigations on visuality of mortality as recalibrated by Angelopoulos. "Now, at my age, I find it necessary to begin to devote some thought to death. In order to rediscover life. In order to see life in a new light, conscious of the fact that you have made peace with the idea of dying" (in Fainaru 2001: 106).

Robert Sinnerbrink concludes his study of Malick and his "cinematic ethic" by exploring in a form of a Platonic dialogue two possible approaches to Malick's work: "one way of articulating some of the nuances and complexities is to frame my responses in a form of a dialogue between a *rationalist sceptic* critic of Malick and a *romantic idealist* defender of his work" (2019: 208). This is a very important distinction to be made, not simply about Malick or other directors (Terence Davies, for example, or Tarr but also Akira Kurosawa and Ozu), but also about the nature and ultimately the purpose and the essence of cinema. With Malick, for example, we go way beyond the traditional behaviourist, functionalist, and mechanistic idea that something is what that something does – an idea which dominates American film production. Cinema is an extremely *uncanny* technological invention with profound metaphysical implications because *it objectifies the presence of time in time* both materially and conceptually. It duplicates and replicates the real and the imaginary simultaneously—something that deeply fascinated Angelopoulos as we see in many scenes, especially the end of *The Suspended Step of the Stork*, starting with *Voyage to Cythera*, where, as he stated, "the film deals with double identities throughout" (in Fainaru 2001: 39).

Even in *The Weeping Meadow*, where the great escape to America takes place, the first thing we hear in the letter sent back is a statement of intense disappointment: "Is this America? I asked myself." The constant feelings of frustration, disempowerment, and dysphoria in an irrational world coexist in his films with the vague expectation of a liberating action leading to an existential catharsis, to a non-religious redemption of the real and the human psyche. From the closed rooms of Ingmar Bergman, Angelopoulos looked back to the open streets of Sergei Eisenstein: could Elisabet Volger and her nurse, in Bergman's *Persona*, ever be able to experience the explosive temporality of a revolutionary opening, as seen by all ordinary and anonymous protagonists in *Battleship Potemkin*? And what happens when the revolutionary project is lost and the self defines its existence not as transcendence and disclosure but as lack and loss, as opaque negation? Can the self be and not be at the same time?

Such *asymmetric conjunctions* have caused considerable consternation to many thinkers who have engaged with Angelopoulos's work. For example, the Greek philosopher and theologian Stelios Ramfos accused him of "cinematic somnambulism" and claimed that "we encounter 'the mytho-construction of gaze, conscious-unconscious combination of atemporal oriental and post-modernist seeing.'" Ramfos went even further and claimed that "in his misty landscapes with cold colours and grey atmosphere of inhospitable places hovers the melancholy for the nostalgia of emotions that remain unexpressed within the self-indulgence of images" (2012: 31–3).

The charges are serious, albeit un-cinematic and essentialistic, and cannot only be attributed to specific cultural agendas or personal politics. (What is indeed oriental or occidental within the wide and fluid networks of communication structured around cultural diffusion?) Angelopoulos constructed reflexive images that caused uneasiness to many viewers; to some because they were confronted by the implied perplexing interiority, and others because they never expected that the 'Dionysian' Mediterraneans would have been tormented and bedevilled by such confusing and darkening *introspective conscience*. Angelopoulos's images challenged the well-established belief going back to Nietzsche in the dichotomy between the Apollonian and the Dionysian spirit in Greek culture, and recalibrated the semantics of such oppositions. Beyond the Germanic dichotomy, referring mostly to the works of Richard Wagner, Angelopoulos saw the contemporary human condition as made of both elements, symbiotically coexisting within each other. Within the accomplished immobility of classical art, he could depict the restless and disastrous entropic forces that are "deep down" embodied in ancient Greek aesthetics.

His cinematic images construct an *intermediate space* of formally colliding temporalities in which the human eye can see itself in the act of making and see the outcome of what is being made, like in certain Byzantine icons. It both presents and represents: it is mimetic and anti-mimetic at the same time. Students of history know that both tendencies co-existed since the beginning of all visual arts, as a conflict between presentational and representational tendencies, or what Wilhem Worringer defined as the oscillation between "abstraction and empathy." In the elements comprising this art, as Worringer observed, we see a "return to the plane surface, suppression of the organic, crystalline-geometric composition [. . .] a purely abstract habitus" (Worringer 1997: 104).

Angelopoulos was not an auteur like John Ford, Howard Hawks, or Federico Fellini; he was aware of the visual *self-questioning* at the heart of visuality, and he was addressing the *negative* character of cinematic images when he stated,

> images exist in our mind before we reproduce them. Even when we chose a place for filming, that place already existed in our mind. The same happens with the shades of colour. They are internal colours which come to the surface, and we struggle to find them again. And, when we fail, we paint them . . . I have done so much painting all over Greece . . .
>
> ARCHIMANDRITIS, 2013: 70

The idea of image as illusion and reality simultaneously goes back to Plato's *Republic* and the Parable of the Cave (so ingeniously yet unevenly employed in Wachowski Brothers' *The Matrix* (1999) but not in its rather overblown sequels).

Plato distinguishes between knowledge and opinion but, for him, the prisoners in the cavern experience such shadows as their own everyday reality. They define themselves through them even when someone who has seen the real sun informs them about the falsity of their belief. But it is a false belief based on actual experience. Their mental reality is a mixture of both, illusion and pragmatics, and the human condition is precisely about the interstitial, *metaxy* dimension of the human mind, in which the boundaries between illusion and reality are not always distinguishable. Plato's Parable of the Cave essentially refers to the exposure of the human eye to the unmitigated and unchallenged revelations of light, and what the light reveals to the perceiving mind about itself. Cinema raises, as Nathan Andersen has argued, "questions of the relation between appearance and reality, questions of ethics, questions of knowledge and interpretation, questions of aesthetics" (2014: 8).

Death in *Eternity and a Day* is the question of ultimate concern but must be answered within the experiential limits of material existence framed by cinematic visuality. Not as illusion or reality but as simultaneously both. Temporal simultaneity leads to the convergence of the dimensions of time and frames a completely different philosophical problematic about its essence. If the central question of time is about becoming, then in *Eternity and a Day* the question of becoming, the transition to different modes of being, is addressed as the ontological grounding of finitude. The interstitial nature of images, both material and immaterial, makes this film paradoxical in the way that it deals with its own questions. We die because we create and vice versa: this serial and cyclic perception of time, like the rather spiritualistic theories of J.D. Dunne or P.D. Ouspensky, is vaguely articulated by Angelopoulos in this film. In order to set out this problematic in terms of his conceptual framework, he had to test the limits of his own iconosophy and explore the ways in which what philosophy is saying about death does enunciate death as a problematic for living through images.

On Philosophical Visuality

How do we visualize death and dying cinematically? What images can we construct to enunciate the question of death as the philosophical question par excellence? In *Eternity and a Day*, all cinematic elements indicate that the question of death is at the heart of its philosophical project: "nothing is nothing" is the song heard in the underground basement where small children are sold (Angelopoulos 1998: 33). Nothingness is the ultimate ground for the final celebration of life. The concept of death as nothing, which appears also before one's own death, raises the acute epistemological question: is the unexperienced expressible? Can we conceptualize and make words and images about the experience of death we will never have? We will definitely die but can we be conscious of our death? The well-known anecdote about Proust who just before dying wanted to correct his description of Comte de Charlus's death is highly relevant. Angelopoulos visualizes portents of death, omens indicating that physical reality is always shadowed by unknowable messengers, by uninvited shadows that want to destroy the organic. In *Eternity and a Day* these portents are foreshadowed through colors, yellow in particular. Three cyclists follow the strange journey on the bus and return to where they began—in front of a big ship that will take the child to the wide world and the poet to his death.

Why yellow, however? The color has appeared also in *Landscape in the Mist* and *The Suspended Step of the Stork*. When Angelopoulos wants to point out the proximity of the *unheimlich*, he employs yellow as an opening to a completely unknowable realm of experience. Angelopoulos's films negotiate and recalibrate the relation between the human eye and natural light in an almost anti-Newtonian manner, closer to Goethe's theories of color:

> colour may have a mystical allusion, [. . .] for since every diagram in which the variety of colours may be represented points to those primordial relations which belong both to nature and the organ of vision, [and] there can be no doubt that these may be made use of as a language in cases where it is proposed to express similar primordial relations which do not present themselves to the senses in so powerful and varied a manner.
>
> GOETHE, 2006 [1810]: 193

Colors form a language, expressing the primordial relation between vision and luminosity and pointing towards the corporeal materiality of the images themselves. Colors evoke spaces where the unseens can leave their vestigial presence. Finally, colors define modes of being and moods of relating: under the eyes of death, thinking itself becomes a reflection of an unexperienced immanence. In a monologue over the body of his mother, Alexandros confesses:

> Why mother? Why did nothing come while we waited for it? Why? Why must we rot helpless between pain and desire? Why did I live my whole life in exile? Why the only moments I came back were when still I was

given the grace to speak my language . . . my own language . . . When I still could find or retrieve again lost or forgotten words from silence? Why only then I could hear the echo of my footsteps in my home?

ANGELOPOULOS 1998: 76

Silence was always the great protagonist in Angelopoulos's films; it denoted a philosophical aporia, a dead-end, but also the liberating project of clearing the mind from noise and distraction. The most important image that Alexandros sees when he "enters the cities" is the vision of the revolving galaxies, with the inexplicable cosmic music of spheres, at the beginning of *Voyage to Cythera*, probably the most arcane codified message ever given to viewers by any modern filmmaker. At this point, we are reminded of Maxim Gorky's reflections after attending the early screenings of the Lumière cinematograph in 1896:

Last night I was in the Kingdom of Shadows. If you only knew how strange it is to be there. It is a world without sound, without color. Everything there – the earth, the trees, the people, the water and the air – is dipped in monotonous grey. Grey rays of the sun across the grey sky, grey eyes in grey faces, and the leaves of trees are ashen grey. It is not life but its shadow, it is not motion but its soundless spectre.'

1999 [1896]: 10

Gorky's dread in front of the Kingdom of Shadows expresses the same existential ambivalence that many have felt towards cinema ever since: from the original viewers of the train coming to the station, to Jacques Derrida's rejection as the token of "elementary spectrality" of what he characterized thus:

Cinema thus allows one to cultivate what could be called "grafts" of spectrality; it inscribes traces of ghosts on a general framework, the projected film, which is itself a ghost. It's a captivating phenomenon and theoretically, this is what would interest me in cinema as object of analysis. Spectral memory, cinema is a magnificent mourning, a magnified work of mourning.

2015 [1998/2000]: 27–8

Angelopoulos had a completely different and probably oppositional stance to Derrida's fear of ghosts and shadows, although this film in particular visualises the work of mourning which tends to de-realize experience. Cinema tames the fear of shadows and liberates the mind from the panic of its own creations. Angelopoulos's films rail against such logic of perceptual conditioning by mostly *spectral* ways of thinking and challenge the viewer's resistances against "the kingdom of Shadows." The cultural element might be also relevant here. Maybe it is also a linguistic question as the Greek language connects *phantasia* (imagination) and *phantasma* (ghost). For Aristotle, *phantasia* functions as an intermediary between thought and perception, and as Martha Nussbaum said: "*Phantasia* ties abstract thought to concrete perceptible objects or situations" (Nussbaum, 1986: 265). According to Aristotle, *phantasia* is "different from either perceiving or thinking, though it is not found without perception, nor judgement without it" (*De Anima*, 166, 3.3.427b. 14–16). Visual *phantasia* is the link between all brain faculties, indeed the loom that weaves all things together as mental images constructing together a *theoria* about the cosmos, a *weltanschauung* which culminates with the ultimate questions of both epistemic and epistemological nature. Can we find a language to talk about loss and death?

For Angelopoulos, cinematic images create a critical form of reality, indeed articulate a critique of *relational reality*, that connects and conjugates objects and subjects: images constitute links between the material and the symbolic. As such they have a meaning beyond themselves. They belong to the ability of the mind to construct mental forms even when something is not sensed or experienced. Aristotle indicated that *phantasia* "occurs when [either sight or seeing] is present, as when objects are seen in dreams" (*De anima*, 3.3.428a.1–8). Angelopoulos's images are like the *phantasias* that transform the real into hyper-real presence: they do not dematerialize or deterritorialize it. They stress the primacy of the sensible and the sensory while extracting the invariable parameters to integrate them into a set of interpersonal connections. Images consist of underlying geometric structures that unite Aristotelian materiality and the thought forms of Platonic pragmatism. Like Byzantine icons, they link form and symbol and, through them, foreground the principal feature of iconography, "a presence of the unspeakable that springs from matter" (Sendler, 1988: 82).

The unspeakable, which is the presence of the unfilmable in Angelopoulos, becomes the final project in his cinematic language—with a new perspective. "Anyway," he stated, about *Landscape in the Mist*, "I deeply wish that people would learn to dream again. Nothing is more real than our dreams" (in Fainaru, 2001: 120). The oneiric quality of his films, which has nothing to do with repressed sexual fantasies or transferred orgasms, is about the transcendental ethics that Wittgenstein talked about, bringing out into the world of complex social realities the symbols of shared civic reality. In many of his films, symbols of shared civic reality. In many of his films, the movement of the camera indicates something extremely significant, as it is the forms and the objects that move towards the camera and not the other way around. The objects and the forms see the camera and establish a connection not simply because they are reflected in it. Returning to an observation by Bazin, the camera is not only a mirror, but also a window: we look through the window into something which is both out there and in here. The introspective consciousness of viewers and the inner life of their existence stare back at us. The director is the author of such an encounter, framing the parameters of their gaze and focusing it on specific images.

Angelopoulos filled his works with signs of an *oneiric transubstantiation of reality*: the first filmic images as *phantasies* of unlived experiences can be seen in *The Voyage to Cythera*, when the film becomes self-referential. A poster of *The Travelling Players* in the office of the director makes the film itself an *archive* of its own genealogy: Angelopoulos is filming Angelopoulos—the camera records the camera. In *Landscape in the Mist*, the broken film reveals what cannot be seen and cannot be articulated. We can mention here the actual cinemas in Angelopoulos's films: abandoned, used as storage, or a railway line made in front of their entrance, or gone underground. Ultimately, as in the past people believed in religion through the sublime masterworks of great artists, cinematic heroes look upon history from the annals of modern cinema either as photographs or as painted portraits. The whole adventure of humanity in *Ulysses' Gaze* ends with an unfilmed cinematic frame, with the sound of the projector indicating the birth of a new reality—better or worse we are not told, but it is up to the viewer to discover. In *The Dust of Time*, the icons we see everywhere are those of actors, actresses, and singers; they look upon the characters and through them look at viewers with the dispassionate gaze of their created fragile eternity. Cinema records a dreaming humanity, the dreams that reveal the authentic presence of individuals.

It is obvious that as a filmmaker Angelopoulos privileged vision and the primacy of visual encounters. For him, cinema plays the crucial and important role that in the past only literature could perform, through the genre of *ekphrasis*; yet how could the polysemy of language capture the prismatic multiplicity of visual fields? Cinema retrieves the lost synchronicity between past and present, the severed thread between incongruous and somehow random connections. For him, cinema is a social ritual of creative bonding. In 1998 he disclosed:

> My generation was born in a cinema theatre and that was a ritual. That's the most significant thing. Today we are losing that element of ritual, not only in cinema but also in our everyday life, and I feel sad for what is lost. This is the reason that I have so many scenes with dancing. Because I have the impression that dance vanished from our lives. It was part of a full ritual. These rituals are lost gradually, and I think that this is also a loss of emotions and sensibilities. Things become so rationalised today.[2]

Angelopoulos formed gradually his *iconosophy* as the philosophical framing of such loss and the absence of positive rituals about the real through the discovery of the oneiric as a mode of presenting and representing inner life, the psyche. Already in 1984, after his own "turn," he understood that the language of cinema embodied itself a philosophy of existence. "The cinema is a disease. It outlasts the time when one is not accepted, as well. I have had a very difficult time in the past. But the cinema is very strong – one cannot live without it. It's not just a medium of expression, it's a form of life" (Fainaru, 2001 [1984]: 35). The concept of "form of life" of course refers to Ludwig Wittgenstein's suggestion in his *Philosophical Investigations*: "So you are saying that human agreement decides what is false and what is true? – It is what human beings *say* that is false and true; and they agree in the *language* they use. That is not agreement in opinions but in form of life" (2009: § 241).

The idea that philosophical cinema, like any natural language, is a *Lebensform* reflecting the structures and the experiences that give meaning to life is probably Angelopoulos's most pertinent theoretical belief. Philosophical cinema is neither entertainment nor education. Regarding *Landscape in the Mist*, he responded:

> I am not a missionary. I don't want to educate people; I try to find a way from chaos to light. We live in confused times where values do not exist any longer. Melancholy goes along with confusion and disorientation. But the questions people ask themselves are still the same. Where do I come from? Where do I go? Questions about life, death, love, friendship, youth and age.
>
> In FAINARU, 2001 [1998]: 120

His answer has too many epistemological consequences to be ignored. It expresses a deep undercurrent in his work that the cinematic is a new form of self-structuring, of self-fashioning, of personalized subjectivity, in a technologized society in which images are rhetorical devices that can be manipulated, manufacturing identities and identifications. Angelopoulos's images break the rhetorical force of illusory identifications. In his images we experience the minimalistic renunciation of the superfluous, and the creation of a "humble art" according to Seferis, or indeed a new *arte povera* according to the Italian artists of the 1960s. The emergence of *emotional primordiality*, in his later films, constitutes his most relevant approach to the medium, especially after the 1980s. In this aspect Angelopoulos is close to what Paul Schrader defines in his *Transcendental Style in Film* as "the desire to express the Transcendent in art and the nature of the film medium" (1972: 3), but differs substantially and in the understanding of its essence from Ozu, Bresson, and Dreyer, despite his continuous homage to them. (In the recent new edition of his book, Schrader mentions the sense of slow time in Angelopoulos (2018 [1972]: 12) without really foregrounding the central element of its function.) Angelopoulos stressed that he didn't believe in the metaphysical or the transcendent. And when he said the transcendent, he meant divine revelation, despite the constant presence of religious iconography and sometimes religious language in his films. But he searched for the transcendent in the medium itself and how it transforms "personal experiences into poetry" (in Fainaru, 2001[1998]: 120).

Within a secular world, he looked for transcendence through the *poesis* of images and words, in the evocative impact on the viewer's eyes when both either converge or diverge. The appearance of the poet in *Eternity and a Day*, in the enigmatic bus scene, is one such moment of divergence and emergence: historical time is suspended, and another dimension emerges. Nobody expects that Dionysios Solomos, dead since 1857, would appear in a bus, reciting his poems while leaving incomplete the final line, framing the most *terrible* and *awe-inspiring* presence in the whole movie, which also remains invisible and unfilmed: death. He speaks from the realm of death, yet invites the mind to confront the real now.

Solomos's poem is completed later in the film by the paraphrased verse of Paul Celan about "the other shore" or "*Dein Hinübersein heute Nacht*" (1988: 164), which we see in the last scenes of the movie when the sea absorbs the human form in an act of symbolic rebirth. "Your / having crossed over tonight. / With words I brought you back, here you are, / all is true and a waiting / for the true," says Celan's poem adapted by Angelopoulos for his poet before being lost into the sea. *Thalassa* in Greek, a name used by Sándor Ferenczi for the need for replication through regression to the original womb, or indeed in Jacques Lacan's semantic transposition "from a present sign (*la mer*) to an absent (*la mère*)" (Stoltzfus, 1996: 97), indicates absence and ultimately death—a motif repeated at the end of *The Weeping Meadow* and the waters in the Spree River of Berlin in *The Dust of Time*. Autobiography, essentially *biomythography*, re-signifies and intensifies the construction of images: the imminent death of his mother back in 1998 caused the profound confrontation with mortality that we see in this film, which represents the principal problematic of his mature work—especially for someone like him, who accepted no pre-existing philosophical, psychological, or theological foundational theory to anchor his cinematic thinking.

The answer was given by his friend Rafailidis who, talking about *Ulysses' Gaze*, wrote:

In a film, nothing is dead, not even the dead. In a film, all living things remain alive for ever. It is certain that in a 1920s film all protagonists and extras, whom I see today fully alive on the screen, are dead by now, but this does not give any mournful ideas. Humans died but their gaze is fully alive in front of me, captured on the screen. The only known form of immortality is the one that cinema can present us with. Here the creator imitates more successfully the Creator. If he wants, he graces you with spectral immortality; if he doesn't, he throws you into frameless hell.

RAFAILIDIS, 1996: 9

The ancient Greeks believed that the most important task of knowledge is to "save the phenomena" and thus maintain the *aletheia* of their being. *Aletheia* in Greek means not only truth, but as Rafailidis also points out, "deprivation of oblivion, negation of oblivion" (1996: 20). The purpose of cinematic images in the field of cinematic visuality, according to Angelopoulos, is to save the phenomena from disappearance and oblivion: images immortalize the ephemerality of the fragile and vulnerable human body.

The cinematic is a dimension of being and thinking which saves the phenomena from oblivion: Angelopoulos's cinematic *aletheia* is precisely about the truthfulness and the objecthood of forms. Drawing from one of his beloved poets, we could claim that Greek art had as its central concern to preserve and save forms: as C.P. Cavafy said: 'But we have lost the most precious—his form, / that was an Apollonian vision' (Cavafy, 1961 [1914]: 50). The word "precious" in the original is *timion*, which also means honest and pure. In his best films, Angelopoulos captured the visual purity of forms in their unique luminosity and unrepeatable radiance. The language to address the un-representability of death is given by studying the uniqueness and the singularity of human forms.

Plato in *Phaedo* made the bold claim, after the death of Socrates, that philosophy reveals what "other people are likely not to be aware of, that those who pursue philosophy study nothing but dying and being dead," and the whole project of philosophy is that "the true philosophers practise dying, and death is less terrible to them than to any other men" (Plato 2005: 223, 235 (64a3–4)). The original expression that philosophy is *melete thanatou* is at the heart of Angelopoulos's iconosophy, indeed at the heart of all philosophical endeavor. As Bradatan aptly observed: "philosophy is an art of living only to the extent that it offers us an art of dying" (2018: 5). Therefore, given the polysemy of the term in Greek, *Melete thanatou* means both a study of death but also a rehearsal for dying—and *Eternity and a Day* is framed by this ambiguity.

Eternity and a Day is therefore a philosophical essay on death and dying without anti-natalist tendencies: it expresses the practice of dying as the basis of a moral theory of anthropodicy. Furthermore, it has nothing to do with spiritualism, hermeticism, or rejection of the body—and it does not question the morality of procreation. The ontological comprehension of dying is much more important than the reality of death as such, or its religious understanding as a meeting with God. Despite its existentialist leaning, there is place neither for Kierkegaard nor for Pascal in Angelopoulos's universe. Neither fear nor dread but also not Pascal's wager and therefore not probabilistic metaphysics. Living is self-contained and autotelic: it justifies the givenness of existence by enhancing the uniqueness of presence. In the final scene of the film, Alexandros is absorbed by the sea and returns to the source, the origin, that *alma mater* of being. The trauma of birth is healed through the giving back of the most important element of human presence: the enigma and the paradox of human existence.

Within the Platonic framework, Angelopoulos articulates a vitalistic approach, parallel to the one articulated by Henri Bergson in his *Creative Evolution*. Paul Celan's paraphrased poem sums up Angelopoulos's response to the question of anthropodicy: why is there something and not nothing? Angelopoulos himself re-imagined Celan's poem, as we saw earlier: "My passage tonight to the other shore / I brought you back with words. And you are here. / And everything is true and premonition of the true." (Angelopoulos 1998: 109). Because there is something, the *Real* as an order of experience and form of life, we can ask similar questions, and therefore life can only be justified as a metaphysical manifestation of *élan vital*, a Bergsonian reformulation of the question which can be the only response to the aestheticization of existence proposed by Nietzsche. But what is metaphysics for Angelopoulos?

Excursus on Tarkovsky

We cannot understand the specificity of Angelopoulos's ontology and anthropology without contrasting him with the mystical and religious cinema of Andrei Tarkovsky. Their comparison and contrast have been attempted on many occasions, albeit in a brief and rather fragmented manner. Despite their analogies, however, there are profound asymmetries between them which show the different *space* occupied by each of them within the realm of cinematic thinking. Tarkovsky's slow and unhurried narrative pace paves the way for the presentation of cinematic images as "a second reality" (Tarkovsky, 1989: 176), and of the image as a religious, or spiritual, revelation. The temporal and the eternal exist, supplanting each in the specific image. It is precisely that complementarity of temporalities which make Tarkovsky's films so open to semantic transignification according to different contexts or approaches. In his best films there is a suspension of historical time, even a reversal of natural order: religion for Tarkovsky is the ultimate *telos*, the end of all ends when, in meeting face to face with God, we will find our authentic self, our archetypal image, and true home.

Reality, however, was always problematic for Tarkovsky. Within the space of temporal openness—which means that at the moment we realize that an image is not reducible to its specific cultural encodings, or even more so, deducible from them—we have to deal with the most pertinent "impression" of an image as its oneiric character. In this aspect Angelopoulos's iconosophy and Tarkovsky's iconology are very close and overlap. We can imagine Tarkovsky and Angelopoulos together disputing the origin of the word "nostalgia"; one claiming that it was altogether Russian, and the other attributing it to Homer. (This quintessentially uber-Greek word was coined by the Swiss mercenary Johannes Hofer in 1688 to describe his anxiety away from home, while translating into a proper cultural language the uncouth German word *Heimweh* or homesickness.)

The time they shared together in Rome coincides with the radical changes in Angelopoulos's turning towards his existential films and the rise of nostalgia as a dominant trope and mood in his work. 'I love Tarkovsky's *Stalker*; *Nostalghia*, I like less; *The Sacrifice*, I do not like it at all. As far I am concerned, the Holy Trinity—that of the actor, the landscape, and the camera—is perfect in *Stalker*' (in Fainaru, 2001[1988]: 64), Angelopoulos hints that the "expansion of the dimension of time" that we find in his own films is closer to Tarkovsky's early films, especially to *Stalker* than the later ones. Tarkovsky never speaks about Angelopoulos's work, although the differences are too obvious, even for a perceptive and meticulous scholar of Tarkovsky's work like Jeremy Mark Robinson.

Robinson argues that "in some ways, Angelopoulos has taken Tarkovsky's cinema and developed it more than any other director" (Robinson, 2006: 550). He observes that they both explore the "same psychological, social and political territory" producing "a cinema of displacement, migration, exile, history and spiritual anxiety" although "Angelopoulos has much more to say than Tarkovsky about the contestation of national and cultural borders, about the agony of exile, about the effects of politics on people's lives" (Robinson, 2006: 549). Robinson also contrasts their use of the long take, suggesting that Angelopoulos makes a much more effective use of the device by condensing more actions and events into a single shot, in "magnificently realized cinema," as he points out (2006: 550). In a way, Robinson finds Angelopoulos's use of Tarkovskyan devices is more successful than in Tarkovsky himself.

The truth, of course, is that this is not simply a difference in style or image-making: Tarkovsky had strong metaphysical beliefs which Angelopoulos tried to avoid, or even rejected, throughout his life. Tarkovsky made, according to Robinson,

> sacred cinema; and he always stressed the importance of his religious beliefs as an integral part of his filmmaking. The symbolism, the setting, even the dialogues as we see in *Nostalghia* is between the transcendental realm of the Deity and the created world after it was punctuated by the Incarnation. "My films," Tarkovksy said, express ". . . the ideal and man's aspiration towards the infinite".
>
> TARKOVSKY, 1989: 238

Infinity is understood as transcendental extinction of personality, but not through the empathic identification with the existential agony of a distinct character, like in Bresson's *Diary of a Country Priest* (1951) or its contemporary reincarnation in Schrader's *First Reformed* (2017). Tarkovsky makes films about the post-lapsarian individual, the Everyman, or, as he pointed out, "about a Man who lives on the earth, is a part of the earth and the earth is a part of him, about the fact that a man is answerable for his life both to the past and to the future" (Tarkovsky, 1989: 9).

On the other hand, there is no religion in Angelopoulos; and wherever it appears, in *Megalexandros* for example or at the beginning of *Ulysses' Gaze*, it is a structural indicator or a marker of rural realities, indeed an evasion and a distraction. In Angelopoulos, the aesthetic, the religious, and the moral realms are reversed and have at best an anthropology of the divine darkness, as articulated by Pseudo-Dionysius—especially in *Landscape in the Mist*. As I argued elsewhere:

> Despite his disenchantment and nihilism, Angelopoulos succeeded in visually articulating a *negative theology*, an apophatic depiction of the traces of numinosity as found in the realm of historical change and existential impermanence. The eyes of the children transform the cruelty of history into a tale of restoration and return to the ground of being. Its filmic space, both oneiric and material, framed an imaginative revelation of the inner conscience of the individual trying to come to terms with the fallen nature of humanity as a historical event.
>
> KARALIS, 2014[3]

Angelopoulos's divergence from Tarkovsky, and also Bresson, is both aesthetic and ontological: he insists on the social, indeed political, function of films and the mind's capacity to enhance and intensify praxis as positive self-realization. He also focuses on the self-sufficiency of visible phenomena; even his most metaphysical film, *Voyage to Cythera*, "offers the Greek audience a possibility to face the future without the traumas of the past" (Fainaru, 2001 [1985]: 41). The traumas are not only the traumas of history; they are also the traumas of a self that can observe its own silence and invisibility. For Angelopoulos, cinema frames these questions in such a way that they can be answered by its own structure and within its own conceptualizations.

Cinema produces the symbolic space where existence becomes visible to itself: it objectifies its being and turns its own gaze inwards. However, the existential background is not one of harmonization or appeasement. Despite the slow take and the incorporation of silence, what is significant is "the confrontation between the real world and the dream world, a world unsullied and still pure which exists only in memory" (Fainaru, 2001 [1985]: 42). Angelopoulos's films are precisely about that confrontation between the trauma of reality and the redemptive closure offered by memory. Following Marcel Proust, he "seeks to understand Being by exploring the obscurities of Time" (Kristeva, 1993: 6–7), as Julia Kristeva has pointed out. In a way his films invite their viewers to address "the felt time of their subjective memories" (Kristeva, 1993: 7), where the sacred ultimately abides. Tarkovsky's films are consecration liturgies of the real attempting to save reality form self-occlusion. Angelopoulos has a completely different *ontological entelechy* when he is searching for redemption in history through history.

From Abstraction to the Aniconic

Probably the spectator's response to Angelopoulos's filmmaking has nothing to do with his cinematic images as such but with the way they point towards the aniconic, the imageless, the unfilmed. The Aristotelian word entelechy indicates that the purpose and destiny of anything, its *telos*, is within it, as both its prime mover but also as its own entropic death wish. No film by Angelopoulos, like certain films by Antonioni, bears the culminating caption of all films, the word that indicates closure or postponement of closure—the word "end" (*telos* in Greek). "This is the reason," he stated, "you will never find the word 'End' at the end of any of my films. As far as I am concerned, these are chapters of one and the same film that goes on and will never be finished, for there is not ever a final word on anything" (Fainaru, 2001 [1999]: 135).

The Greek word *telos*, in its absence, is more apt to describe Angelopoulos's effort to create an invisible narrative thread from one film to the other. In Greek, *telos* means end and closure but also purpose and direction. But it is never used by the Angelopoulos, who invites viewers to add their own *telos* to the films or wait for the sequel that will complete it. He never manipulates or emotionally blackmails his viewers with premonitions of redemptive closure; his images are connected through intertextual or inter-filmic references and converse with each other through their formal analogies in specific settings and storylines. Such open-endedness in Angelopoulos's films creates a semantic surplus, or a margin of indeterminate significations, which emerges as a rupture within the imaginary of the viewer, especially at moments of historical, social, or indeed individual implosion. The context is part of the filmic text: when *Ulysses' Gaze* was made, the Yugoslav wars were still raging, or earlier when *Days of '36* was released, the Dictatorship was dominating the reception of the film. One could claim that metaphysics in Angelopoulos's images emerges out of the finality of the entelechic process: at the moment that a physical event completes its narrative trajectory, archives its historical realities, and unifies its formal possibilities, then it becomes metaphysical, the event completed, part of the reality of symbols and a symbol of the realities it epitomized.

Because of the fierce battle against mimetic imagination, going back to Aristotle, Angelopoulos's visual fields do not depict spaces of stable and fixed references; their pragmatics are not found in the actual objects and forms but in other images, and ultimately in the way that he intentionally puts them together, gathering them under the gaze of a unique confluence of time through his camera. This happened especially after his transition from Brechtian theatricality to Proustian temporality: the discovery of cinematic slowness changed the relation between his films and their viewers and his films with their structuration processes.

In *The Suspended Step*, the camera depicts a camera looking at another camera and all of them looking back at the viewer (or perhaps through the viewer?). Who is holding the camera of cameras? The ambiguities of sight, through the negative capabilities of imagination, are at the heart of such a cinematic project of reinventing visual fields and the semantics they presuppose. Angelopoulos's films *work* intensely in the unconscious of their viewers, on the process of abstracting out of figures and objects the formless invariants that transcend the specificities of space and time. The cinematic image *gathers* potentialities, both semantic and formal, figurative and abstract; and, in Heidegger's approach, "the gathering itself builds a dwelling and therefore founds a thinking" (2013: 151). In such a *gathering* function of different thinking possibilities Angelopoulos constructs his own ontological entelechy as a response to Tarkovsky's religiosity; the purpose of living, especially under the perspective of death, is not returning to God, but our reconciliation with the limitations of our human nature.

The depiction of the reconciliation of such a gathering is probably one of the most significant elements in Angelopoulos's project. Its visual structure is equally important. Here we must revisit J.J. Gibson's ecological optics and the suggestion that "the perceptual system does not respond to stimuli but extracts invariants." In his analysis of images, Gibson went even further, stressing that each image captures what he calls "formless invariants," that is "alignment or straightness, perpendicularity, or rectangularity, parallelity as against convergence intersections, closures and symmetries" (Gordon, 1989: 167). This is a re-articulation of the geometric neo-Platonic tendency towards abstraction and the aniconic, as also found in Byzantine iconography.

The significance of Angelopoulos's *visual gathering* resides precisely in the structural invariants of what is seen and what can be seen, of the invisible colors within the visible forms, and the material foundations that make possible the corporealization of an image. The image itself expresses the experience of seeing as a mental and physical event: it constructs an ontology of its own as it frames existential elements which emerge, as ongoing translations and transmutations of reality into symbolic visual maps of self-consciousness. Through them we can reconcile ourselves with the strictures and the restrictions of our existence. These are not the passions inflicting the psyche but the passions within the psyche—that cause our psyche to change and confront its own structure. Images of passions in the psyche define how we relate to the external world and how we manifest our existential anxiety to others. Angelopoulos's moral theory leans heavily towards Stoicism as endurance and temperance, but also as self-sufficiency and attunement to natural order.

The purpose of civic life is what Stoics called *oikeiôsis*, the gradual appropriation of the real. By living in "agreement with nature," the self recognizes its presence as material and social reality; therefore it develops a sense of belonging. We are our body and therefore we belong to it: belonging means oikeiôsis (appropriation) of our existential passions. According to the Stoics, by appropriating them we control them rationally and avoid the falsification of our being, our *allotriôsis*, alienation. In the final scenes of the film, Alexandros gathers his passions together, overcomes his limitations and transcends the drive for self-preservation, delivering himself to the eternity of being through artistic sublimation. The cruelty of dying is gradually apprehended and becomes part of self-awareness. Being towards death means regaining self-awareness at every moment, not falling into the deleterious entropy of panic. The future lasts an eternity and a day, as is repeated in crucial moments of the film: it happens every day and every day is lost.

The depiction of "eternity and a day" as emotional reality and existential entelechy can be seen at the very end of the film. In the beginning of Raúl Ruiz's adaptation of Marcel Proust's *Time Regained* (1999), the eye follows the normal flow of a dark river moving upstream towards one direction with ripples and small eddies moving erratically within its dominant flow. Suddenly, the imperceptible movement of the camera seems to reverse the flow and the spectator watches the river moving backwards, like an ebb which returns the water to its source, or soon moving in many directions, as if the center is lost and new ones emerge. This visual depiction by Ruiz of what is the actual theme of Proust's great novel constitutes an apt metaphor about the most important aspect of the cinematic image—its condensed and fluid temporality, indeed its tendency to stream heterogeneous experiences together under a common pattern of perception in order to capture the moment of time regained.

This is an apt metaphor of how the tendency towards abstraction, as total *oikeiôsis of the real*, works in Angelopoulos's images. In the final freeze frame, as with the end in *Ulysses' Gaze*, we see all images condensed into a formless void: the icons of life are transformed into the invisible forces that create them. Hence, we can understand the entelechy of his images and the various questions that their very poetics entail in order to save the phenomena and, as the theorist of the cinematic image Eric Rhode said, to "release the object into its own autonomy" (2003: 12). Rhode, a notable historian of cinema, explored how "the unknowable, or ontological, thinks the thinker; the aniconic generates the iconic" (2003: 12–13). Each image presupposes its absence and its very negation. The icon is a trace of the invisible. It exists to point towards the aniconic, the fields of being that are beyond experience and seen only through intuition and imagination. The aniconic generates its own presence, its integration into the visual system of potential forms of recognition, of forms that *gather* together disparate and incongruous elements establishing patterns of recognizability. In Heidegger's vocabulary, to gather means to create the ontological convergence by *enframing* and therefore calling forth a form and indeed a *presence*, making thus possible the elucidation of formless invariants as cognitive realities. What we see in the final frame of *Eternity and a Day* is the fecund void, the void of all possibilities, which started the history of Being and unconceals the existence of Beings. This happens because of the film itself and the ultimate raison d'être of all activities of imagination, to *save the phenomena*.

Saving the phenomena means precisely to *extract* the ultimate deep structure of all mental *gestalten* that allows us to recognize our humanity. The ancient commentator Simplicius commenting on Plato used this expression (to save the appearances σώζειν τά φαινόμενα) to indicate how astronomers, through their imaginative hypotheses, their presentations of celestial phenomena, make the invisible stars visible and also, by association, how the irregularities in movements can be inferred and visualized" (Duhem 2015: 6). Owen Barfield also stressed that, because of the imaginative form of such representations, such theorizing about what is not experienced constitutes "a new theory of the nature of theory: namely that, if a hypothesis saves all the appearances, it is identical with truth" (1957: 51).

This is what Angelopoulos achieved in his subtlest and most enduring images: the creative replication of reality through hyper-realistic images as seen at the end of *The Suspended Step of the Stork*, the final scene in *Landscape in the Mist*, or the beginning of *The Weeping Meadow*, which replicates the truth of the phenomena or even more so constitutes their essential truth. The double geometry of such scenes, with their kinetic immobility, one aspect still and the other trembling, creates an archetypal network of connections that we find in the most important works of Byzantine, Islamic, Chinese, and Japanese art through their underlying *eurhythmic* geometry of aniconic representation. The center of an image is depicted through its absence: the rhythms of history are traces of the past in the experience of today. Letters, photographs, monuments, or even trees and stones all represent the continuous presence of the past. The phenomena are saved because their composite events, experiential and imaginary at the same time, are mental and physical. What is presented implicitly is equally significant as what is actually represented. As the Greek writer Nikos Kazantzakis wrote regarding Japanese art: "You feel that the painter loves the external form but loves still more the mystic forces that gave birth to that specific form" (1964: 109).

Angelopoulos's ontological entelechy is precisely based on how his images can save the phenomena from *allotriôsis* first, from alienation, and then from oblivion. Contemporary philosopher Byung-Chul Han argues that "the task of art is *the saving of the other. The saving of beauty is the saving of the other*. Art saves the other by 'resisting its identification with its givenness' [*Vorhandeinbeit*]" (2018: 68). Angelopoulos's poet wants to complete a poem from the nineteenth century which is both a Promethean impossibility and a form of diabolical usurpation. The great ambition to complete Solomos's incomplete third draft of his poem *Free Besieged* is something similar to a contemporary poet trying to complete Friedrich Hölderlin's *Elegiac Fragments*, written during his incarceration in a mental asylum. Despite the differences in their circumstances and vocation, poetry transcends time and history. Ultimately the poet admits his failure. He must start afresh the human adventure that never ends. The creative imaginary absorbs the past and reimagines it. So, the poet vanishes speaking scattered words which make no sense. In the end, his confession to his dying mother reveals the ontology of creative imaginary: "Why did I live my life in exile? Why the only moments I returned were when I was only given the grace to speak my language . . . My own language . . . When I could find again lost or retrieve forgotten words from silence?" (Angelopoulos 1998: 76).

His only poetry was through the language he articulated in the letters to his wife. The *oikeiôsis* of reality means its ultimate integration and completion. Unlike Tarkovsky, Angelopoulos suggests that the only redemption we can have in the secular modernity of self-alienation comes through the words of others who relate to us with the foundational principle that annuls the death wish and all entropic tendencies—namely love, *agape*. His final three films are precisely about the ontological entelechy emerging in us not through the determinism of forces outside ourselves or the metaphysical predestination of religious belief, but through our positive appropriation of otherness. After "the failure of the philosophies of death," as Luc Ferry wrote, love is the only experience that "transcends the split between the particular and the universal, between nature and spirit" (2013: 172). In a sense, we return to Marx's observation that love is a *specific expression* of our real individual life. If there is no reality in our individual existence, then "your love is impotent—a misfortune" (Marx 1988: 140). Do we have images of love beyond the usual banalities of Hollywood? Can we express symbolically our real self as manifested through love? Angelopoulos's attempt to restart the morphoplastic potential of cinema finds in his last films its most ambitious and most ambiguous expression.

Images of Love

Angelopoulos's images of love are also images searching for their enunciation of the feeling they invoke: they create their own horizon of expectation. Cinematic visuality of emotions creates its own regimes of perception and interpretation: Georges Didi-Huberman observed that every image is an act and "every image act saves itself from the impossibility of describing the real" (in Saint & Stafford, 2013: 4). What Angelopoulos always does is to embody the hyper-real, the intensified condensed temporality of the oneiric, and their complex web of evocations and references. Angelopoulos's anti-realism is probably the most accurate visual language for the *dreaming* of the human love which he never stopped exploring, even in a political film like *The Hunters*. The ultimate confrontation in the semantics of his language is with the representability of love as a metaphysical principle sustaining individual existence and creating the gathering bridge to otherness. And how does he see love? Despite his anti-religious stance, Angelopoulos stands very close to Simone Weil's ideas. "Belief in the existence of other human beings, writes Weil, is *love*" (2005: 291). Love in Angelopoulos is not a subjective or personal emotion: in its mutuality, it entails the recognition of others in their concreteness, materiality, and specificity. Love is *isness*. Weil points out that

> to love and to be loved only serves mutually to render this existence more concrete, more constantly present to the mind. But it should be present as the source of our thoughts, not as their object. If there are grounds for wishing to be understood, it is not for ourselves but for the other, in order that we exist for him.
>
> 2005: 293

Angelopoulos's final answer to the *telos* of Images of love came through several questions uttered in absolute despair over the bed of the dead (or maybe not-dead-yet) mother in *Eternity and a Day*. In that scene, the film dramatizes the quest for an icon, an ontological ideogram, beyond all images. Probably his visual answers can be found in the end-less final scenes of his films: all vision immersed into light or drowned in darkness: "When could I find again lost or retrieve forgotten words from silence? Why only then could I hear again the echo of my footsteps in my home? Tell me. Why didn't we know how to love? Why, mother?" These questions can be considered ethical postulates for his future viewers—and "hopefully it will not end here," as he said. Angelopoulos was a thinker who avoided certainties and dogmas—he re-negotiated persistently the boundaries of his philosophy: "I am always, endlessly, searching, searching," he stressed (Fainaru, 2001[1997]: 102).

The answer to such profound questions cannot be a definition or an axiomatic principle. It can only be an experience, an intensification of experience: "Love needs reality," states Weil again (2005: 292). In Angelopoulos, images of love concern the absolute materiality of the real and the concrete. It is not about illusions, obsessions, or imaginary bodies; on the contrary, it is about our need for belonging and creating. "Love," concludes Weil, "is a sign of our wretchedness. God can only love himself. We can only love something else" (2005: 290). In a God-less world, loving each other reaffirms the primacy of existence, its unrepeated nature and endless phenomenality. The politics of love are about the rediscovery of the *polis* in a privatized and atomized world. After *Voyage to Cythera*, different forms of love, friendship, affection, intimacy, and desire all alternate in different degrees in Angelopoulos's imaginary. We can infer that love, as communal *agape*, was the sole thematic thread that linked all his different styles, poetic forms, and visual patterns.

This indicated the dominant presence of a strong *romantic humanism*, focused on his faith that humans can transform themselves into creative individuals, poets as he called them, through love, in their own everydayness, and be imaginative within the prose of their own life. Such feelings have also their historical horizon as collective and individual projects. Socialism, or social solidarity, was for Angelopoulos and his generation a project that came out of the ashes of World War II and the Greek Civil War, galvanized by projects of social justice and emancipation. After the new millennium and the rise of instrumentalized rationality as part of market liberalism and consumer capitalism, emotions as collective and individual realization became a thing of the past. However, without the validation of emotions "we become too rigid. Too rigid for life the way it really is. We fight it with wrong methods, the wrong self-protection," he stated (Fainaru 2001: 110).

Love was replaced by possession or obsession, or even by self-destructive proclivity, because of the inability to love. We can see Angelopoulos as a *skeptical humanist*, questioning the individualism of hypermodernity and the fetishization of love images in the era of total spectacle. Images of love led to the images concerning love as incapacitating anxiety, as grief for the potentialities that were never actualized, as we see in *Taxi Driver*, *Last Tango in Paris*, or more recently in Spike Jonze's Heideggerian *Her* (2013) or Wong Kar-wai's *In the Mood for Love* (2000). Angelopoulos's last film *The Dust of Time* is precisely about such lack of meaning and, in a way, it is pessimistic and bleak—something we haven't seen in his earlier films. Nevertheless, he juxtaposed creativity, innocence, and love with the dominant feelings of despair, grief, and anomie. He kept thinking in terms of the possible as his characters evolve into different degrees of self-awareness. In his last work, he tried to form images about growth through insecurity and uncertainty, through existential groundlessness. The temptation of nothingness became then an actual mode of being, experiencing human finitude as incomprehensibility and meaninglessness.

Despite all, however, he maintained a radical and somewhat Marcusean perception about the function of eros as a liberating project and as a creative minority against the current in a technocratic society. As Marcuse pointed out, "the task and duty of the intellectual [is] to recall and preserve historical possibilities which seem to have become utopian possibilities—that it is his task to break the concreteness of oppression in order to open the mental space in which this society can be recognized as what it is and does" (1969: 95). In order to historicize the utopian possibilities as envisaged by the Left and to combat the resurgence of occluding regimes of authoritarianism, Angelopoulos tried to *intensify* the psychological impact of images: in the 1970s he stressed their critical function; in the 1980s their existential self-questioning; in the 1990s, their restorative myth-making capacity; and in the last decade of his life, their emotional power.

Although he flirted with the aestheticization of experience as the only way out of nihilism and skepticism, he argued also that the most important duty of filmmakers was to become *mythmakers*, to compose a mythopoeia for their people and their adventure in history. After the success of *Ulysses' Gaze*, he experienced the melancholy of the end of the century and the absence of a new project of renewal: "We must all search for an elsewhere," he said, "for a utopia. I always believed that the world moves on, or moved on, through small or grand utopias. Now, I don't know I am rather lost in the modern world. I have no right to be pessimistic. I would like being superficially pessimistic. But I do worry" (in Archimandritis, 2013: 93).

Who were his *people*, however? His last short film of 2012, *Céu Inferior/Under the Sun*, ends with the optical illusion of the continuity between life and art in the form of graffiti wall-painting expressed by the caption: "The people have been deceived." The frustration over a whole movement for change converged with personal frustration about the gradual commodification of cinema in contemporary consumer society and the spectral function of images, establishing regimes of inauthenticity and bad faith. Angelopoulos's utopian *polis* was the visual refuge of people who realized themselves through the act of narrating their own life. The autobiography of his symbolic existence, his interaction and confrontation with the grand symbols of tradition, against the cruelty and nightmare of contemporary history, were the central concerns of his late cinematic conscience, and the principal elements of his iconosophy. His films give us his spiritual autobiography, as he stated, the ultimate biography of his psyche in collision with the forces that have shaped it, visualizing deep down the conflict with his own self. However, despite his frustration and melancholy, he remained always a humanist both romantic and skeptical at the same time.

Consequently, Angelopoulos stands close to Hannah Arendt's humanism, as he privileges the fundamental event of *natality*, as the ontological foundation for a "specifically human life [. . .] which ultimately can be told as a story, [and] establish a biography" (1958: 97). His films were the biography of the rebirth of consciousness in cinema and through cinema; a visual narrative full of reversals and counter-reversals, without closure or catharsis, and of course without end, which must be experienced by their viewers, every time they find the time to watch them.

In *The Suspended Step of the Stork*, he included an answer to the question, "What do you want from me?" in the form of a poem:

> I wish you health and happiness, but I can't take part in your voyage. I'm just a visitor. Everything I touch hurts me deeply. And then it doesn't belong to me. There is always someone to say: "That's mine!" I don't have anything that is mine . . . I arrogantly said one day. Now I've learned that nothing . . . is nothing. That we don't even have a name. And that each time we need to borrow one. Give me a place to look at. Forget me in the sea. I wish you health and happiness.

This idea of a perpetual traveler, of a vulnerable ideologically homeless individual, without faith, name and orientation is probably one of the most interesting elements of his late philosophical anthropology as seen in *The Weeping Meadow* and *The Dust of Time*.

Angelopoulos intuited and anticipated the feeling that there was a problem with history and its Hegelian cunning: the change happened in the 1980s, a decade which started with optimism and good omens and yet ended with radical collapse and a profound implosion. Because of these epochal changes it was obvious that Angelopoulos, like many "believers" of his generation, inaugurated a flight towards utopia, as history had become the dwelling of dystopia. In that respect, the gradual fusion in his movies of existentialism and Marxism started taking form and simultaneously disintegrating. Marx's early ideas became more visible in his works as a profound meditation on mortality, but also on embodied presence in the history of an individual.

"Man," wrote Marx, "as an objective, sensuous being is therefore a suffering being—and because he feels what he suffers, a passionate being. Passion is the essential force of man energetically bent on its object" (1988: 155). Angelopoulos's characters develop this *passionate* and suffering interiority which until then, in the famous Althusserian expression, were impersonal institutional "practices" and not individuated realities. From then onwards Angelopoulos, entered the realm of recognizing what it means to become mortal, a realm that can be detected in many other intellectuals of the period. By recognizing its own "unbeing," its own "nullity" according to Marx, the act of knowing itself reveals "the objective being, as its self-alienation; because it knows that it exists as a result of its own self-alienation" (1988: 157). By othering your existence you recognize the other in you and the objective relation you form with all others around you. If being-towards-death became the catalyst to relive the profound emotion of love, then the ultimate confrontation with self-alienation motivates Angelopoulos to investigate the actuality and the unthinkability of dying.

The Realm of Conscious Mortality

As we have seen since the 1980s, history itself started becoming problematic. The problematization of historical experience led to a new form of historical awareness which coincides with the rise of postmodern subjectivism and cultural relativism. The problems were not simply personal, they were collective concerns leading to a sense of an ending. Cornelius Castoriadis called it "the rise of insignificance," which led to the domination of postmodern solipsism renouncing all claims to the truth. Castoriadis stated that the reason of such domination was a profound decomposition and "dilapidation," as he described the European imaginary. "The specificity of Western civilization," he continued, "is this capacity to call itself into question and to undertake self-criticism" (n.d.: 142). At the moment that the self-critical ability is deferred or renounced, the only project that can imagined and acted upon is that of self-dismemberment and self-oblivion.

Angelopoulos addressed this question in *Eternity and a Day*, when his central character is confronted by his imminent death; mortality becomes the only way to define his own historicity. Philosophically the film stands next to Proust's *In Search of Lost Time*, Leo Tolstoy's *The Death of Ivan Ilyich*, and Martin Heidegger's *Being and Time* in its attempt to bring together all the questions and dilemmas of his engagement with thinking cinematically. Historically, Kurosawa *Ikiru* (1952) addresses the question of imminent death not in the Kierkegaardian dread and anxiety that it supposedly entails but as a dynamic re-evaluation of all lived and imagined experience. The text which encapsulates the transformative atonement that we see at the end of the film comes from Tolstoy's unsurpassed novella:

And suddenly everything was clear to him: what had been oppressing him and would not go away was now going away, all at once, on two sides, ten sides, all sides. He felt sorry for them, and he must do something to stop hurting them. Set them free, and free himself from all this suffering. "So nice, and so simple," he thought. "But what about the pain?" he wondered. "Where's it gone? Hey, pain, where are you?"

He listened and waited.

"Oh, here it comes. So what? Bring on the pain."

"What about death? Where is it?"

He was looking for his earlier, accustomed fear of death, but he couldn't find it. Where was death? What death? There was no fear whatsoever, because there was no death.

Instead of death there was light.

"So that's it!" he said suddenly, out loud. "Oh, bliss!"

TOLSTOY, 2008: 134

This revelation in Tolstoy's work is what made Heidegger leave his magnum opus unfinished. Heidegger's being-towards-death seems to underestimate the singularity and necessity of mortality, the fact that we exist with the feelings that we have lost something; the unity with the mother, the connection with ourselves, or the image and likeness of God in us. The fear of death was one of the central characteristics of modernity, trying to cover the loss, which promised immortality of some sort by "technologizing" and "medicalizing" the body. The idea of Angelopoulos's film is about precisely the transformative redemption of thinking when visualizing and conceptualizing death as an event in the symbolic order of existence. "My little flower, stranger, I, very late"— the dying poet's scattered, meaningless words, which are yet full of evocative resonances, indicate how culture helps us regain the only paradise we can experience, the paradise offered by our mortality. The voice of the sea which is also the maternal voice inviting him to the beginning is heard coming out of the gray waters.

The image that can answer the philosophical question that Plato sought is given with the elusive title of the film which is repeated throughout: eternity and a day. It is an image, adapted from Shakespeare's *As You Like It*, about the time and temporality of loving, about complete self-awareness in mutuality in its absolute and unmediated manifestation. It is both a paradox and a contradiction, an enigma that cannot and should not be answered. "Dying could appear as the very condition of our being born and mortality as a chance for the human being—no longer an obstacle, but rather the springboard from which the human can then leap into existence," as Françoise Dastur pointed out. Beyond the fear and dread both religious and psychological, death as self-awareness intensifies the experience of "the essential transitoriness and precariousness of our being but is also what allows us to be open to ourself, to others, and to the world. Death would no longer appear as a scandal, but rather as the very foundation of our existence" (Dastur 2012: 44).

Death in Angelopoulos's films reveals the truth of Shakespeare's verse: "Rosalind: Now tell me how long you would have her, after you have possess'd her. / Orlando: For ever and a day."[4] It is about the supratemporal for ever, the "always" of lovers, offered by images in an era when eternity has ceased to be attractive or even believable. Yet the nostalgia for the absolute or for a desired face-to-face encounter with the ineffable still permeates the entire cultural imaginary, from Eisenstein to Kubrick, from Lars von Trier to Denis Villeneuve. As in the end of *The Beekeeper*, the images "are invocations to an unknown god," whose face only history can reveal. "I would like to believe the world will be saved by the cinema," Angelopoulos stated. "Cinema is my world, and it is the scope of all my journeys. I am always searching for secret little utopias what will enchant me" (in Fainaru, 2001: 64). It seems that the greatest little secret utopia for Angelopoulos was filmmaking itself as an act of interpreting the past, elucidating the present, and foreshadowing the future, or indeed saving the phenomena from their own ephemerality and the oblivion caused by our finitude.

Chapter 6

The Risk of Being Tempted by *Déjà Vu*

Or On the Ontological Sublime

The Destiny of Images

In conclusion, philosophically speaking, the filmmaker Theo Angelopoulos articulated a theory of visual mythopoetics with complex ethical, political, and finally ontological implications. Based on his iconosophy, he succeeded in re-invigorating a long-standing tradition of theoretical conceptualizations about the nature of images and took cinematic praxis out of an introverted exceptionalism, incorporating it firmly within the currents of global visualities and their philosophical underpinnings. *Ontological universalism* is probably the most important characteristic of his "ocular poetics" because of the comprehensive, "thick" texture and multilayered iconographic formalization constructed in his films. His images *philosophize* through their very structure: their structure discloses the argument and the conceptual references of the film. When in *Voyage to Cythera*, the film starts with an image of the celestial spheres and lands down on earth during the German Occupation, we understand that the images seek to formulate a certain relation between the cosmic and the terrestrial. The juxtaposition itself indicates that viewers must think about the link emerging out of such collision of significations which is not stated explicitly and is abandoned in the rest of the film.

It is true that his images encapsulate, indeed embody, mostly propositions of problematization about politics, temporality, and mortality. I leave aside here all aesthetic and formalist aspects of his images which refer to the filmic aspect of his project. However, in their philosophical formulations, his images constitute a sustained series of *synecdoches* implying a visual theorization about the concreteness and the objecthood of the experienced world. As Irving Singer indicated concerning the philosophical function of cinema, a film "is always a product of formalist techniques and creative innovations that enable some filmmaker to express what he or she considers *real* in the apparent world" (1998: xii). With Angelpoulos's cinema, the visual potentialities of the ontology of moving images found a new, complex articulation and elaboration by privileging the concreteness and the objecthood of the real. Imagination frames and localizes the real: only through the ability to construct images, the real becomes comprehensible.

Angelopoulos constantly makes connections with previous attempts both in cinema and in thinking by directors and thinkers alike; his iconosophy is *palimpsestic* and multilayered, producing a challenging conceptual problematization of the real in the phenomenal world. In a way, his work creates its own genealogy, reordering the history of the medium as culture, form, and industry; the special concern for him was centered on cinematic images as the philosophical diagnostics of contemporary disorientation and deracination, in a world without solid or common hermeneutical horizons.

If in Sergei Eisenstein's cinema images collide with their own visual formation enhancing the political and logical contradictions of the presumed real, or in Andrei Tarkovksy's films images stand as iconographic traces of an "eternal" temporality that can be experienced in miraculous moments of disclosure, in Angelopoulos's work cinematic images foreground the specificity of objective reality, the energetic presence of the past, through memory and imagination, breaking through the occluding regimes of *aphanisis* and absence.

Certainly, in his iconosophy there is an element of what we have called *asymmetrical dissonance*; it is obvious that with his images Angelopoulos interrogates fields of visual disclosure which presumably, on certain occasions, are not compatible with each other. I attribute this to his sustained attempt to visually construct a space in which the *sublime* could emerge as ontological disclosure, justifying the failed projects of individual lives or self-conscious collectivities of the recent past; his insistence on the Greek Civil War has nothing to do with defeatism or antiquarianism. Angelopoulos depicts the existential anxiety of the defeated as the ontological substratum of all self-conscious historicity today. (This is similar to the way that the Spanish Civil War is the ontological background of contemporary Spanish cinema or the Soviet experiment in contemporary Russian films.)

Drawing from Rosa Luxemburg, Angelopoulos could also claim that "the road to socialism is paved with defeats . . . from which we draw historical experience, understanding, power and idealism"; but the defeats, as Luxemburg noted, create an order "built on sand. Tomorrow, the revolution will 'rise up again, clashing its weapons,' and to your horror it will proclaim with trumpets blazing: *I was, I am, I shall be!*" (Luxemburg, 1919). In a way, most of Angelopoulos's heroes are desperate idealists, tragic Don Quixotes of modern politics, who desire their redemption through personal engagement in projects that look doomed from their very inception. Yet, through their failure, they proclaim the ontological testimony of their existence: the verb *ego eimai* which appears so emphatically in *Voyage to Cythera* becomes the link between the real and the utopian, the anxiety for the new and the dread of the old. The assertion of existential autonomy of the individual is the ultimate philosophical postulate of his images. The link between individual freedom and collective responsibility was an unintended consequence of his project.

It is true that such tense dialectical oppositions didn't always lead to the cinematic or indeed ontological disclosure he was looking for; but Angelopoulos's horizon is replete with fragments or intimations of its emergence in everyday existence, even when his images are full of pessimism and dejection. *Landscape in the Mist* and *Ulysses' Gaze* are the ultimate examples of this unpredicted emergence. The ordinary generates the luminosity of life as a unique and unrepeatable experience and also as a liminal condition of being. Some would think of it as the Buddhist *satori* that we find in Ozu, for example, or, more recently, in the films of Apichatpong Weerasethakul; or like the Christian *immanent grace* in the movies of Federico Fellini, Martin Scorsese, or Paolo Sorrentino, or the thinking of Jean-Luc Marion and Alain Badiou. Yet, Angelopoulos visualizes the emergence of such *disclosure* as "an ecstatically extended timeliness" (Heidegger 2010: §410) through an ontology of material presence. Objects, bodies, and interactions are linked in space through the manifestation of emotions and desires, and through them "the phenomenon of the most primordial truth in the mode of authenticity" (Heidegger 2010: §221) is actually represented. It is the realm of emotions, the invisible world of attachments, yearnings, and impulses, that keeps people *resolutely* together, as individuals and society, despite their exile in Siberia, their social alienation, or their long separation. Emotion as the network of invisible links that sustain *political* life and individual existence is the ultimate conclusion to his work.

Desires and especially libidinal wishes are absent from his films, despite their brief appearance in *Landscape in the Mist* or *The Beekeeper*, as failed or frustrated sex. Philosophically, sexuality has no existential content for Angelopoulos, and that's probably his response to the hypersexual obsessions of Bertolucci's films, for example, or the histories of sexuality that became *en vogue* after Michel Foucault. After *Megalexandros*, his cinema became the most anti-Freudian and anti-Foucauldian visual essay in contemporary Europe. Although there are some hints of Freud's late cultural pessimism, his main theories of sexuality seem to be invalidated in Angelopoulos's films through their persistence on lifelong and usually self-destructive love attachments and passions. In films like *The Suspended Step of the Stork*, *Ulysses' Gaze*, or *The Weeping Meadow*, sex is an act of self-oblivion, of self-effacement, the recognition of a profound lack and loss at the very core of human existence. In a way, the image of the divided primeval unities that we encounter in Plato's *Symposium*, always looking for the other half but always failing to find it, is at the heart of the erotic mythography of his films.

As Aristophanes expressed it: "So it is really from such early times that human beings have had, inborn in themselves – Eros, the bringer together of their ancient nature, who tries to make one out of two and to heal their human nature" (Plato, 2001: 20). In Angelopoulos's early works, sex is associated with violence and death, as in the late Pier Paolo Pasolini or the early Terence Davies. Gradually his cinematic images expel all sexual bodies from their framing and expose the vulnerability and the fragility of the human body. The episode of the most brutal rape of the young girl in *Landscape in the Mist*, which is not seen and not even heard, is the most emblematic symbol of how sexuality functions in his films: as a void, dark amorphous space of self-negation, violent domination, and self-destruction. Even the love of two men for the same woman in his last film creates a strange triangle of possession, resentment, and rejection that adds to an extreme confusion of emotions. In Freudian terms, sex is the death wish, the entropic principle within the body, the invitation of Thanatos, which humans cannot resist. Nevertheless, love remains in Angelopoulos the "bringer together" of ancient nature and the "healer" of the current one: if sex destroys human relations, love weaves them inextricably together in a common inescapable destiny. Only being together makes them live their temporality authentically, as Heidegger suggested.

Such understanding of sexuality brings Angelopoulos into conflict with the dominant trends of queer cinema or the French or German violent extreme cinema of the last years. However, thanks to his marginal position, which ultimately is the great privilege of his visual idiom, he offers the opportunity to reassess the development of the cinematic representation of such emotions from the vantage point of its liminal borders and not of its presumed centers, or indeed something more common, of its fashionable trends. In a way such an approach to his work corroborates E.H. Gombrich's statement that "there really is no such thing as Art, there are only artists" (1990: 5); indeed, we can positively state that there is no cinema as a general category—there are only filmmakers and the audience they create or attract.

Angelopoulos's artistic adventure culminates with a concerted attempt to construct shared regimes of visuality, under conditions of radical self-alienation that seem impossible to transcend by any project of emancipation. In a way, this justifies Walter Benjamin's prediction that our society today "can experience its own annihilation as a supreme aesthetic pleasure" (2008: 42). Since the early twentieth century, the rise of modernism led to the growing fragmentation of all codes of common ways of seeing, perceiving, and conceptualizing the optical phenomenology of moving images. We must not forget that images depict something, they are photographic traces of something in front of the camera and not simply expressionistic spaces as we see in the paintings of Jackson Pollock or the abstract films of Stan Brakhage.

Angelopoulos is neither a painter nor a photographer; despite his allusions to both arts his films are total works of *pure cinema*, all-embracing artworks, more like Wagnerian symphonies in the tradition of the *Gesamtkunstwerk* and less like isolated lyrical episodes. Despite his early structuralist tendencies, his films, culminating with *Landscape in the Mist*, *Ulysses' Gaze*, and *Eternity and a Day*, even *The Dust of Time*, aspired to articulate *integrated* visual discourses about mortality, memory, death, and ultimately about human nature itself. As they explored the emergence of the cinematic disclosure of the sublime it became obvious to Angelopoulos that it could exist only if there was an *ontological sublime*: if living creation could become an opening to the transformed cosmos of existential redemption.

Re-focusing his camera from the cinematic to the ontological sublime, Angelopoulos explored the disclosure of being, the self-anagnorisis of consciousness existing in his most challenging and accomplished films. The foundational ontology of his films was given, as I have stressed, through Plato's statement posited at the beginning of *Ulysses' Gaze*, but also in the way that the poet George Seferis employed it in his poetry: "and a soul if it is to know itself must look into its own soul; the stranger and enemy, we've seen him in the mirror" (Seferis, 1995: 6). The last verse, which does not exist in Plato's *Alcibiades*, indicates that the great unknown of our thinking, the stranger and the enemy of us, is our *own self*, because the very essence of our being remains unknown and unknowable. The Socratic quest to *know thyself*, through *ascesis*, which means ideologies, politics, and personalities, is implicitly rejected by Angelopoulos.

On the contrary, following an older stipulation by Pindar, so superficially used by Nietzsche and Foucault, Angelopoulos's quest is always to "Become such as you are, having learned what that is" (*γένοι', οἶος ἐσσὶ μαθών*) (Pindar, 1997: 238). Angelopoulos sees the self as an ongoing, incomplete and constantly recreated project. The self is not a given: it is a becoming, in constant transmutation, in search of the concrete images that bespeak it. The self of the repatriated refugee in *Voyage to Cythera* is elusive and unlocatable. He has multiple selves as he has many children; but in the end, he remains out in the open sea, without center of reference or point of orientation. For Angelopoulos, the self-knowing consciousness is the failed project of European modernity because it is center-less and direction-less: there are no projects of self-realization anymore. The more we pretend to know who we are, the less likely it becomes for us to be authentic and true to our own self.

In the later films, the self exists, intermittently and somehow spasmodically, only if there is a project at hand: we exist as individuals if something outside us is intended to be done and be materialized.

When the project is completed, then the accomplished self changes into another form of self-perception, and is transformed into a spectral ghost of the past, into an immaterial illusion. When the project remains incomplete, as we see in the last two films, the self succumbs to its own entropic forces: it vanishes together with the rituals that formed it. Byung-Chul Han observed that all rituals that gave meaning to our world have disappeared today; and 'what are rituals?', he asks: "We can define rituals as symbolic techniques of making oneself at home in the world. They transform being-in-the-world into a being-at-home. They turn the world into a reliable place. They are to time what a home is to space: they render time habitable. They even make it accessible, like a house" (2020: 2). The existential *anomie* of living in a world destined to be unhabitable, through the disappearance of rituals, was the final concern of Angelopoulos's iconosophy.

After the Self, What?

Angelopoulos tried to synthesize elements of all arts in order to construct a complete vision of a new creative self, with a comprehensive *theoria* of human destiny in the time characterized by Byung-Chul Han as "the burnout society," that is a society "stripped of all its narrativity" (2015: 50). Angelopoulos's effort aspired to transform cinematic presentation into the most "condensed" narrative about what he called, in the final scene of *Ulysses' Gaze*, "the complete human adventure, the adventure that never ends." Persistently in his films, he constructed a contemplative vision of cinematography by taking the rhetoric out of the story. Trying to avoid the sensationalism of the Hollywood tradition but also the hyper-emotionalism of mainstream melodrama, he created a visual narrative without conflicts or upheavals; in a sense, he achieved the cinematic equivalent of what Roland Barthes defined as the degree zero of writing, since "writing is precisely this compromise between freedom and remembrance, it is this freedom which remembers and is free only in the gesture of choice, but is no longer so within duration" (1970: 16). The flatness of most of Angelopoulos's scripts, except for the final ones, makes the philosophical case for the existential reality of aloneness in contemporary societies, of the thrownness of existence, exacerbating the confrontation between individual independence and social oppression, knowing that "one cannot achieve this perspective alone, but only in the mirroring or confrontation of what Aristotle calls the friend" (Cavell 2005: 173). Friendship as the force that creates civic bonds, in the way that Aristotle claimed in his *Politics*, is the ultimate categorical imperative and moral duty implicitly foregrounded by Angelopoulos's final films.

Eternity and a Day is the most exceptional experiment in elliptical visualization, through the flattening of emotional reactions and the obliteration of romanticized discord. In the psyche of his main character, the real is like a musical monotone, leading almost imperceptibly to the return to the womb. The incidents around him are distractions and indeed temptations to deviate him from his main destination, which defines his destiny: "What can a poet do?" asks the child. "He has to sing the revolution, cry for the dead and invoke the lost face of freedom" (Angelopoulos 1998: 51). In a challenging way, Angelopoulos denuded his cinematic script of all emotionalism and sensationalism, allowing the image of the poet Solomos to function at a subliminal level and articulate a nonverbal *theoria* of living poetically in a world of violence and war. Solomos abandoned his studies and life in Italy and returned to his country in order to enunciate the event of the Revolution. His personal sacrifice indicated that he wanted to stress that life is not justified as an aesthetic phenomenon (Nietzsche 2000: 38), but *only as creative activity and existential engagement*. The ontology of living reality is not necessarily the Heideggerian being-towards-death. As Wittgenstein observed, death is not an event of life: we do not live out death. So, the only ontology we can articulate, as Angelopoulos does in this film, is the ontology of creativity, the platonic understanding of the creative act as *tokos en kalo*, as birth in beauty, even under the circumstances of war, brutality, and death.

How can we "create" beauty in the era of hyper-fragile subjectivism? Angelopoulos's kinetic images brought together the efforts of many filmmakers from Robert Bresson to Alexander Sokurov to emancipate the art of filmmaking from facile sentimentalism and seductive individualism (so systematically and persistently promoted by Hollywood). His visual language became the general *gestalt* which functioned as the springboard of visual representation for the self as the creative act itself, as a project of constant *re-imaging* of the state of being. The self as a work of art becomes an implicit but never completely articulated project in his films. Coining words or images means to crystallize new modalities of being:

naming is calling into existence, the act of gathering the untold possibilities and transporting them into their unique linguistic dwelling. To achieve this, he had to experiment with formal studies of his central theme, which was also the mythopoetic thread that links all his works. Mark Cousins defined this as "schema plus variation," arguing that "for an art to evolve, original images can't always be copied slavishly. They should be adjusted according to new technical possibilities, changing storytelling fashions, political ideas, emotional trends . . ." (2011: 12). The visual possibilities of cinematic representation are also existential modalities of understanding: we make forms (*gestalten*) to give order to the multiplicity of experiential information.

From within his own abstract schemata, Angelopoulos *potentialized* the cinematic language into a wide variety of representational codes incorporating formal variations that were previously unthinkable in the visual language of filmmaking. Within cinematic history, Angelopoulos's position remains liminal, at the edges of European cinematic tradition, as he stands at the moment of transition, when local or transregional cultures were challenged by external factors (the rise of global cinemas) and internal ones (the rise of television). Other filmmakers both from his country and elsewhere in Europe can be seen in an oppositional stance vis-à-vis his work, dismantling and deconstructing the grand narrative of his palimpsestic language by visual idioms of individualized or even private visions. (As already mentioned, Geoff Dyer obviously missed the point in *Ulysses' Gaze*.) His perception of cinematic images and understanding of the self can be refuted and negated by the younger generation of filmmakers facing different challenges, especially in their specific imaging and imagining towards a contemporary representation of the self.

Angelopoulos's project to construct the ontological foundations for the new autonomous individual conflicts with the dominant regimes of fragmentation and privatization that became dominant after the rise and demise of postmodernism. The pastiche character of modern cinema, from Quentin Tarantino to Luc Besson, indicates that ontological fragmentation has become the dominant gaze over human existence, or indeed the only path of self-definition. Defining the self through heterogeneous fragments without an integrating axis is probably one of the greatest philosophical challenges of contemporary thinking. As Charles Taylor observed: "Authenticity can't be defended in ways that collapse horizons of significance. [. . .] Horizons are given" (1991: 38).

In an unexpected twist of the cunning of history, Angelopoulos became the father figure that had to be assassinated, dismembered, and devoured by the younger generation, struggling for funding and visibility, while failing to produce a mythopoetic visual narrative on whose space individual and collective expectations might converge as Angelopoulos's did. We see the collision between a grand totalizing narrative against a sequence of micro-histories with their ontological and philosophical preconditions and consequences. Nevertheless, his iconosophy had a wider scope that was not to be limited by the restrictions of an era or an ideology. Angelopoulos's cinematic ideology can be located in the same symbolic territory inhabited by Bresson, Antonioni, Godard, Tarkovsky, Ozu, Mizoguchi, and Malick. It is about a vision of life and not an interpretive scheme of political or activist origins. His visual language reinvents its own genealogy as it becomes the spatial-temporal embodiment of different trends that all converge on his unique cinematic frame. Angelopoulos created a *universalizable visual philosophy* by becoming post-political and meta-ideological, and by critiquing, implicitly, the very foundations of his visuality.

It was a painful and prolonged process as he had to reconsider the "dreams of his youth" without betraying or denouncing them. The existential questions, visually articulated in his films, were fundamental questions of his own life. He succeeded in transforming 'history' into an imaginary cinematic landscape, a visual space of signs and omens framing the search for an ecstatic or transcendental sublimity, through an anthropocentric redemption, and therefore by imagining an ideal *polis* in the Platonic tradition or in the sense of a new utopia for a civic society. The New Atlantis of human emotions and the Newfoundland of interiority appear to carry into the future all human capacity for transformation and introspection, in an era that externalizes psyche and commodifies its workings, disfiguring its creative and morphoplastic potential.

Harvey Keitel, one of the most popular actors who worked with him, observed: "Angelopoulos is a man of conscience, who amazingly goes to these places and tells a story about what it's like for us to try to evolve as human beings, the mistakes we make, the death we bring to us, if we don't venture into the unknown" (in Fine 1997: 233). Keitel's points are truly pertinent as he points out the central element of Angelopoulos's work to transform viewers and then transport them into the realm of the unknown, or even of the unknowable.

It is true that in his early films he was more drawn towards the intriguing silence of static and abstract presentations; but, as he moved on, the rhythm became internalized and psychologized because the images and their stories "opened up" to an intuitive articulation for intensified expressiveness. Ultimately, Angelopoulos's images construct a space of symbolic correspondences that we must take seriously as cinematic language, or indeed as cinematic philosophy. Following Andrew Sarris, we can argue that what matters in his work is the struggle for a style of visual philosophizing and not the romantic anxiety of the director as an individual. Beyond the political aspects of his work, he was also a mythmaker with the archetypal temporality of myth as the organizing principle of cinematic movement, close to many other directors of world cinema. As Sarris observed about John Ford, he was "a director who could draw pictures on the screen without clogging up the continuity with mere pictorialism" (1976: 8).

This was achieved through the meticulous construction of *trans-signifiable* visual morphemes which we see evolving throughout his films, on some occasions into new forms or in other cases being totally or partially discarded. The Brechtian style of acting becomes superfluous and an impediment. Empathy and identification are the two postulates of his late style. When we find residual Brechtian elements in *Ulysses' Gaze* or in *The Weeping Meadow*, they appear as self-parody or self-conscious pastiche, slightly ironic or more specifically self-ironic. Their very dissimilarity is *dialogic*: they indicate the latent autobiographical mythopoeia articulated through different philosophical questioning. The poet discusses with his self about the process of articulating the self.

Angelopoulos stood opposed to visual strategies which neutralize the critical faculties of spectators and, more importantly, the abiding power of the image to be a self-contained unity. Strange as it sounds, his dilated introspective temporality is much more *real* than the dominant specular sense of time we see in Yorgos Lanthimos's *The Favourite* or Denis Villeneuve's *Blade Runner 2049*, movies based on visual illusionism, awkward self-referentiality, and seductive subterfuges which mean pure sensationalism and "mere pictorialism." What we find in these films is the *suspension of time*, indeed the introduction of non-time, a perceptual strategy of de-centering and self-othering for the audience and the director which in the end becomes mere escapism, un-thinking deterritorialization. Despite their strong pictorialism, they are cinematically anti-iconic: they contrive illusory unities and continuities in iconographic patterns which we never experience in everyday life, enlarging and blurring the boundaries between reality and illusion.

In Angelopoulos's films the dilated sense of time, of elongated time-span and delayed or off-stage action, represent an actual way of being in time and being here now, bringing together the Heideggerian principles of *Dasein* and *Sein*. For Angelopoulos, *seeing* a film is an anthropological opening to the multiplicity of beings, especially in the privatized world of the contemporary society of the spectacle and the mentality of instantaneous gratification imposed by consumer capitalism. In his unique understanding of visuality, Angelopoulos suggested that the omniscient source of meaning in a film is not the director, but the viewer, and the filmmaker has to reconstruct what is happening in the viewer's mind, re-enacting and re-living emotions of dialectical oppositions: fear and awe, confusion and wonderment, hate and love. Through such dialectical oppositions, a new understanding of human psyche and human nature takes form as a philosophical argument.

On certain occasions, Angelopoulos overestimated the ability or the willingness of spectators to *think* cinematically, but that was his main strategy to break down the 'fourth wall' and create a meta-cinematic epistemology of viewing. By making the camera the eye that looks back to the spectators and through them, Angelopoulos experimented, not always flawlessly, with a holistic understanding of cinema as a new hyper-human, but not anti-human, semiotic system of perceiving reality. In another sense, what Angelopoulos hoped for was a *synergistic* model of viewing in which the filmmaker articulates the spatial-temporal parameters of visual fields while spectators populate them with stories, desires, hopes, phantasies, or more obviously with words and images. He wanted to restore the emotional force of the lived or imagined experience through evocative iconographies drawing from the dilemmas of human interiority and the complexities of psychological inwardness.

Ultimately, Angelopoulos was consciously reflecting on the function and nature of images while constructing them as sites of understanding of the radical elucidation of selfhood. His cinematic images are *open spaces* for creative re-thinking and re-assembling: he is still a director's director, letting the images philosophize as images instead of projecting an ideological agenda onto them. On many occasions, it is the epistemology of his images that implies a philosophical constructivism of the real and the hyper-real. His multi-perspectival *mise-en-scène* presented both immobility within the cinematic frame and movement in its pictorial space, creating a visual language of philosophical aporias and dilemmas. His famous long takes are exactly about this project: how can we incorporate the unseen, the unknowable, and the unspeakable in the same frame as the visible concreteness of existential materiality? His ocular poetics brought together multifarious and occasionally incongruous experiments with time, visuality, and ultimately his continuous attempts to capture the ontological sublime as emergence in history. If there are verses that express the function of his images, we can find them in T.S. Eliot's *Four Quartets*: "At the still point of the turning world" (Eliot 1963: 179). His images are *topoi* of convergence of movement and immobility in an attempt to present the foundational collisions in their structure and then the profound ambivalence we feel in front of the mysteries of life and death, for the inability of the mind to find an answer or, as in the case of cinema, to construct a symbol for the existential aporia of being here now.

Without espousing Eliot's Christianity, there are definitely some traces of mysticism in Angelopoulos's work; but it is a mysticism emanating from nature, from the awe and wonder that we feel innately and instinctively, what Robert S. Corrington has called "ecstatic naturalism." Angelopoulos in his approach also evoked a long tradition of thinkers going back to Thales's foundational ontological statement "everything is full of gods," followed by Aristotle, Averroes, Thomas Aquinas, Spinoza, Emerson, Einstein, and Whitehead amongst others. In his last films the human phenomenon is seen and presented holistically: history is not disconnected from nature and every act of existential redemption is mirrored by a corresponding natural event. The weather plays a significant role semantically in his films, as well as the landscape. In an almost epic manner, action is defined by natural seasons, especially winter and spring, with the notable absence of summer in his films. Angelopoulos sees nature as both *natura naturans* and *natura naturata*, creating an enormous web of interconnected potencies enabling "nature to create itself out of itself alone," as Corrington defined it (2015: 3).

Through such total "encompassing" we encounter even the primary nothingness that envelops all things and, as Corrington concludes his analysis, "this nothingness is the Same as the Encompassing and gifts nature with all of its riches, terrors, potencies, and powers" (2015: 110). The sea at the end of *Eternity and a Day* and *The Weeping Meadow* encompasses the full existence of the dying individual, his nature and creativity, his historical consciousness, and his symbolic thinking. This *encompassing* happens by returning the individual to the *urgrund* of what Julia Kristeva defined as "the material maternal," which precedes all established interpretations and haunts all cultural engagement with its memory, through its *forgetting*. The descent into the maternal sea brings out the uncanny within us, the eternal stranger in us, the main theme of Angelopoulos's existential anthropology. "The foreigner is within me, hence we are all foreigners. If I am a foreigner, there are no foreigners" (1991: 192) states Kristeva, and this is what links the ontology of *Eternity and a Day* with the existential problematics of his late period.

After winning the Palme d'Or at Cannes in 1998, Angelopoulos stated: "There is no such a thing as the Angelopoulos phenomenon. I am the product of this place; but I simply had more stubbornness, endurance and persistence to realise my ideas" (in Soldatos, 2004 [1998]: 590). The uniqueness of his vision was made up of diverse challenges confronted by all those who found the time to watch his films everywhere. "The eternal game of time between present, past and projection to the future is continuous in my films. [. . .] But memory alters everything. Yet there is a sweetness of things that comes out of memory, which makes them softer and yet dilates them because we need this dilation," he clarified in the same interview (Soldatos, 2004: 591). One of his beloved poets, Rainer Maria Rilke, gave the answer to the "eternal game" he foregrounded in his films: "and ousting them, filling their place: an act without image" (2011: 335).

Constantly searching for the image that would name and locate the act, Angelopoulos went through the different shades and nuances of the iconographic process, which he didn't simply see in terms of formal figuration but the temporalization of the authenticity of the real. Historical temporality is the permeating problematic of his movies, defining tone and mood, marking an essential moment in the continuum between Kierkegaard and Bergson as mediated by Arendt's *vita activa* and, in cinematic terms, between Antonioni and Tarkovsky mediated by

Kurosawa. His work shows that cinema can reflectively re-think itself and respond to various challenges raised by its very nature: technological, compositional, mythopoetic, and ultimately anthropological. Because of its limitations and potentials, cinema presents visibly the act and the art of self-reflection and self-invention; hence it is probably the most socially crucial event of philosophy's articulation of reality. This is what Keitel means when he claims he claims that Angelopoulos films are "ventures into the unknown."

The construction of an anthropology of temporality, the Being and its Chronos, establishes the foundation of a new philosophical *theoria* of visible reality: *a theoria* that leads ultimately to an ontology reaffirming historical praxis and prefiguring a new symbolic order. His oeuvre foregrounds in the mind what Weil called *attention*: it makes us look carefully and *attentively* at the real. The real encapsulates the fecund promises of natality and presents humans with the ability to give birth through beauty: "Whatever is born . . . is born in darkness . . . Flowers and roots that grow . . . Nature hides more than humans . . ." as Angelopoulos wrote in the script of one of his films (Angelopoulos 1984: 11).

Angelopoulos talked about "the risk of being tempted by *déjà vu*" (in Fainaru, 2001: 143), indicating that the unhappy role of the sociopolitical reality of today is to create illusions through repetition, risking the danger of us being transformed into complacent, conformist followers. He struggled to make cinema again as "the means for keeping in contact with life around us and [as] one of our few creative options" (Fainaru, 2001: 55). His philosophical cinema was focused on the elucidation of reality by pointing out the illusorily character of contemporary technologized self and its occluding images. In a way, his iconosophy consists of what he saw after he escaped Plato's cave; it contains both the astonishment of the real and the confusion of the blinding light. The distance from Plato to Angelopoulos is a few verses translated into visual frames.

Postscript

It would be unfair to finish a philosophical reading of Angelopoulos's work without a brief mention of his last incomplete film *The Other Sea*, which poses the postmodern question of existential and transcendental homelessness. It is a film that never happened, a hypothetical *mise-en-scène* of light and sound, that never experienced disclosure. From what we can gather, Angelopoulos tried to visually articulate one of the most disturbing and unsettling questions of communal life, aptly and decisively stated in the Gospel of Luke with the lawyer's question: "Et quis est meus proximus?" (Who is my neighbor?) (Luke 10, 29).

Angelopoulos brought together people from different religious, social, and cultural backgrounds all united under the reality of displacement and exile, exploring the ontology of hearth-less existence, of a life dissociated from land and ancestry. Memory is suspended and all links between past and present are severed. The experience of an absolute imprisonment in the moment without an opening to the future, existing precariously in no man's land, a being without political ontology, is at the heart of his new vision of being. After the skepticism and pessimism of the previous decade, Angelopoulos's philosophical concerns focus on the precarious existence of the margins and homelessness.

The film was meant to be a visual essay on the profound crisis of self-perception and self-definition that encompassed Europe in the beginning of the decade, a crisis that debunked the myths and the certainties of the previous twenty years, especially after the collapse of socialism and the gradual erosion in the certainties of the nation-state. Francis Fukuyama had predicted the end of history with the prevailing of liberal societies whose capitalist consumer-based economies imposed new strategies of security and power. However, security was based on strategies of control and power, the constant surveillance not simply of human activity and political action but ultimately of the human mind.

Angelopoulos had already made this an essential part of his previous movie, as human bodies are stripped naked electronically and examined by state authorities in their most personal particulars: the body itself becomes an inorganic digital trace. The journey, which in the past was an escape to adventure and freedom, has now become a regulated activity: you are being watched even when you think that you are free. Furthermore, the stories of older generations become the background for escapist legends and obfuscating fairy tales, as contemporary life is based on power relations of submission and subjugation. In this last film, the famous proclamation by Albert Camus—"There is but one truly serious philosophical problem, and that is suicide. Judging whether life is or is not worth living amounts to answering the fundamental question of philosophy" (2005: 6)—is answered and memorialized.

Furthermore, from what we can infer from the existing script of *The Other Sea*, Angelopoulos wanted to explore an ontology beyond the identification with place or language, a closed ontology of being relegated to the social and legal position of the perennial foreigner, defining their identity through their liminality. An abandoned factory in Piraeus, the ultimate symbol of the failed industrial revolution, becomes the *threshold and the border* where new realities and connections are made. All refugees are restricted in the same space and, despite, their proximity, are and remain aliens. They try to learn other languages, sing foreign songs, assume false identities. For Angelopoulos, this is ambiguous and dangerous, as he had earlier indicated in *The Suspended Step of the Stork*. The symbiosis of different existential potentialities stimulates a new horizon of meaningful but potentially also dangerous encounters.

However, the de-territorialization of existence, being in no man's land, is a confronting visual challenge. There are two films situated in the pure space of psychological realities: Tarkovsky's *Stalker* and Kurosawa's *Dreams*. The no-place of transitory existence cannot create existential realities or ontological foundations. It leads to what Marc Augé called "the emptying of consciousness" as the main characteristic of "supermodernity," an emptying that leaves "no room for history unless it has been transformed into an element of spectacle, usually in allusive texts. What reigns there is actuality, the urgency of the present moment" (Augé 1995: 103–4). Being suspended in time and place becomes the new precondition of future humanity, leading to the anthropology of lost centers, hence to an anthropology of absolute and incommunicable solitude. A song, composed by Angelopoulos himself, is heard in the film: "I live on the edge of the sky / I don't know what will happen to me / in the darkness of your hair / I lost and then found love."[1] If in his previous films the vicissitudes of history established a strong and resistant self, in this last project, deterritorialization and deracination create a completely new perception of a *missing* self, of a self without coordinates and therefore existential axis, a self that can never be found. In this film an ontology of deracinated existence is elaborated, an ontology of people "in a state of stupor and [. . .] at war with society," as Simone Weil had observed (2002: 46).

The grim project of an existence without any awareness of past or future, of an existence imprisoned by its circumstantial *nowness*, seems to have been the focus of his final project—and its translation into the *wisdom of images* was never completed.

Chapter 7
Visual Essay

The Discovery of the Psyche

1 & 2 From Metaphysics to Physics. *Landscape in the Mist* (1988) directed and written by © Theo Angelopoulos. All rights reserved. Produced by Greek Film Centre, Greek Television (ERT-1), Paradis Films (Paris), Basicinematografica (Rome), and Theo Angelopoulos Productions.

3 The Challenge of Modernity. *Megalexandros* (1980), directed and written by © Theo Angelopoulos. All rights reserved. Produced by: R.A.I., Z.D.F., Greek Film Centre, and Theo Angelopoulos Productions.

4 The Call of Secular Mystery. *Landscape in the Mist* (1988) directed and written by © Theo Angelopoulos. All rights reserved. Produced by Greek Film Centre, Greek Television (ERT-1), Paradis Films (Paris), Basicinematografica (Rome), and Theo Angelopoulos Productions.

5 Out of Plato's Cave. *Eternity and a Day* (1998) directed and written by © Theo Angelopoulos. All rights reserved. Produced by Theo Angelopoulos Productions, Greek Film Centre, Greek Television ERT-1, Paradis Films, Intermedia S.A, and La Sept Cinema.

6 The Question of Suicide. *The Beekeeper* (1986) directed and written by © Theo Angelopoulos. All rights reserved. Produced by Greek Film Centre, ERT-1 TV (Greece), Paradis Films (Paris), Basicinematografica (Rome), and Theo Angelopoulos Productions.

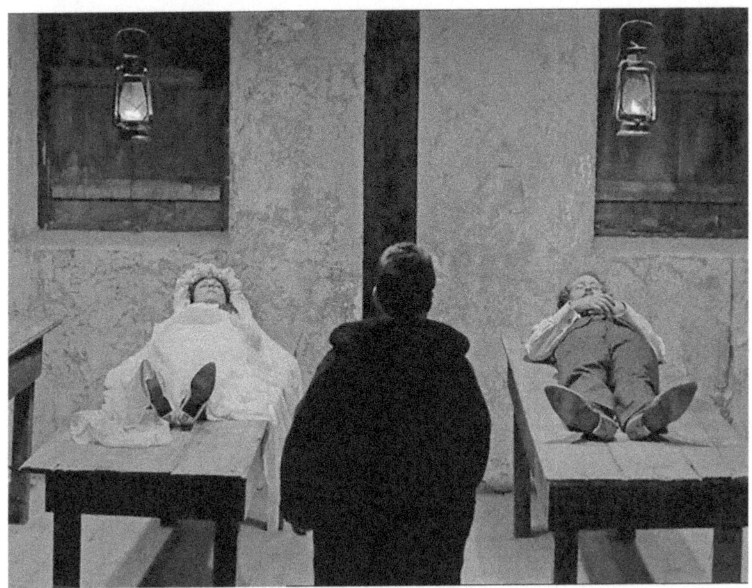

8 The Redemption of Poetry. *Eternity and a Day* (1998) directed and written
by © Theo Angelopoulos. All rights reserved. Produced by Theo
Angelopoulos Productions, Greek Film Centre, Greek Television ERT-1,
Paradis Films, Intermedia S.A, and La Sept Cinema.

9 At the Still Point. *The Weeping Meadow* (2004) directed and written by © Theo Angelopoulos. All rights reserved. Produced by Theo Angelopoulos, Greek Film Center, Hellenic Broadcasting Corporation ERT S.A., Attica Art Productions (Athens), BAC Films S.A, Intermedia S.A, and Arte France.

10 The Gathering Gaze. *Ulysses' Gaze* (1995) directed and written by © Theo Angelopoulos. All rights reserved. Produced by Theo Angelopoulos Productions, Greek Film Centre, MEGA Channel, Paradis Film, La Generale d'Images, La Sept Cinema, with the participation of Canal+, Basicinematografica, Istituto Luce, RAI, Tele-Muenchen, Concorde Films, Herbert Kloider, and in association with Channel 4.

Notes

2 On First Encountering Theo Angelopoulos

1 Aris Davarakis in an interview with Dionysis Savvopoulos in 1983: https://
antifono.gr/%CF%83%CF%85%CE%BD%CE%AD%CE%BD%CF%84
%CE%B5%CF%85%CE%BE%CE%B7-%CF%83%CE%B1%CE%B2%
CE%B2%CF%8C%CF%80%CE%BF%CF%85%CE%BB%CE%BF%
CF%85-%CE%B4%CE%B1%CE%B2%CE%B1%CF%81%CE%AC%C
E%BA%CE%B7-1983-%CF%84%CE%B1%CF%87/ (accessed on July
23, 2021).

3 On Seeing Films Philosophically

1 https://www.criterion.com/current/posts/974-the-taking-of-power-by-louis-
xiv-long-live-the-cinema (accessed December 20, 2021).

5 On Redemption

1 My translation but for the complete text in the famous translation by Byron
Raizes, see Solomos (1998: 101).

2 Theodore Angelopoulos, Comments on his films, Cinephilia.FGr, in
http://www.cinephilia.gr/index.php/prosopa/hellas/606-agelopoulos-6
(accessed September 3, 2021).

3 http://filmiconjournal.com/blog/post/35/religion_and_greek_cinema

4 William Shakespeare, *As You Like It, Act IV, Scene I, lines 1916–17*. See
https://www.opensourceshakespeare.org/views/plays/play_view.php?Wor
kID=asyoulikeit&Act=4&Scene=1&Scope=scene (accessed December 2,
2021).

6 The Risk of Being Tempted by *Déjà Vu*

1   I would like to thank Ms. Eleni Angelopoulou for providing me with a copy
     of the unpublished script.

References

Agamben, Giorgio, 1998, *Homo Sacer: Sovereign Power and Bare Life*, trans. Daniel Heller-Roazen. Stanford: Stanford University Press.

Althusser, Louis, 1969, *For Marx*, trans. B. Brewster. London: Verso.

Althusser, Louis, 1971, *Lenin and Philosophy and Other Essays*, trans. B. Brewster. London: New Left Books.

Althusser, Louis, 1993, *The Future Lasts a Long Time: A Memoir*, ed. O. Corpet and Y.M. Boutang, trans. R. Veasey. London: Chatto & Windus.

Andersen, Nathan, 2014, *Shadow Philosophy: Plato's Cave and Cinema*. London: Routledge.

Angelopoulos, Theodoros, 1977, *The Hunters, the Script*. Athens: Themelio Publications.

Angelopoulos, Theo, 1984, *Voyage to Cythera*, the Script. Athens: Aigokeros.

Angelopoulos, Theo, 1986, *The Beekeeper*, the script in collaboration with Dimitris Nollas. Athens: Aigokeros.

Angelopoulos, Theo, 1993, *Landscape in the Mist, the Script*. Athens Aigokeros

Angelopoulos, Theodoros, 1995, *Ulysses' Gaze, the Script*. Athens: Kastaniotis Publications.

Angelopoulos, Theo, 1997, *Scripts, Vol. One, 10¾*. Athens: Aigokeros.

Angelopoulos, Theodoros, 1998, *Eternity and Day, the Script*. Athens: Kastaniotis Publications.

Archimandritis, Yorgos, 2013, *Theodore Angelopoulos: With Naked Voice*. Athens: Patakis Publications.

Arendt, Hannah, 1958, *The Human Condition*. Chicago: Chicago University Press.

Aristotle, 1924, *Metaphysics*, trans. W.D. Ross. Oxford: Clarendon Press.

Aristotle, 1998, Politics, transl. by C.D.E. Reeve, Indianapolis/Cambridge: Hackett Publishing Company.

Augé, Marc, 1995, *Non-Places: Introduction to an Anthropology of Supermodernity*, trans. John Howe. London: Verso.

Axelos, Kostas, 2015, *Introduction to the Future Way of Thought: On Marx and Heidegger*, trans. Kenneth Mills. London: Meson Press.

Barfield, Owen, 1957, *Saving the Appearances: A Study in Idolatry*. London: Faber and Faber.

Barthes, Roland, 1970, *Writing Degree Zero*, trans. Annette Lavers and Colin Smith. New York: Beacon Paperback.

Baudrillard, Jean, 1984, *The Evil Demon of Images*, trans. Paul Patton and Paul Foss, Sydney: Power Institute Publications.

Baudelaire, Charles, 1993, *The Flowers of Evil*, trans. James McGowan. Oxford: Oxford World's Classics

Bazin, André, 2005, *What Is Cinema?, Volume 1*, trans. H. Gray. Berkeley: University of California Press

Benjamin, Walter, 1998, *The Origin of the German Tragic Drama*, trans. John Osborne, London: Verso Books.

Benjamin, Walter, 2008, "The Work of Art in the Age of Its Technological Reproducibility" (Second Version), in *The Work of Art in the Age of Its Technological Reproducibility and Other Writings on Media*. Cambridge, MA: Harvard University Press.

Bergson, Henry, 1911, *Creative Evolution*, trans. Arthur Mitchell. New York: The Modern Library.

Bergson, Henri, 1946, *The Creative Mind*, trans. Mabelle L. Addison. New York: Dover Philosophical Library.

Biro, Yvette, 2008, *Turbulence and Flow in Film: The Rhythmic Design*, trans. Paul Salamon. Bloomington: Indiana University Press.

Bordwell, David, 2005, *Figures Traced in Light, On Cinematic Staging*. Berkeley: University of California Press.

Boule, Jean-Pierre & McCaffey, Enda, 2011, *Existentialism and Contemporary Cinema: A Sartrean Perspective*. New York: Berghahn Books.

Bradatan, Costica, 2018, *Dying for Ideas: The Dangerous Lives of the Philosophers*. London: Bloomsbury Academic.

Bresson, Robert, 1986, *Notes on the Cinematograph*, trans. Jonathan Griffin, introduction by J.M.G. Le Clezio. New York: New York Review of Books.

Camus, Albert, 2005, *The Myth of Sisyphus*, trans. Justin O'Brien. London: Penguin Books.

Caryl, Christian, 2013, *Strange Rebels: 1979 and the Birth of the 21st century*. London: Basic Books.

Castoriadis, Cornelius, n.d., *The Rising Tide of Insignificancy*, translated from the French and edited anonymously as a public service. http://www. notbored.org/PSRTI.pdf.

Castoriadis, Cornelius, 1997, *World in Fragments, Writings on Politics, Society, Psychoanalysis and the Imagination*, trans. David Ames Curtis. Stanford: Stanford University Press.

Castoriadis, Cornelius, 2011, *Postscript on Insignificance: Dialogues with Cornelius Castoriadis*, trans. Gabriel Rockhill and John V. Garner. London: Continuum.

Cavafy, C. P., 1961, *The Complete Poems*, trans. Rae Dalven. London: Vintage.

Cavell, Stanley, 1981, *Pursuits of Happiness: The Hollywood Comedy of Remarriage*. Harvard: Harvard University Press.

Cavell, Stanley, 2005, *Cities of Words: Pedagogical Letters on a Register for the Moral Life*. Harvard: Harvard University Press.

Celan, Paul, 1988, *Poems*, trans. Paul Hamburger, New York: Persea Books.

Cioran, E.M., 2012, *The Temptation to Exist*, trans. Richard Howard. New York: Arcade Publishing.

Cohen, G.A., 2000, *Karl Marx's Theory of History: A Defence* (expanded version). Princeton: Princeton University Press.

Collingwood, R.G., 1958, *The Principles of Art*. London: Oxford University Press

Corrington, S. Robert, 2015, *Deep Pantheism: Towards a New Transcendentalism*. New York: Lexington Books.

Cousins, Mark, 2011, *The Story of Film*. London: Pavilion Press.

Cox, Damian & Levine, Michael P., 2012, *Thinking Through Film: Doing Philosophy, Watching Movies*. London: Wiley-Blackwell.

Dastur, Françoise, 2012, *How Are We to Confront Death? An Introduction to Philosophy*, trans. Robert Vallier, Foreword by David Farell Krell. New York: Fordham University Press.

Debord, Guy, 1995, *Society of the Spectacle*, trans. Donald Nicholson-Smith. New York: Zone Books.

Delacampagne, Christian, 1999, *A History of Philosophy in the Twentieth Century*, trans. M.B. DeBevoise, Baltimore: Johns Hopkins University Press.

Derrida, Jacques, 2015, "Cinema and its Ghosts: An Interview with Jacques Derrida," by Antoine de Baecque and Thierry Jousse. Trans. Peggy Kamuf, *Discourse*, 37.1–2, Winter/Spring 2015, pp. 22–39.

Duhem, Pierre, 2015 [1908], *To Save the Phenomena: An Essay on the Idea of Physical History from Plato to Galileo*, trans. Roger Ariew and Peter Barker. Indianapolis: Hackett Publishing Company.

Dyer, Geoff, 2013, *Zona, A Book about a Film about a Journey to a Room*. Edinburgh: Canongate.

Eilenberger, Wolfram, 2020, *Time of the Magicians: The Invention of Modern Thought 1919–1920*, trans. Shaun Whiteside. London: Allen Lane.

Eisendrath, Rachel, 2021, *Gallery of Clouds*. New York: New York Review of Books.

Ekardt, Philip, 2018, *Toward Fewer Images: The Work of Alexander Kluge*, An October Book, Cambridge, MA: The MIT Press.

Eliot, T.S., 1970, *Collected Poems*. London: Faber and Faber.

Eliot, T.S., 1975, *Selected Prose*, edited with an introduction by Frank Kermode. London: Faber and Faber.

Elsaesser, Thomas, 2019, *European Cinema and Continental Philosophy: Film as Thought Experiment*. New York: Bloomsbury Academic.

Engels, Friedrich, 1972, *The Marx–Engels Reader*, ed. Robert C. Tucker. New York: W.W. Norton and Company.

Estevez, Manuel Vidal, 2015, *Theo Angelopoulos*. Madrid: Ediciones Catedra.

Fainaru, Dan (ed.), 2001, *Theo Angelopoulos Interviews*, Jackson: University Press of Mississippi.

Falzon, Christopher, 2002, *Philosophy Goes to the Movies: An Introduction to Philosophy*. London: Routledge.

Ferry, Luc, 2013, *On Love: A Philosophy for the Twenty-first Century*, trans. Andrew Brown. Cambridge, UK: Polity Press

Ferry, Luc & Renaut, Alain, 1990, *French Philosophy of the Sixties: An Essay on Antihumanism*, trans Mary Schnackemberg Cattani. Amherst: University Press of Massachusetts.

Fine, Marshall, 1997, *Harvey Keitel: The Art of Darkness*. London: HarperCollins Publishers.

Foucault, Michel, 2001, *Essential Works of Foucault 1954–1984: Power*, vol. 3, ed. and trans. James D. Faubion. New York: New Press.

Freud, Sigmund, 1995, *Five Lectures on Psycho-Analysis*, trans. James Strachey. London: Penguin Books.

Freud, Sigmund, 2001, *New Introductory Lectures on Psycho-analysis and Other Works*, trans. James Strachey, vol. 22. London: Penguin Books.

Fromm, Erich, 1966, *Marx's Concept of Man*. New York: Frederick Ungar Publishing.

Fukuyama, Francis, 1992, *The End of History and the Last Man*. New York: Simon & Schuster.

Goethe, J. W. von, 2006, *Theory of Colours*, trans. bCharles Locke Eastlake. New York: Dover Publications.

Goh, Robbie B.H., 2022, *Christopher Nolan: Filmmaker and Philosopher*. London: Bloomsbury Academic.

Goldmann, Lucien, 1977, *Lukács and Heidegger: Towards a New Philosophy*, trans. William Q. Boelhower. London: Routledge & Kegan Paul.

Gombrich, E.H., 1990, *The Story of Art*. London: Phaidon Press.

Gordon, Ian, E., 2004, *Theories of Visual Perception*. London: Routledge.

Gorky, Maxim, 1999, "The Kingdom of Shadows," in *Movies*, ed. Gilbert Adair. London: Penguin Books, pp. 10–13.

Guinard, Paul, 1956, *El Greco*, trans. James Emmons. Lausanne: Skira Press.

Han, Byung-Chul. 2015, *The Burnt-Out Society*, trans. Erik Butler, Stanford: Stanford University Press.

Han, Byung-Chul, 2017, *Psychopolitics: Neoliberalism and New Technologies of Power*, trans. Erik Butler. London: Verso.

Han, Byung-Chul, 2018, *Saving Beauty*, trans. Daniel Steuer. London: Polity.

Han, Byung-Chul, 2020, *The Disappearance of Rituals: A Topology of the Present*, trans. Daniel Steuer. London: Polity Press.

Heidegger, Martin, 1968, *What Is Called Thinking?* trans. J. Glenn Gray. New York: Harper & Row.

Heidegger, Martin, 1971, *Poetry, Language, Thought*, trans. Albert Hofstadter. New York: HarperPerennial.

Heidegger, Martin, 1992, *The Concept of Time*, trans. William McNeill. Oxford: Blackwell Publishers.

Heidegger, Martin, 2010, *Being and Time*, trans. Joan Stambaugh, revised by Dennis Schmidt. New York: SUNY.

Heidegger, Martin, 2011, *Introduction to Philosophy—Thinking and Poetizing*, trans. Phillip Jacques Braunstein. Bloomington: Indiana University Press.

Heidegger, Martin, 2013, *Poetry, Language, Thought*, translations and Introduction by Albert Hofstander. New York: HarperPerennial.

Hendrix, John, 2004, *Platonic Architectonics: Platonic Philosophies & the Visual Arts*. London: Peter Lang Publishing.

Heraclitus, 1987, *Fragments*, a text and translation with a commentary by T.M. Robinson. Toronto: Toronto University Press.

Hobbes, Thomas, 2006, *Leviathan*, ed. G.A.J. Rogers & Karl Schuhmann. London: Bloomsbury Publishing.

Horton, Andrew (ed.), 1997, *The Last Modernist: The Films of Theo Angelopoulos*. Westport: Praeger Publications.

Horton, Andrew, 1999, *The Films of Theo Angelopoulos, A Cinema of Contemplation*. Princeton: Princeton University Press (1st ed. 1997).

Karalis, Vrasidas, 2006, "The Disjunctive Aesthetics of Myth and Empathy in Theo Angelopoulos' Ulysses' Gaze," *Literature & Aesthetics*, 16(2), December, pp. 252–68.

Karalis, Vrasidas, 2012, *A History of Greek Cinema*. London: Continuum.

Karalis, Vrasidas, 2014, "Religion and Greek Cinema," *Filmicon*, December 28, http://filmiconjournal.com/blog/post/35/religion_and_greek_cinema (accessed July 25, 2021).

Karalis, Vrasidas, 2017, *Realism in Post-War Greek Cinema*. London: I.B. Tauris.

Karalis, Vrasidas, 2021, *The Cinematic Language of Theo Angelopoulos*. New York: Berghahn Books.

Kazantzakis, Nikos, 1960, *The Saviors of God: Spiritual Exercises*, trans. Kimon Friar. New York: Simon & Schuster.

Kazantzakis, Nikos, 1964, *Japan and China*, trans. George C. Pappageotes. New York: Simon & Schuster.

Kierkegaard, Søren, 1983, *Repetition, A Venture in Experimental Psychology*. trans. Howard V. Hong and Edna H. Hong. Princeton: Princeton University Press.

Kluge, Alexander, 2015, "Foreword," in *The Cinema of Theo Angelopoulos*, ed. Angelos Koutsourakis and Mark Steven. Edinburgh: Edinburgh University Press.

Kristeva, Julia, 1991, *Strangers to Ourselves*, trans. Leon S. Roudiez. New York: Columbia University Press.

Kristeva, Julia, 1993, *Proust and the Sense of Time*, trans. Stephen Bann. New York: Columbia University Press.

Kumar, Krishan, 1987, *Utopia and Anti-Utopia in Modern Times*. Oxford: Blackwell.

Lipovetsky, Gilles, 2005. *Hypermodern Times*, trans. Sebastian Charles. London: Polity Press.

Lukács, György, 1971, *The Theory of the Novel*, trans. Anna Bostock. Cambridge, MA: The MIT Press.

Lukács, György, 2010, *History and Class Consciousness: Studies in Marxist Dialectics*, trans. Rodney Livingstone. London: Merlin Press (1st ed. 1923).

Luxemburg, Rosa, 1919, "Order Prevails in Berlin," Luxemburg Internet Archive, https://www.marxists.org/archive/luxemburg/1919/01/14.htm (accessed December 12, 2021).

Marcuse, Herbert, 1958, *Soviet Marxism: A Critical Analysis*. New York: Columbia University Press.

Marcuse, Herbert, 1978, *The Aesthetic Dimension: Toward a Critique of Marxist Aesthetics*. Boston: Beacon Press.

Marcuse, Herbert, 2005, *Heideggerian Marxism*, introduced by Richard Wolin and John Abromeit. Lincoln: University of Nebraska Press.

Mars-Jones, Adam, 2011, *Noriko Smiling*. London: Notting Hill Editions.

Marx, Karl, 1988, *Economic and Philosophic Manuscripts of 1844 and The Communist Manifesto*, trans. Martin Milligan. Amherst: Prometheus Books.

Murdoch, Iris, 1987, *Sartre: Romantic Rationalist*. London: Chatto & Windus.

Nietzsche, Friedrich, 2000, *The Birth of Tragedy*, trans. Douglas Smith. Oxford: Oxford University Press.

Nietzsche, Friedrich, 2006, *On the Genealogy of Morals*, ed. Keith Ansell-Pearson, trans. Carol Diethe. Cambridge: Cambridge University Press.

Nussbaum, Martha C., 1986, *The Fragility of Goodness: Luck and Ethics in Greek Tragedy and Philosophy*. New York: Cambridge University Press.

Ollman, Bertell, 1977, *Alienation: Marx's Conception of Man in Capitalist Society*. Cambridge, UK: Cambridge University Press.

Panofsky, Erwin, 1951, *Gothic Architecture and Scholasticism*. Cleveland: Meridian Books.

Panofsky, Erwin, 1997, *Three Essays on Style*, ed. Irving Lavin. Cambridge, MA: The MIT Press.

Pike, Burton, 2004, Introduction to the translation of J.W. von Goethe's *The Sorrows of Young Werther*. New York: Modern Library.

Pindar, 1997, *Olympian Odes & Pythian Odes*, ed. and trans. William H. Race. Cambridge MA: Harvard University Press.

Pippin, Robert B., 2017, *The Philosophical Hitchcock: Vertigo and the Anxieties of Unknowingness*. Chicago: University of Chicago Press.

Pippin, Robert B., 2020, *Filmed Thought: Cinema as Reflective Form*. Chicago: University of Chicago Press.

Plato, 1977, *Timaeus and Critias*, trans. Desmond Lee. London: Penguin Books.

Plato, 2000, *The Republic*, trans. Tom Griffith, ed. G.R.F. Ferrari. Cambridge: Cambridge University Press.

Plato, 2001, *Symposium*, trans. Seth Benardete, commentaries by Allan Bloom and Seth Benardete. Chicago: University of Chicago Press.

Plato, 2005, *Euthyphro, Apology, Crito, Phaedo, Phaedrus*, trans. Harold North Folwer. Cambridge, MA: Harvard University Press.

Proust, Marcel, 1987, *On Reading Ruskin*, trans. Jean Autret and Philip J. Wolfe. Yale University Press.

Rafailidis, Vasilis, 1996, *Film-Construction*. Athens: Aiyokeros Publications (1st ed. 1984).

Rafailidis, Vasilis, 2003, *Journey to Myth through History and to History through Myth: The Cinema of Theodore Angelopoulos*. Athens: Aiyokeros Publications.

Ramfos, Stelios, 2012, *Time Out*. Athens: Armos.

Rhode, Eric, 2003, *Notes on the Aniconic*. London: Apex One.

Richie, Ronald, 2007, *A Tractate on Japanese Aesthetics*. Berkeley: Stone Bridge Press.

Rilke, Rainer Maria, 1995, *Ahead of All Parting: The Selected Poetry and Prose of Rainer Maria Rilke*, trans. Stephen Mitchell. New York: Modern Library.

Rilke, Rainer Maria, 2011, *The Poetry of Rilke*, trans. and ed. Edward Snow. New York: North Point Press.

Rising, Tilo, 2008, *Jenseits von Mythos und Melancholie Philosophisch-theologische Überlegungen im Anschluss an das Kino von Theo Angelopulos*. Berlin: Schuren Verlag.

Robinson, Jeremy Mark, 2006, *The Sacred Cinema of Andrei Tarkovsky*. Maidstone: Crescent Moon Publishing.

Saint, Nigel & Stafford, Andy, 2013, *Modern French Visual Theory: A Critical Reader*. Manchester: Manchester University Press.

Sarris, Andrew, 1976, *The John Ford Movie Mystery*. London: Secker & Warburg in association with the British Film Institute.

Sartre, Jean-Paul, 1985, *Existentialism and Human Emotions*, trans. Hazel Barnes. New York: Citadel Press.

Sartre, Jean-Paul, 2007, *Existentialism is a Humanism*, trans. Carol Macomber. New Haven: Yale University Press.

Sartre, Jean-Paul, 2016, *What Is Subjectivity?*, trans. David Broder & Trista Selous. London: Verso.

Saussure, Ferdinand de, 2011, *Course in General Linguistics*, trans. Wade Baskin, ed. Perry Meisel and Haun Saussy. New York: Columbia University Press.

Schopenhauer, Arthur, 2004, *Essays and Aphorisms*, selected and translated with an Introduction by R.J. Hollingdale. London: Penguin Books.

Schrader, Paul, 2018 [1972], *Transcendental Style in Film: Ozu, Bresson, Dreyer*. Berkeley: University of California Press.

Seferis, George, 1995, *Collected Poems*, trans. Edmund Keely and Philip Sherard. Princeton: Princeton University Press.

Sendler, Egon, 1988, *The Icon: Image of the invisible*, trans. Fr Steven Bigham. Oakwood Publications.

Shaw, Daniel, 2008, *Film and Philosophy: Taking Movies Seriously*. London: Wallflower.

Singer, Irving, 1998, *Reality Transformed: Film as Meaning and Technique*. Cambridge, MA: The MIT Press.

Sinnerbrink, Robert, 2019, *Terrence Malick: Filmmaker and Philosopher*. London: Bloomsbury Publishing.

Soldatos, Yannis, 2004, *History of Greek Cinema, vol. 5, Documents 1970–2000*. Athens: Aiyokeros.

Solomos, Dionysios, 1998, *Faith and Motherland: Collected Poems*, trans. Marios Byron Raizis. Minneapolis: A Nostos Book.

Stallworthy Jon and Potter, Jane, 2011, *Three Poets of the First World War*. London: Penguin Classics.

Stoltzfus, Ben, 1996, *Lacan and Literature: Purloined Pretexts*. New York: State University of New York Press.

Tarkovsky, Andrei, 1989, *Sculpting in Time: Reflections on Cinema*, trans. Kitty Hunter-Blair. London: Faber and Faber.

Taylor, Charles, 1991, *The Malaise of Modernity*, Toronto: House of Anansi Press.

Tolstoy, Leo, 2008, *The Death of Ivan Iliych and Other Stories*, trans. David Mcduff and Ronald Wilks. London: Penguin Classics.

Traverso, Enzo, 2017, *Left-Wing Melancholia: Marxism, History, and Memory (New Directions in Critical Theory)*. New York: Columbia University Press.

Turovskaya, Maya, 1989, *Tarkovsky: Cinema as Poetry*, trans. Natasha Ward. London: Faber & Faber.

Vattimo, Gianni, 1988, *The End of Modernity: Nihilism and Hermeneutics in Post-modern Culture*, trans. Jon R. Snyder. London: Polity Press.

Voegelin, Eric, 2000, *Modernity Without Restraint*. Columbia: University of Missouri Press.

Wade, Chris, 2021, *Theo Angelopoulos: The Film Guide*, World Cinema Series. London: Lulu Press.

Warehime, Marja, 2006, *Maurice Pialat*. Manchester: Manchester University Press.

Weil, Simone, 2002, *The Need for Roots*, trans. Arthur Wills. London: Routledge.

Weil, Simone, 2005, *An Anthology*, edited and introduced by Siân Miles. London: Penguin Books.

West, David, 2010, *Continental Philosophy: An Introduction*. Cambridge: Polity Press.

Wittgenstein, Ludwig, 1958, *Tractatus Logico-Philosophicus*, transl. D.F. Pears and B.F. McGuinness. London: Routledge & Kegan Paul.

Wittgenstein, Ludwig, 2009, *Philosophical Investigations*, trans. by G.E.M. Anscombe, P.M.S. Hacker, and Joachim Schulte. Rev. 4th ed. London: Blackwell Publishing.

Wolin, Richard, 2001, *Heidegger's Children, Hannah Arendt, Karl Löwith, Hans Jonas and Herbert Marcuse*. Princeton: Princeton University Press.

Worringer, Wilhelm, 1997, *Abstraction and Empathy: A Contribution to the Psychology of Style*, trans. Michael Bullock. Chicago: Elephant Paperbacks.

Index